CONSUMER PRODUCT GUARANTEES

To Bev

Consumer Product Guarantees

CHRISTIAN TWIGG-FLESNER
Institute for Commercial Law Studies, University of Sheffield

ASHGATE

Published by
Ashgate Publishing Limited
Gower House
Croft Road
Aldershot
Hants GU11 3HR
England

Ashgate Publishing Company
Suite 420
101 Cherry Street
Burlington, VT 05401-4405
USA

Ashgate website: http://www.ashgate.com

British Library Cataloguing in Publication Data
Twigg-Flesner, Christian
Consumer product guarantees
1.Warranty - Great Britain 2.Warranty - European Union countries 3.Consumer protection - Law and legislation - Great Britain 4.Consumer protection - Law and legislation - European Union countries
I.Title
343.4'1'08

Library of Congress Cataloging-in-Publication Data
Twigg-Flesner, Christian, 1975-
Consumer product guarantees / Christian Twigg-Flesner.
p. cm.
Includes bibliographical references and index.
ISBN 0-7546-2186-3 (hbk)
1. Warranty--Great Britain. 2. Consumer protection--Great Britain. 3. Warranty--European Union countries. 4. Consumer protection--European Union countries. I. Title.

KD1654.C6T88 2003
343.4107'1--dc21

2003041877

ISBN 0 7546 2186 3

Printed and bound in Great Britain by MPG Books Ltd, Bodmin, Cornwall

Contents

Table of Cases

English Cases

Abu Dhabi National Tanker Co v Product Star Shipping [1993] 1 Lloyd's Rep 397
Adams v Richardson&Starling Ltd. [1969] 1 WLR 1645
Alexander v Comet Group plc [1995] *Consumer Policy Review* 29
Andrews v Hopkinson [1957] 1 QB 229
Ashington Piggeries Ltd. v Christopher Hill Ltd. [1972] A.C. 441, HL.
Ashley v London Borough of Sutton (1995) 195 JP 631
Associated Provincial Picture Houses v Wednesbury Corp. [1948] 1 KB 223
Bernstein v Pamson Motors (Golders Green) Ltd. [1987] 2 All ER 200
Bowerman v Association of British Travel Agents Ltd. (1995) 145 New Law Journal 1815
Breed v Cluett [1970] 2 All ER 662
Brown v Sheens and Richmond Car Sales [1950] 1 All ER 1102
Carlill v The Carbolic Smoke Ball Company [1892] 2 Q.B. 484, [1893] 1 Q.B. 256 (CA)
Chappel & Co. Ltd. v Nestle Co. Ltd. [1960] A.C. 87
De la Bere v Pearson Ltd. [1908] 1 K.B. 280
Director-General of Fair Trading v First National Bank plc. [2001] UKHL 52
Dixons Ltd. v Roberts (1984) 184 JP 513
Donoghue v Stevenson [1932] AC 562
Drury v Victor Buckland Ltd. [1941] 1 All ER 269
Esso Petroleum Co. Ltd. v Customs and Excise Commissioners [1976] 1 WLR 1.
Gan Insurance Ltd v Tai Ping Insurance Co. Ltd. [2001] 2 All ER (Comm) 299
L.Gent & Sons v Eastman Machine Co. Ltd. [1986] BTLC 17
Grant v Australian Knitting Mills Ltd. [1936] A.C. 85, PC
Harlingdon & Leinster Ltd. v Christopher Hull Fine Art Ltd. [1990] 3 WLR 13, CA
Heilbut, Symons & Co. v Buckleton [1913] AC 30
Lambert v Lewis [1982] A.C.225
Newell and Taylor v Hicks (1984) J.P. 308
Nash and others v Pararagon Finance Plc [2001] 2 All ER (Comm) 1025
Nishika Corporation v Goodchild [1990] Fleet Street Reports 371
Partridge v Crittenden [1968] 2 All ER 421
Pharmaceutical Society of Great Britain v Boots (Southern) Ltd. [1953] 1 Q.B. 401
Philips International BV v British Sky Broadcasting (unreported, 19 October 1994)
Reardon Smith Line Ltd. v Yngvar Hansen-Tangen [1976] 1 WLR 989
Rogers v Parish [1987] 2 All ER 232
Shanklin Pier v Detel Products LD [1951] 2 KB 854
Sony K.K. v Saray Electronics (London) Limited [1983] Fleet Street Reports 302

St Albans City and District Council v International Computers Ltd. [1996] 4 All ER 481
Stevenson v Rogers and another [1999] 1 All ER 613, CA
Thain v Anniesland Trade Centre [1997] SLT (Sh C) 102
Wells (Merstham) Ltd. v Buckland Sand and Silica Ltd. [1965] 2 QB 170
Williams v Carwardine (1833) 4 B. & Ad. 621; 110 E.R. 590
Wood v Letrik (1932) Times, 12 January (KB)

European Cases

C-373/90 *Criminal Proceedings against X* [1992] ECR I-131
C-31/85 *ETA Fabriques D'Ebauches S.A. v DK Investment S.A.* [1986] 2 C.M.L.R. 674
C-86/82 *Hasselblad (GB) Limited v Commission* [1984] ECR 883
C-376/92 *Metro SB-Großmärkte GmbH & Co.KG v Cartier SA* [1994] ECR I-15

European Commission Decisions

Constructa, Competition Report EC 1974, point 109
Ford, EC Competition Report 1983, para 104
Moulinex and *Bauknecht* EC Competition Report 1980, point 121
SABA (1976) O.J. 128/19
Sony, EC Competition Report 1987, point 67
Zanussi (1978) O.J. L 322/36

Office of Fair Trading Decisions under the Unfair Contract Terms Regulations

Adorn Supplies	(OFT, 1999b, p. 9)
Aspen Windows Group	(OFT, 1999a, p. 7)
The Babies Paradise Nursery	(OFT, 1999a, p. 14)
Comet Group Plc	(OFT, 2001a, p. 13)
Dampco (UK) Ltd.	(OFT, 1999a, p. 34)
Dyno-Rod Plc	(OFT, 2000a, p. 16)
East Yorkshire Aluminium	(OFT, 1997b, p. 37)
Emanuel Spence Ltd.	(OFT, 2000b, p. 21)
Ford Motor Company	(OFT, 1996d, p. 24)
Garland Electronics Ltd.	(OFT, 1998, p. 32)
Glass and Glazing Federation	(OFT, 1999c, p. 20)
Goodalls Caravans Ltd.	(OFT, 1996c, p. 30)
Haygate Engineering Ltd.	(OFT, 2000c, p. 25)
Hidden Hearing	(OFT, 1999a, p. 43)
Hidden Hearing	(OFT, 2001a, p. 33)

ISL Renosystems Ltd.	(OFT, 1999a, p. 47)
Kenwood Damp Proofing Plc	(OFT, 2000a, p.22)
Laport Garage Doors	(OFT, 1999a, p.51)
Microsoft UK	(OFT, 1998, p.54)
Multiyork Furniture Ltd.	(OFT, 2000c, p.45)
Nationwide Security Blinds	(OFT, 2002a, p.39)
Olympic Warranties	(OFT, 1996d, p.30)
Rimacroft Ltd.	(OFT, 2000b, p.28)
Timberland Flooring Co. Ltd.	(OFT, 2002a, p.58)
Town and Country Driveways	(OFT, 2001b, p.52)
Vauxhall Motors Ltd.	(OFT, 2000a, p.29)
R C Woodhouse	(OFT, 2000c, p.51)
Yakamoto Futon Centre	(OFT, 2001a, p.61)

Preface

Consumer Product Guarantees have been topical for almost a decade now, ever since the European Commission published its *Green Paper on Guarantees for Consumer Goods and After-Sales Service*, which eventually resulted in Directive 99/44/EC on Certain Aspects of the Sale of Consumer Goods and Associated Guarantees. The main objective of this Directive is to introduce a minimum level of consumer protection by establishing the "conformity with the contract" requirement, together with a detailed remedial regime. Inevitably, academic commentary on the *Green Paper* and the Directive itself has concentrated on those aspects. However, the Directive also contains a provision on voluntary guarantees given free-of-charge, usually by a manufacturer. I was surprised to discover that very little had been written about such guarantees. Curiosity therefore lead me to look into this further, eventually producing a Ph.D.-thesis and, finally, this book.

I would have found this process a considerably more difficult task without the support and encouragement by a number of people. Colleagues both at the University of Sheffield and the Nottingham Trent University (where I worked before returning to Sheffield in August 2002) endured my enthusiastic ramblings with great patience. Particular mention should go to John Adams, Robert Bradgate, Roger Brownsword and Geraint Howells. Angela Donaldson (Library Information Services, Nottingham Trent University) proved to be a life-saver on several occasions when she managed to deal with my requests for obscure journal articles in record time.

I am also grateful to a number of people who were willing to respond to my requests for information at various times: Ken Wilson and Lindsey Addison at Domestic & General plc., John Sherwood of IMG group, Professor Jean Braucher (Arizona State University), and the numerous manufacturers who were kind enough to send me copies of their various guarantee documents.

Finally, my thanks go to Ashgate for their support and patience as I kept delaying submission of the final manuscript in anticipation of the implementation of the Directive into English Law. Particular mention should go to Val Saunders and Carolyn Court.

However, none of this would ever have come together without the support given to me by my family, and Bev and Sophie in particular. Thank you!

Christian Twigg-Flesner

Chapter 1

Guarantees, Product Quality, and Consumer Protection

1.0 Introduction

This book is about consumer product guarantees. The most common consumer product guarantee is the manufacturer's guarantee. This is a voluntary undertaking given by a manufacturer[1] (hereinafter "the guarantor") without charge to provide a remedy, should the product covered by the guarantee become defective as a result of poor workmanship or the use of faulty materials in the manufacturing process during a specified period of time after purchase. Similar guarantees are often also given by retailers. However, for the sake of simplicity, this book will generally only refer to manufacturers' guarantees.

Crucially, consumers[2] are not required to pay for such a guarantee in addition to the overall purchase price of the product covered by the guarantee, because it is an "integral part of the bundle of satisfactions" (Udell and Anderson, 1968, p.1) obtained by the consumer when he buys the product. Guarantees are given on most consumer goods,[3] especially cars[4] and consumer durables such as hi-fi systems or washing machines. For some consumers, a guarantee may be an important part of the overall package, i.e., of considerable significance in the purchasing decision-making process. Such consumers may regard the guarantee as an assurance of product quality and value and as protection against the risk of product failure. For others, a guarantee may also be regarded as redress mechanism, should the product break down, or be of a lower quality than promised (Kelley and Conant, 1991). The purpose of this book is to investigate the legal issues of, and to develop a legal framework for, manufacturers' guarantees. The theme running through this book is that that manufacturers' guarantees could be one route by which to obtain redress informally, and that a legal framework for such guarantees should be designed to facilitate this.

1.0.1 A lack of discussion of manufacturers' guarantees

Although guarantees are very common, the legal issues to which they give rise have not been investigated systematically by legal scholars in the United Kingdom. A glance at the standard consumer law textbooks reveals that guarantees are given a rather brief treatment.[5] In essence, most books refer to various theories of the consumer guarantee and the only detailed examination of these, in particular (Priest, 1981).[6] Editions published after 1999 generally also provide a brief summary of the changes to be introduced by Directive 99/44/EC on Certain Aspects of The Sale of Consumer Goods and Associated Guarantees (hereinafter "the Guarantees Directive"), which was adopted by the European Community (E.C.) in May 1999.[7]

There is hardly any commentary or analysis of the English or European Community law on manufacturers' guarantees in the law journals, either. Although there is a reasonable body of literature in U.S. journals, particularly in the wake of the adoption of the Magnuson-Moss Warranty Act in 1975,[8] this is now rather dated. There were a number of English articles in the early 1990s when a Private Member's Bill was introduced to enact reform proposals modelled on the U.S. legislation and put forward by the National Consumer Council (NCC, 1989b), notably three papers by Willett (1991; 1992; 1993). Howells examined some of the proposals and considered the tension between a desire to regulate guarantees on the one hand, and the potential that competition on guarantees might offer on the other hand (Howells and Bryant, 1993; Howells, 1994). Palle-Bo Madsen produced a general introduction to the topic in the wake of the E.C. *Green Paper* (Madsen, 1995) and highlighted some of the aspects that are particularly relevant from a European point of view. The Competition Law aspects of manufacturers' guarantees have received slightly more attention (Astola, 1984; Fine, 1989; Goyder, 1996), but this has mainly been in response to decisions in this field by the European Court of Justice.[9]

In short, there has not yet been a systematic analysis of the legal aspects of manufacturers' guarantees. One might suggest, perhaps somewhat cynically, that this must be so because there is nothing much to say about manufacturers' guarantees. This book will demonstrate that there are, in fact, numerous issues that are raised by manufacturers' guarantees and that there is a considerable amount to say about them.

1.0.2 Scope of analysis

The central task for this book is to identify the function of guarantees and the shape of the legal framework that should be adopted. It is assumed that it is desirable to put into place a legal framework for guarantees. To some, this may be begging the question, and it might be suggested that it is not necessary at all to intervene. For present purposes, it is assumed that it is desirable to create a legal framework for guarantees, but it remains necessary to examine what this framework should cover. That there is such a desire is evident from the string of reform proposals put forward over the last decade or so, and the legislation that eventually emerged in the form of the Guarantees Directive.

An important consideration is the point at which consumers are most likely to be interested in the existence and substance of a guarantee. If this is the case before they commit to a purchase, then the central purpose of a guarantee may be to aid the consumer in reaching a purchasing decision. If it is after purchase, then the guarantee may be there to provide redress when a product does not work. The findings of the examination of guarantees in subsequent chapters will lead to the conclusion that guarantees are better regarded as a means of obtaining redress and that the legal framework on guarantees should enhance this function.

It will also be considered in how far the existing legal framework on manufacturers' guarantees reflects the framework developed in this book. This will involve a detailed analysis of the relevant provisions of English and European Community law.

1.0.3 A word on methodology

Much of chapters 3 and 4 draws on research from non-legal fields, such as economics, business studies and consumer complaining behaviour. However, the present writer does not claim significant expertise in these fields. This book will focus on the conclusions reached by those who carried out research in these non-legal disciplines, but there will be no examination of the methodology employed. The interest is in the conclusions reached in those areas and their implications for a legal framework for guarantees. The risk with this approach is that arguments are based on findings which may subsequently be proved incorrect. In order to minimise this risk, account has generally been taken of research which has been cited subsequently without its accuracy or correctness being doubted. However, with some of the recent research in the field of consumer complaining behaviour, this was not possible because this is very much an evolving area of study. The analysis in this book is therefore based on the state of the research in these fields in the autumn of 2002.

Considerable reassurance of the value of this approach is derived from Hugh Collins' recent examination of the law of contract (Collins, 1999). He too adopted an interdisciplinary approach in his exploration of the purposes and effects of the legal regulation of contractual relationships. He conceded that:

> It must be admitted, however, that [the available evidence about the effects of legal regulation of markets and contracts] is patchy and susceptible to rival interpretations ... (p.359).

The evidence relied on in this book leads to the claim that guarantees can have a particular function and that the legal framework should be designed to support this. Arguably, some of the specific evidence that is available in the context of manufacturers' guarantees may be as patchy and susceptible to rival interpretation as the evidence on the effects of the more general regulation of contracts relied on by Collins (1999). Yet, it is possible to identify evidence which supports the conclusions reached in this book, although it would have been desirable to have available more conclusive and less equivocal evidence. Still, it is submitted that the conclusions put forward in this book can be defended successfully, on the basis of a careful scrutiny of the available evidence.

1.1 Quality defects and consumer protection

In the introduction, it was noted that manufacturers' guarantees are given against defects in workmanship and materials which become apparent within a specific period after the consumer has bought the corresponding product. Guarantees are therefore given against quality defects. Before guarantees are examined further, it is necessary to examine two issues: first, there is the problem of quality defects generally, and second, the extent to which consumers are protected against such defects under relevant legislation. The objective for the remainder of this chapter is to analyse more closely the nature of quality defects and the problems consumers face in this context. Furthermore, the rights of consumers in English Law and under relevant provisions of E.C. Law will be examined. It is important to gain a fundamental understanding of these aspects to appreciate the context within which manufacturers' guarantees are provided. This will form the background for the analysis and discussion in the following chapters.

1.2 The nature of "quality defects"

1.2.1 What is "quality"?

One of the most common difficulties that consumers encounter is that something they have bought fails to work as promised. A new refrigerator may fail to chill food to the appropriate temperature, a new personal computer may refuse to boot up to allow an academic to complete an important paper, or a television set may not show a colour picture. Such problems are all grouped together under the broad heading of "quality defects". They are not uncommon. The Office of Fair Trading estimated that in 1999,[10] there were some 85.8 million consumer complaints and concerns in the United Kingdom per year (OFT, 2000, p.9). It was found that nearly half of those related to defective goods or substandard service.[11] More specifically, adding together the number of problems reported by individual categories (major household appliances; TV, videos, hi-fi, radios, personal stereos; computers; other household goods; new cars; second hand cars; camera, video cameras and camcorders), there were some 8.7 million problems with these product groups alone. Almost 52% of consumers who encountered a specific problem in 1999 reported that a product they had bought was in some way defective, i.e., either it did not work at all, or it did not work as specified.

There are therefore numerous instances of consumers having bought defective goods, but when can a product be said to have a quality defect? To answer this, it is necessary to examine the aspects of "quality".

Broadly speaking, there are two categories of "quality. The first relates to basic functionality. A product should perform as intended for a reasonable period of time. In this sense, quality defects could be a result of a lack of durability, or reliability, or both. These are two distinct concepts, and the difference is explained succinctly by Jarmin (1994):

> Reliability ... is the term used to describe the ability of a product to continue to perform its function or simply to work. It relates to the operating 'mechanism', whatever it may be. Typical mechanisms may be mechanical, electrical or increasingly electronic to name but three (p.60).

Thus, the "reliability" of a product is that the product will perform as it should. It refers to the basic functionality of a product.

> Durability [-] Often confused with reliability, this is how long a product or specific components of the product endure when used both normally and abnormally. It is about design and use of materials appropriate to the application and use of the product (*ibid.*).

"Durability" thus denotes the period during which a particular product can be used before it requires attention. Such attention may include routine maintenance, or the need to repair a component of the product which has deteriorated to the extent that the product as a whole can no longer function. However, the distinction between the two should not be overstated. A product which is not sufficiently durable is likely to have been defective when supplied to the consumer. This defect may be located in the "operating mechanism" and would then also be a reliability problem.[12] It is nevertheless important to appreciate that the two concepts are not identical.[13]

The second category of quality relates to product appearance and performance. Although durability and reliability are fundamental aspects of product quality, there are other matters that are also relevant, particularly in a consumer context. A consumer will not only be interested in the functionality of a product, but also its appearance and finish. A consumer is likely to expect a new product to be free from cosmetic defects, unless these have been pointed out to him before making a purchase.[14] Moreover, the performance of a product will matter. A car may well be suitable for driving from A to B, but if a consumer buys a top-of-the-range car, then he will expect more than simple functionality - he will wish to travel in comfort and have as pleasant a journey as possible (cf. *Rogers v Parish* (1987)).

1.2.2 What can cause a quality defect?

Quality defects can be the result of a problem at one or more of the following stages.[15] First, a particular product type may have inherent weaknesses in its design. As a result, every unit of this product may fail to perform as intended (a design defect). Second, there may be a small number out of many units of one product which fail to work as intended (a manufacturing defect). Third, a quality defect may be caused by the way the product is handled between leaving the producer and being delivered to the consumer.

Design defects may affect products made by a particular manufacturer, or they may affect a particular product sector. In the latter case, it may be that the technical knowledge in the particular sector is not yet sufficiently advanced to produce goods that will work without trouble. In essence, the design of the product is such that a breakdown is inevitable.

In the case of manufacturing defects, the product itself may generally be regarded as being of good quality, but there may be a problem with the particular unit purchased by a consumer. Such a manufacturing defect may only affect a small number of individual units within a product category. Thus, 999 out of 1,000 Brand A Model 1 MP-3 players perform as intended, whereas one does not. It is rarely possible to identify this problem prior to purchase. Consumers therefore buy products without knowing how reliable and durable the particular product will be. Often, quality defects will not manifest themselves until after the consumer has used the product for some time:

> If, for example, as part of the design of a washing machine, a component is used which will inevitably wear out quickly and require a repair, then the first the consumer will know of this defect in quality is when the machine breaks down (Collins, 1999, p.298).

The difficulty for most consumers, therefore, is that most product defects will only become known when the product has been used for some time. It is usually not possible to identify the likelihood of a product breakdown before purchase.

1.2.3 A problem for consumers: Imbalance of information about product quality

The predominant problem, therefore, is that consumers are unable to establish the level of quality of a particular product before purchase. This is because most consumer goods are "experience" goods rather than "search" goods. The attributes of "search" goods can be determined before purchase, whereas those of "experience" goods can only be established during use (Hadfield, Howse and Trebilcock, 1998, n.17). It is difficult, if not impossible, to discover quality defects in "experience goods". They are technically complex, and consumers are usually not able to examine the product and to assess its likely performance, or to discover any defects, simply by inspecting the product.

It is generally assumed that there exists an imbalance in the distribution of information about product quality between consumer and seller:

> Consumers may often lack adequate information on the reliability, durability and running costs of products, and sellers will generally have superior information on these matters (Ramsay, 1989, p.415).

Ramsay regards this lack of information on the consumer side regarding the durability and reliability of products as the primary problem in this area.

This lack of information can also produce a more general problem. In a seminal paper, Akerlof (1970) argued that the inability of consumers to identify whether a particular product is a low-quality or a high-quality item, together with the inability of sellers and manufacturers to communicate the level of quality of their products,[16] may result in a drop of the overall standard of quality in a particular product sector. If consumers cannot ascertain the level of quality before purchase, there is no incentive for a seller to offer high quality products. There is also no encouragement for manufacturers to avoid design and manufacturing defects. As a result, low-quality products ("lemons") will push high-quality products off the market.

This may lead to a downward spiral for product quality. Akerlof suggests that the overall level of quality in a market may decline if consumers cannot establish the quality of goods before purchase. However, in order to be able to establish whether a particular product is of high or low quality, consumers need to be aware of the general level of quality to be expected in a particular product market in order to compare a particular product to the general level of quality. This general level may decline because consumers cannot make this comparison.

Therefore, the inadequate distribution of information about product quality presents two challenges, one with regard to the quality to be expected of a particular unit, and a further one in respect of the overall level of quality that may be anticipated in a product sector.

There are sources from which consumers can obtain information about product quality. It is very common today for consumer associations to carry out product testing in order to provide general guidance to consumers with regard to the level of quality they might be able to expect from a particular product. In the United Kingdom, the Consumers' Association (CA) publish their findings in their monthly magazine *Which?*. Consumers can utilise such information to distinguish better between products of higher and lower quality. The informational imbalance regarding the overall level of quality may therefore be less significant today, and the main problem will be the difficulties consumers face in establishing the level of quality of a specific product they wish to acquire.

This informational imbalance has been a major factor in the adoption of rules to protect consumers in the sale of goods. It is generally recognised that consumers are entitled to expect that goods meet a certain level of quality. At the very least, products should be functional, but consumers may have expectations beyond reliability and durability. There are numerous factors that may influence the exact expectations of consumers, such as price, brand image and statements made in advertising. The law generally gives effect to these expectations through a flexible quality standard. In English law, this is the requirement that goods must be as described, of satisfactory quality and fit for a particular purpose required of the goods by the consumer. The Consumer Guarantees Directive requires goods to be in conformity with the contract, aspects of which are similar to those found in English law. Both refer to a number of variables which can be taken into account in determining whether a particular product has met the standard of quality required by law.

The legal rules relating to the quality of goods, both in English law, and under the E.C. Directive on Certain Aspects of the Sale of Consumer Goods and Associated Guarantees ("the Guarantees Directive") will be discussed in the next section. It is important to be aware of the extent to which these rules seek to address the problems associated with quality defects. Furthermore, throughout this book, consideration will be given to the relationship between these rules (which will be referred to as "statutory rights" for the sake of simplicity) and manufacturers' guarantees. It will be seen that both the statutory rights and guarantees offer protection to consumers against defects which exist when the consumer purchases a product. However, there are differences in the scope of protection, with guarantees largely limited to manufacturing defects, whereas the statutory rights may also include cosmetic defects as well as a failure to perform at a sufficiently high level.

1.3 An overview of the legal rights of consumers in relation to product quality

This section will present an overview of the legal rules on quality defects. This is divided into two parts. The first will outline the relevant provisions of the Guarantees Directive. The second part will examine the corresponding rules in English law, following the implementation of the Directive in December 2002. The discussion in this section is selective and does not provide an exhaustive and detailed account of the relevant rules, but rather a broad overview.[17]

1.4 The guarantees directive

In this section, the salient features of the Directive will be examined.

1.4.1 Scope

The Directive only applies to contracts for the sale of consumer goods[18] to consumers,[19] and only where goods are sold by a seller within the meaning of the Directive.[20] A "seller" is "any natural or legal person who, under a contract, sells consumer goods in the course of his trade, business or profession" (Article 1(2)(c)). This encompasses situations in which a person sells goods that are ordinarily part of that person's business. It seems that irregular or one-off transactions may therefore not be covered by the Directive.

1.4.2 The quality standard: Conformity with the contract

Article 2(1) of the Directive states that the seller must deliver goods to the consumer which are in conformity with the contract of sale. Article 2(2) provides four criteria for this assessment. Goods are presumed to be in conformity with the contract if they meet these criteria. It is important to note that this merely gives rise to a presumption of conformity. If there were further terms in the contract of sale regarding the quality of the goods, and the goods failed to comply with these, then the goods would not be in conformity with the contract *even if* they met the criteria set out in Article 2(2) (Beale and Howells, 1997, p.28). Conversely, it seems that if the goods fail to meet one of these criteria, they may not be in conformity with the contract. The four criteria will now be examined in turn.

The goods comply with the description given by the seller and possess the qualities of the goods which the seller has held out to the consumer as a sample or model

This criterion contains two separate elements: (a) if goods are sold by description, then they must correspond to that description and (b) if goods are sold by sample, then they must conform to that sample.[21] It is, however, not clear if "description" is to be interpreted narrowly to include, e.g., only the essential characteristics of the goods, and aspects which a consumer could reasonably be expected to rely on in making a purchase.

Furthermore, the description has to be given "by the seller". However, in most consumer transactions, the relevant description will be printed on the packaging and therefore be given by the manufacturer. Thus, if a consumer bought a CD ROM Drive described on the packaging as a "48-speed drive" and the device actually delivered was only a 20-speed drive, there might not be a lack of conformity under this provision.[22] It is not clear why there is an express reference to the seller. In its current form, it is unlikely to be of much relevance in consumer transactions, as the relevant description will, in most cases, be given by the manufacturer.[23]

The goods are fit for any particular purpose for which the consumer requires them and which he made known to the seller at the time of conclusion of the contract and which the seller has accepted

If a consumer has a particular purpose in mind, and he makes this known to the seller, then the product he buys should be suitable for that purpose. Thus, the consumer makes known the purpose and the seller must accept that purpose. This seems to require that the consumer states his purpose expressly, and the seller must similarly state expressly that he thinks the particular product is suitable for that purpose. However, it seems that there could be implied acceptance by the seller if the seller agrees to the sale, being aware of the consumer's particular needs. There is no requirement, however, that is must have been reasonable for the consumer to rely on the seller's acceptance. This is therefore a purely factual criterion, and only requires an assessment of what happened when the relevant sale took place.

The goods are fit for the purposes for which goods of the same type are normally used

This provision emphasises general fitness for normal use. Although only a presumption, a product is unlikely to be in conformity with the contract if it is not fit for all its normal uses.

The goods show the quality and performance which are normal in goods of the same type and which the consumer can reasonably expect, given the nature of the goods and taking into account any public statements on the specific characteristics of the goods made about them by the seller, the producer or his representative, particularly in advertising or on labelling

This aspect of conformity reflects the notion that goods should conform to the consumers' reasonable (or legitimate) expectations (Micklitz, 1997) and gives express recognition to the fact that consumer expectations regarding the quality of products are shaped by public statements, notably advertising, brochures and catalogues. However, under Article 2(4), a seller will not be liable for a lack of conformity based on public statements if he is able to show that:

1. he was not, and could not reasonably have been, aware of the statement in question. This could happen where the producer had made claims in a regional advertising campaign of which the consumer was aware, but not the seller
2. by the time of conclusion of the contract the statement had been corrected, or
3. the decision to buy the consumer goods could not have been influenced by the statement.

The burden of proof is on the seller. It may be very difficult for a seller to show that the consumer was not influenced by a particular statement. It may be assumed that most of the "public statements" referred to in this paragraph will be advertisements, and the dominant purpose of advertising is to encourage consumers to buy the product advertised (see generally Ramsay, 1996) and therefore intended to influence consumers.

There is no set of criteria that expand on which aspects to focus on in assessing the quality a consumer may reasonably be entitled to expect.[24] It is likely that domestic courts applying the implementing provision of this paragraph will have regard to other factors such as freedom from minor defects, safety or durability. Moreover, the Directive does not expressly refer to the price of the goods, nor the circumstances surrounding the contract of sale, as aspects of establishing conformity. This is unfortunate - consideration of the price may, for example, raise the standard to be met by a product if it is particularly expensive.

The Directive also acknowledges that the consumer cannot legitimately expect a product to meet the quality standard if the consumer is provided with information which makes it clear that the product is defective in some way. If the consumer is aware of the lack of conformity, or could not reasonably have been unaware of such a lack, then the seller will similarly not be liable (Article 2(3)). This provision covers the situation where the seller informs the consumer that there is a problem with the particular product, or where there is a notice next to the product informing the consumer of the lack of conformity and which the consumer can be expected to have read.

Furthermore, if the lack of conformity is the result of the materials (such as fabric to be made into a suit) supplied by the consumer, then the seller will similarly not be liable.

This provision is significant, because it reveals that the statutory rights of consumers only operate to the extent that the consumer was completely unaware of the standard of quality of a particular product. Once the consumer is made aware of a shortcoming, he cannot complain about this subsequently. The Directive therefore creates a basic quality standard, but this can be displaced by disclosing to the consumer any quality defects that exist.[25]

1.4.3 The remedial scheme[26]

Only the final seller is liable to the consumer for any lack of conformity (Article 3(1)). The seller is liable for a lack of conformity that becomes apparent within two years[27] from delivery of the goods. This is not a limitation period, but rather a period during which the lack of conformity must manifest itself.[28] The lack of conformity must have existed at the time of delivery. There is a presumption that any lack of conformity which manifests itself within six months of delivery of the goods existed at the time of delivery unless this presumption is incompatible with the nature of the goods or the nature of the lack of conformity (Article 5(3)). Member States may provide that, a consumer must inform the seller of the lack of conformity within a period of two months from the date on which he discovered this lack of conformity.[29]

Recital 12 to the Directive acknowledges that the seller can offer the consumer any of the four remedies of repair, replacement, price reduction or rejection, but if there is no agreement between seller and consumer, the remedial scheme in Article 3 will apply. In essence, this provides for a two-stage hierarchy of remedies. Thus, in the first instance, the consumer will be able to ask the seller to repair[30] or replace the goods free of charge.[31] Either of these can only be provided if it is not impossible or disproportionate. A remedy will be disproportionate if it imposes costs on the seller which, in comparison with the alternative remedy, are unreasonable, taking into account the value the goods would have if there were no lack of conformity, the significance of the lack of conformity, and whether the alternative remedy could be completed without significant inconvenience to the consumer.

The wording of the Directive indicates that repair and replacement are the only two remedies to which the "proportionality and impossibility" tests apply. These are applied in order to establish when one or the other remedy is available. However, it does not seem to apply when determining whether price reduction/rescission should be favoured over repair/replacement.

When applied, the test reveals that the favoured remedy under this regime is "repair". Repair would only then not be available if it was deemed "impossible". Some goods are so defective as to be beyond economic repair. Others may by the nature of their design be impossible to repair. For example, a faulty disposable camera would not be repaired, but a replacement would be offered instead. Repair may also be impossible where goods fail to meet their description. Again, replacement would be the appropriate remedy. Yet, the circumstances in which repair would be "impossible" are limited. Replacement would be possible in most cases, but there are exceptions to this, as well. Recital 16 to the Directive gives the example of second-hand goods. It states that "the specific nature of second hand goods makes it generally impossible to replace them". It is important to appreciate that this is only a general statement of principle, not an outright exclusion of second-hand goods from the remedy of replacement. A further example for when "replacement" may be impossible is offered by *Alexander v Comet Group* (1995). In this case, it was not possible to replace a faulty product (under a manufacturer's guarantee) because the particular model had been discontinued, and the model that came closest to the faulty product was significantly more expensive. However, it was possible to repair the product. There will, therefore, only be limited circumstances when either remedy will be "impossible".

The focus is likely to be on whether one of the remedies, compared to the alternative, is disproportionate. The overriding criterion appears to be that of cost. In particular, it is the cost to the seller, rather than the consumer, of providing the particular remedy, as confirmed in Recital 11:

> In order to determine whether the costs are unreasonable, the costs of one remedy should be significantly higher than the costs of the other.

There will be cases of low-cost items where replacement would be less expensive than repair, but in most cases, the cost of repairing a product will be lower than that of providing a replacement. If a defective product is replaced, the seller will be left with the defective item, and although it may be possible to repair this, he would not be able to sell it at its full price. It seems that repair is more likely to be proportionate than replacement, and that is why it has to be regarded as the primary remedy.

It is further provided that any repair or replacement should be completed within a reasonable time and without any significant inconvenience to the consumer, taking account of the nature of the goods and the purpose for which the consumer required the goods. A factor to be taken into account here may, for example, be the time it might take to repair a particular product. If a consumer had to wait for two months for a repair of his washing machine, this would undoubtedly be a significant inconvenience, and a replacement washing machine should be provided instead.

If the seller is unable to repair the product or provide a replacement without significant inconvenience to the consumer, then it would be appropriate to consider price reduction or rescission as alternative remedies.

Moreover, if neither remedy produces goods which are in conformity, then the consumer may also accept a reduction in the price of the goods, or return the goods and obtain a full refund (rescission). This may also be the case where the consumer is not "entitled" to repair or replacement, e.g., if both are impossible, or where the seller is taking longer than a reasonable time to provide a remedy. Thus, if repair of a product takes more than a few days, and a replacement product is not available, then the consumer may ask to have the contract rescinded instead. However, rescission will not be available where the lack of conformity is minor (Article 3(6)).[32] In that case, the only remedy that is available to the consumer is price reduction because repair or replacement will also not be available - if they were, then there would be no question of allowing rescission of the contract.

1.5 The quality standard in English law

This part outlines the quality standard and the relevant remedies in English law. In December 2002, the Sale and Supply of Goods to Consumers Regulations 2002 ("SSGCR") were adopted to implement the Guarantees Directive. The Regulations only made a minor change to the quality standard itself, and introduced a new Part 5A into the Sale of Goods Act 1979 ("SoGA") to incorporate the remedial regime in Article 3 of the Directive.

1.5.1 Goods must be as described

SoGA implies three terms relating to product quality into a contract of sale with a consumer. Under section 13 (1):

> Where there is a contract for the sale of goods by description, there is an implied term that the goods will correspond with the description.

However, the term will only cover aspects of the description which have influenced the consumer in some way in buying the particular product - the consumer must have relied on a particular description (*Harlingdon & Leinster Ltd. v Christopher Hull Fine Art Ltd.* (1990)). It has furthermore been held that the description must relate to the commercial characteristics of the goods (*Ashington Piggeries Ltd. v Christopher Hill Ltd.* (1972)) and, more precisely, identify an essential aspect of the goods (*Reardon Smith Line Ltd. v Yngvar Hansen-Tangen* (1976)).

It has been held that the purchase of goods in a shop is still a sale by description (*Grant v Australian Knitting Mills Ltd.* (1936)), and this is so even where the consumer selects the goods himself (see s.13(3) SoGA). It seems likely that this term is of lesser relevance in shop-based consumer transactions than in contracts concluded at a distance, e.g., through mail-order stores or internet purchases. In a shop, a consumer will usually be able to tell if a product meets its description, but with goods bought on-line, the consumer will not know this until these have been delivered (and usually paid for).

1.5.2 Goods must be of "satisfactory quality"

Perhaps the most significant term on quality is that implied by section 14(2) SoGA. This states that:

> Where the seller sells goods in the course of a business, there is an implied term that the goods supplied under the contract are of satisfactory quality.

This term is only implied into contracts of sale where the seller is dealing in the course of a business. Any sale by a business is done in the course of that business, even if the sale is irregular or an isolated transaction (*Stevenson v Rogers* (1999)). If the seller is not a business, the term that the goods must be of satisfactory quality is not implied into the contract of sale - thus, goods sold by one private individual to another do not have comply with this term.

When are goods of satisfactory quality? S.14(2A) explains that:

> Goods are of satisfactory quality if they meet the standard that a reasonable person would regard as satisfactory, taking account of any description of the goods, the price (if relevant) and all the other relevant circumstances.

The test of whether goods are of satisfactory quality is therefore a flexible one. It is an objective assessment - would a reasonable person, aware of the circumstances of the sale, the description of the goods and the price charged for them, regard the goods delivered to the consumer as satisfactory? It seems that this is assessed generally rather than exclusively from the perspective of the consumer (Oughton and Lowry, 2000, p.182).

It is first necessary to consider how the goods have been described. Thus, goods which are sold as "shop-soiled" or "second-hand" will inevitably give rise to lower expectations of quality than goods described as "brand-new". Indeed, products regarded as luxury brands may give rise to higher expectations of quality than similar goods from more "ordinary" brands (*Rogers v Parish* (1987) - a 'Range Rover' could be expected to be of a higher standard of quality).

Frequently, the description of the goods will also be reflected in their price. Second-hand or shop-soiled goods will normally be sold at a lower price than brand-new goods. Furthermore, goods made by some manufacturers will have a higher price than those made by others, which may reflect a higher standard of quality. Indeed, a consumer may expect a higher overall level of quality if the price of a product made by a particular manufacturer is higher than that of competing products.[33] However, the price is unlikely to be relevant where goods are reduced during an end-of-season sale period (Oughton and Lowry, 2000, p.185).

In order further to facilitate the application of this test, the Act refers to a number of factors which can be taken into account in determining whether goods are of satisfactory quality. Section 14(2B) starts with the general statement that one aspect of quality is the state and condition of the goods. This reflects the fact that the standard of satisfactory quality is not limited to functionality, but covers other aspects of the goods, such as their general appearance. For example, a brand-new top-of-the-range hi-fi system which is badly scratched and soiled would not be in a condition that could be described as satisfactory, even if it still worked properly.

The section then goes on to list a number factors which may also be taken into account in determining whether goods are of satisfactory quality. This is not an exhaustive list, and these factors should be taken into account in appropriate circumstances. There may be factors other than those listed in this section that may be relevant.

Fitness for all the purposes for which goods of the kind in question are commonly supplied If a product has a number of common purposes, then a consumer can expect the product to be fit for all of those purposes. This factor requires a case-by-case consideration of the purposes for which a particular product is commonly supplied. A consumer may have a different opinion regarding the purposes for which a particular product is commonly supplied than the seller or manufacturer.[34] However, if a seller emphasises that a product is not suitable for one of the common purposes for which the type of product would be supplied, a consumer would presumably be unable to claim that the product was not of satisfactory quality.

Appearance and finish This factor falls into the second category of quality identified above.[35] It recognises that consumers look for more than mere functionality in the goods they buy. Thus, a consumer who bought a new suit and discovered that it has a stain that cannot be removed would be able to claim that the suit is not of satisfactory quality, even though he could still wear it and its functionality was not significantly impaired.

Freedom from minor defects This criterion also extends beyond mere functionality. Some products may have minor problems when first used, which could be repaired relatively easily. Yet, depending on other factors such as price and the type of product in question, even such minor problems may render a product as not of satisfactory quality. A number of cases involving motor cars illustrate this point: in *Rogers v Parish* (1987), a new Range Rover suffered from engine noise, leaking oil seals and some scratches to the paintwork. Although the car could still be driven, it was held that it did not meet the quality standard. In *Bernstein v Pamsons Motors* (1987) a car engine had seized after 140 miles because of an obstruction in the oil supply to the camshaft. Although easily repairable, it was held that the car was not of merchantable (now satisfactory) quality.[36]

However, even if a product a consumer has bought is not free from minor defects, it may be that this minor defect does not render the product unsatisfactory. This may be where the defect in question can easily be remedied by the consumer himself, e.g., by tightening the nuts and bolts on a bicycle. In contrast, if there are several minor defects, all of which could be remedied in this way, the product may nevertheless be regarded as unsatisfactory.

Safety Although product safety is a topic treated independently of product quality (see Cartwright, 2001, ch.5), the fact that a product is not safe may also make it unsatisfactory. In *Bernstein v Pamsons Motors* (1987), the defect was minor and easily repairable, yet the consequences could have been disastrous.

Durability The final aspect mentioned in s.14 returns to the first category of quality, functionality.[37] In some circumstances, a lack of durability may therefore make a product unsatisfactory. However, this factor does not constitute a durability requirement, because it does not require products to last for a specific time. Rather, it may be relevant if a product deteriorates more quickly than would ordinarily be expected. It may be difficult to establish when this is so, although in *Thain v Anniesland Trade Centre* (1997), the court observed that a new car could be expected to work trouble-free at least for the duration of the manufacturer's guarantee.

Public statements In accordance with the requirements of the Guarantees Directive, new sections 14(2D) - (2F) provide that public statements made by a seller or producer about the specific characteristics of goods are also to be regarded as relevant circumstances for the purposes of the satisfactory quality test. However, this will not apply if the seller was not aware of the statement, or if it had been corrected, or if it did not affect the decision to buy the goods.

There will not be a breach of the implied term that goods must be of satisfactory quality where the matter which would usually render a product unsatisfactory is specifically drawn to the consumer's attention before he buys the product, or where the consumer examines the product before purchase and where this examination should have revealed the defect (s.14(2C)). This provision confirms that the statutory rules are generally there to compensate for informational inequalities between seller and consumer. If the consumer is made aware of a quality shortcoming, he will therefore not be able subsequently to claim that there has been a breach of the implied terms.

The assessment of product quality under the SoGA thus depends on the factual circumstances of each particular case. Indeed, the court in *Thain v Anniesland Trade Centre* (1997) noted as much in saying that "cases relating to quality tend ... to turn on their own facts". This flexibility makes it very difficult to predict the point at which a particular product ceases to be of satisfactory quality.

1.5.3 Goods must be fit for a particular purpose

Finally, brief mention should be made of s.14(3), which implies a term into the contract of sale that if a consumer makes known to the seller a particular purpose for which goods are required, the goods are fit for that purpose. However, the consumer must have relied on the seller's skill and judgment, and it must have been reasonable for him to have done so. It may be unreasonable for a consumer to rely on the seller's opinion where the latter disclaims any expertise in relation to the consumer's request.

1.5.4 The remedies

SoGA originally provided two remedies: the consumer had the right to return the goods to the retailer and obtain a refund, and he was entitled to claim damages. These remedies continue to be available after the implementation of the Guarantees Directive, and will be examined first.

The implied terms in s.13-14 are classed as conditions. If there is a breach of condition, the consumer is entitled under s.11 (4) SoGA to reject the goods and to treat the contract as repudiated. However, these rights are separate, and the consumer can reject the goods without treating the contract as repudiated (Bradgate, 1995; Bradgate and White, 1995). A consumer who decides to reject the goods can therefore in effect give the seller a further opportunity to perform by providing replacement goods or repairing the original goods. If the consumer rejects the goods and elects to treat the contract as repudiated,[38] the effect is to put the seller in the same position as if he had not delivered the goods to the consumer at all. The consumer's claim for damages will be based on the seller's failure to deliver the goods (s.51 SoGA), and he will be entitled to a full refund of the purchase price.

However, a consumer will no longer be able to reject the goods if he accepts them, or is deemed to have accepted them (s.11(4) and ss.34-35). However, this will only be the case where the consumer has had an opportunity to examine the goods. A consumer will also be deemed to have accepted the goods once a reasonable time has lapsed. Whether a sufficient period of time has passed so as to deem the consumer to have accepted the goods will depend on the nature and complexity of the goods (Per Rougier J. in *Bernstein v Pamson Motors (Golders Green) Ltd.* (1987)). However, the fact that a consumer uses the goods although they are not of satisfactory quality and requires the seller to repair any defects will not be regarded as acceptance (s.35(6)(a)), and the consumer would not lose his right of rejection because of this.

Once a consumer is deemed to have accepted the goods, a breach of the implied terms will be treated as a breach of warranty only. As a consequence, the consumer will not be able to reject the goods, nor will he be able to treat the contract as repudiated. The consumer can still claim damages based on the difference between the value of the goods at the time of delivery, and the value the goods would have had, had they been in compliance with the implied terms (s.53(3)). The measure of damages will usually reflect the cost of repairing the product, but a consumer may also claim for losses which directly result from the breach of the implied terms.[39]

Alternatively, the consumer can set up the breach by the seller (which will only be treated as a breach of warranty) in diminution or extinction of his liability for the price. Thus, the consumer has the option to set-off the lower value of the goods as delivered against the price he is liable to pay under the contract of sale, which is akin to asking for a reduction of the purchase price.

A new Part 5A was introduced by the Sale and Supply of Goods to Consumers Regulations 2002. This applies to consumer transactions only (s.48A(1) SoGA). It replicates the remedial regime in Article 3 of the Guarantees Directive, albeit with some crucial differences. Thus, s.48B sets out the consumer's entitlement to repair or replacement, and s.48C provides for price reduction and rescission. The proportionality test to decide between repair and replacement can be found in S.48B(3). However, in contrast to the Directive, s.48B(3)(c) extends the proportionality test in that repair and replacement may not be available where these would be disproportionate compared to price reduction or rescission under s.48C. It is submitted that by giving this extended scope to the proportionality test, Article 3 has been incorrectly transposed into English law. This is because s.48B(3)(c) undermines the balance between the various remedies defined in Article 3 of the Directive.

S.48D deals with the important problem of the relationship between the original and the new remedies. Both original and new remedies are available concurrently, although a consumer who asks for a remedy under Part 5A can benefit from the six month "reversed burden" (s.48A(3)). However, a consumer who seeks to terminate for breach of condition will have to prove that there was a breach at the time of sale. S.48D(1) provides that a consumer who has asked for a Part 5A remedy must give the seller a reasonable opportunity to provide this before he can exercise the right to terminate under s.11(4). It will remain to be seen if this combination of original and new remedies will work without difficulty in practice.

1.5.5 Only the final seller is liable to a consumer

It must be emphasised that both SoGA and the Directive impose liability only on the final seller. It may seem surprising that a manufacturer is not directly liable to a final consumer. In most cases, the quality defect will be a manufacturing or design defect, and will therefore be the responsibility of the manufacturer, rather than the seller. Furthermore, the consumer is likely to have been influenced in his purchasing decision by the reputation of the particular brand - which is that of the manufacturer. Indeed, many consumers are encouraged to "shop around" for the best price for a product made by a particular manufacturer (Beale, 1996, p.141). In addition, if the manufacturer were directly liable, there would be an added incentive to improve overall product quality in order to reduce the number of instances when a remedy would have to be provided.[40]

Yet, there are advantages to holding the final seller liable. The seller will usually be geographically more accessible to the consumer. Furthermore, the seller is likely to have trained customer service staff, who will be able to deal with consumer complaints effectively. And finally, as noted earlier, the seller may act as a conduit to pass the claim along the chain of contracts, which would result in the person actually responsible for the defect absorbing the loss.

The Directive recognises that this may cause unfairness, particularly where the seller has done nothing to the goods in question. It is therefore provided that the seller may bring a claim against the person in the distribution chain who is actually responsible for the lack of conformity (Article 4). In most cases, this will be the producer himself. However, this right of action is limited in that the conditions of exercising this right as well as the persons against whom this right may, in fact, be exercised, is a question to be determined by Member State law. English law would follow the contracts along the distribution chain, with the result that the seller would only be able to claim against his immediate supplier.[41] Article 4 has not been implemented specifically into English law.

1.6 Evaluation: Consumer protection law and product quality

At the start of this chapter, it was noted that quality defects are a common problem for many consumers. In the case of most consumer products, consumers lack adequate information about product quality. The statutory rules provide some mitigation in that the flexible quality standard reflects the notion that consumers can legitimately expect a certain standard of quality. Remedies are made available if a consumer has bought a product that does not meet this standard.

The statutory standard does not specify a particular standard of quality; rather, it protects consumers against quality defects of which they were not aware at the time of purchase (cf. Hedley, 2001, p.123). A consumer cannot claim that a product does not comply with the statutory standard if the shortcomings complained of by the consumer were drawn to his attention before he decided to purchase the goods.[42] Indeed, because of its flexibility, the statutory standard cannot set a product-specific minimum quality standard. Although it seeks to reflect the expectations of consumers, it is phrased in very general terms. This is inevitable with a standard that applies to the full range of consumer products. A consequence is that it is difficult for consumers to know what exactly to expect of a particular product. Court decisions may offer some guidance as to whether a particular product reached the required level of quality, but there are few reported cases, and most of these involve expensive consumer goods such as cars. Bourgoignie concluded that:

> Court decisions ... lack uniformity, thus creating major uncertainties for buyers and suppliers as to the way risks of defects and cost of repair will be allocated between themselves. Most important, the judicial treatment is made available only to consumers who actually resort to courts in order to solve their [quality] disputes; its effect on the vast majority of consumers is nil (1979, p.268).

Neither the "satisfactory quality" standard, nor the "conformity" standard, therefore help to provide objective guidance on the minimum level of quality to be expected in a product market. This problem is highlighted by Collins thus:

> The general standard of 'satisfactory quality' becomes particularised to an individual case during trial. It is always arguable that another case on slightly different facts should receive a different treatment. The standard now becomes so detailed in its application that it still cannot serve as a guide to market behaviour (Collins, 1999, p.293).

And further:

> Regulation by general standards through particularised adjudication ... is also likely to be ineffective, because it fails to provide determinate standards that can guide participants in the market (ibid., p.295).

Indeed, Adams and Brownsword (1988), in commenting on the Law Commission's Report that lead to the adoption of the satisfactory quality test, observed that the list of factors to be taken into account[43] may "encourage sellers to ensure that their goods are of [satisfactory] quality" (p.489), but then it is possible for a seller to sell goods of low quality provided that he discloses this to the consumer (see also Hedley, 2001). The real use of the statutory scheme would therefore be in the resolution of disputes. The flexibility of the standard and potential for different outcomes in similar cases leads Adams and Brownsword to conclude that:

> the appropriate form for the Act is discretion, not absolute rule; and the principal addressees of the Act are those who are charged with settling sale of goods disputes (p.490).

The statutory quality standard (and the remedies) will therefore be relevant mainly for consumers seeking redress from the seller who sold the faulty product. However, if the seller fails to provide the redress sought, a consumer may be left without any redress. A consumer has, in theory, the opportunity to go to court, but is unlikely to do so.[44]

1.7 A second problem for consumers: Obtaining redress for faulty products

Ramsay (1989) identified a second problem: consumers may find it difficult to obtain redress, should they encounter a quality defect. It was seen above that the statutory quality standard takes account of a number of variables. A consumer may consider that, on the basis of these variables, a particular product he has bought does not meet the level of quality set by this standard, whereas a seller believes that it does. A seller who is dealing with a consumer who complains about a faulty product may therefore refuse to provide a remedy.[45]

Where such disagreement cannot be resolved, or where the seller fails to provide an adequate remedy, a consumer may consider either going to court, or to use an alternative dispute resolution (ADR) mechanism, such as mediation or arbitration.[46] Briefly, arbitration is a process whereby a third party will hear the consumer's complaint and the seller's response and then hand down a binding decision. Arbitration is not dissimilar to court proceedings, but operates outside the normal court system. Mediation is less formal and involves a third party as an intermediary to facilitate a negotiated settlement between the consumer and the seller. The vast majority of consumers who, having encountered a problem, decide to take action will do so informally and without the help of a third party.[47]

Although the statutory standard may counterbalance the informational inequalities between consumer and seller, it does not inevitably resolve the problem of obtaining redress in practice.

1.7.1 Empirical evidence: Consumers' responses to problems

Although formalised redress mechanisms are in place to resolve disputes over product quality, a number of surveys conclude that the vast majority of consumers try to find a solution informally. For present purpose, it is not necessary to examine these formalised mechanisms. Instead, it is more useful to examine how consumers actually react when they have encountered a problem. This section will therefore review recent empirical research on how consumers deal with problems. This analysis will provide important information about consumer behaviour, and its implications are going to be of fundamental relevance in identifying the function of guarantees.[48]

1.7.2 An analysis of recent empirical research in the United Kingdom

Genn (1999) reported the findings of a major survey undertaken in the United Kingdom in the late-1990s. The objective of this survey was to discover the attitudes of the general public to the legal system as a whole. It examined what people did when faced with a problem in one or more of a broad range of different categories of legal problems.[49] Only problems which could be classed as "justiciable" were considered.[50] The study covered instances of such problems over a period of five years preceding the study. One of the general findings was that "consumer problems"[51] were dealt with differently from all other categories examined in this study. This section will examine the findings on "consumer problems" only.

Consumer problems occurred most frequently of all problems. It is estimated that there were about 153 consumer problems per 1,000 adults (p.31), which would be the equivalent of 6,153,132 consumer problems over a five-year period.[52] So what did consumers do when they were faced with a problem?

Some 4% of consumers who had encountered a problem did nothing at all. In about half of those cases, the reason for not taking any action was that the problem was no longer regarded as one, or that it had sorted itself out. Some 17% of those who did nothing consciously decided not to pursue the matter, and another 17% felt that nothing could be done about the problem, or that there was no prospect of successfully doing something.

Most consumers thus took some sort of action to remedy the problem. Around 60% of consumers with a problem took matters into their own hands and did not obtain any outside advice. Most of these consumers (just under three-quarters (73%)) contacted the other party (i.e., the trader), either in writing or orally.

A little over one third (36%) of consumers with a problem obtained advice, which was the lowest rate of advice-seeking for all problem types considered in this study.[53] Of those seeking advice 80% had already attempted to resolve the problem themselves by contacting the other party, but either they had not been able to make contact, or their attempts had been unsuccessful. Around two-thirds of those seeking advice consulted one source only, with almost one-third seeking advice from two or three sources. Only a small minority sought advice from more than three sources.

Initial contact was made with Citizens Advice Bureaux (CABx) by 30% of those who sought advice, solicitors by 21%, trading standards or other consumer advice offices by 14%, insurance companies by 8% or trade associations by 6%. Those consumers who consulted more than one source were usually referred to a trading standards department or a solicitor by a CAB. In total, 18% of all those with a problem obtained legal advice, 12% consulted a CAB and 11% a trading standards department, and 4% contacted a trade association.

Those seeking advice primarily wished to get advice on how to solve the problem (73%), and less than half (47%) sought advice about their legal rights. In a significant number of cases, therefore, specific legal rights of consumers were not an issue.

The advice given to consumers was as follows: 82% were told that something could be done about the problem, most commonly by contacting the other side directly (57%). Threatening legal action was suggested in less than a quarter of cases (23%), and commencing legal proceedings was recommended in only 6% of cases. Mediation and Conciliation were only recommended in 2% of cases.[54] No respondent reported going to mediation (Genn, 1999, p.40). There was also no indication that consumers may have utilised other forms of alternative dispute resolution. Genn suggested that:

> the low rate of advice to take cases to mediation or conciliation demonstrates the slight impact that these alternatives to traditional methods of dispute resolution are currently having on advisers' thinking (p.109).

Legal action was threatened in 18% of all cases, but in only 3% of all cases a court was involved.

Finally, most consumers who took action about a consumer problem were higher income earners, and had better educational qualifications, although some 20% of all consumers reporting a problem had no educational qualifications at all.

The broad conclusion that may be drawn from this analysis is that most consumers with a problem try to resolve matters themselves, and only where this fails will they obtain advice. Less than 1% of cases came to a court hearing, and consumer problems were the least likely to end up in the courts.[55]

The fact that consumers are not as likely to obtain advice as people with other problems may reflect "that the issues involved may be relatively uncomplicated and have less serious implications" (Genn, 1999, p.142). This is probably correct - many instances of faulty goods, for example, are not difficult to identify and to remedy, and are unlikely to have serious long-term consequences. This may be why attempts at informal dispute resolution feature more prominently with consumer disputes.

Consumers were the most successful in coming to some kind of agreement to resolve the problem. This was so in over half (56%) of all cases.[56] In contrast, in 40% of all consumer cases, the problem remained unresolved. This was the case whether or not advice had been obtained. Genn concludes that "it therefore seems that if a direct approach fails, considerable effort is needed to achieve a resolution" (p.157). It is encouraging that 48% of consumers who resolved their dispute without assistance reported that they felt empowered by this.

These figures may be compared with those reported by the OFT (2000). There, it was found that consumers had taken some form of action in around 80% of cases. It was also reported that consumers dealt with their problems directly, without seeking advice or help. In 2.7% of cases, consumers took legal advice; in 2.1% of cases, consumers contacted their local Trading Standards Department (TSD) and in 1.7% of cases, consumers contacted a Citizens' Advice Bureau. The OFT speculates a consumer is more likely to seek advice or to complain to TSDs where the problem is of a high enough value to make the process of formal complaining worthwhile (OFT 2000, para 5.20). The OFT by way of example refer to the used car sector:

> An excellent example of this is the number of reported problems concerning used cars, which amount to an estimated 0.7% of all consumer problems (612,000 out of 85.8 million) but amount to 10.2% of all the cases reported to TSDs in 1998 (92,0000 our of 899,000) (Para 5.20).

The OFT figures vary significantly in respect of the extent to which consumers obtained advice and help. This can be explained on the basis that Genn's study was limited to justiciable problems, whereas the OFT study concerned consumer problems more generally. Not all consumer problems may give rise to a legal cause of action. Nevertheless, a broad trend that most consumers do not involve formal dispute resolution mechanisms can be made out.

Most recently, the DTI (2001a) reported findings which broadly confirm those by Genn (1999) and the OFT (2000). The DTI noted that 38% of all consumers had reason to complain in 2000 and that only 10% of those consumers did not make a complaint. It is further reported that younger and better educated consumers complained more than older consumers. Out of those who complained, the vast majority (87%) did so directly to the supplier of faulty goods. Out of those who took further action after their initial complaint had been unsuccessful, 20% contacted a third party for advice. The findings do not identify the percentage of cases making use of a dispute resolution scheme or the courts.[57]

1.7.3 Implications

These findings are of concern to the extent that the "access to justice" problem is regarded as one that primarily focuses on the institutions for dispute resolution. Consumer problems simply do not end up in court, regardless of the court procedure that would be available. This may be because:

> an individual consumer contemplating litigation is normally faced with a formidably well-organised and experienced opponent and frequently, the amount involved cannot justify the expense and trouble of litigation (Tur, 1982, p.137).

Thus, the fear of costs may provide one explanation of why consumers are more likely to seek redress informally, rather than through formal procedures. Similarly, alternative forms of dispute resolution are not popular with consumers at present.

It may be noted that the lack of utilisation of such procedures is not the result of a lack of awareness. The DTI's *Performance Monitor* (DTI, 2001b) demonstrates that consumer awareness of dispute resolution procedures and sources of advice is high, but that utilisation remains low.

Instead, for present purposes, the findings by Genn, the DTI and the OFT are important for a rather different reason. The results of Genn's study (as confirmed by the DTI and the OFT) strongly suggest that consumers take matters into their own hands.[58] Thus, in every-day life, when a consumer is faced with a problem, the most likely response is to complain without seeking advice. It is submitted that this is something which must be taken into account more seriously when framing consumer protection measures. This is particularly so because the study described by Genn concentrated on problems which had been classed objectively as "justiciable", and are therefore more than banalities about which some people may complain in the hope of gaining some sort of advantage.

1.8 Conclusion

This chapter has provided the background that is necessary for the discussion in the remainder of this book. It was demonstrated that there are two main problems for consumers in the sphere of product quality: (a) the inability to gauge product quality before purchase and (b) the difficulty of obtaining redress if a product falls short of an acceptable level of quality. The relevant legal rules create a flexible standard that reflects the expectations of consumers that products should be of satisfactory quality, but does not lay down any definite requirements.

The statutory standard is therefore only of limited help in addressing one of the main difficulties in the context of product quality, i.e., the divergence in the amount of information available to the consumer about the quality of a particular product before purchase. It encourages disclosure of faults and imposes liability on the seller only where there has not been sufficient disclose of these faults (Hedley, 2001). However, consumers still cannot be sure that a particular product will be of satisfactory quality until they have bought and used the product. Furthermore, with most consumer products, the seller (and even the manufacturer) may not be aware that a particular items is defective, because many defects are latent and may only manifest themselves after a period of using the product.

Having thus examined the nature of quality defects and the extent to which relevant legislation seeks to protect consumers against such defects, it is now possible to consider how manufacturers' guarantees fit into this picture. In particular, it will be considered whether guarantees could help to reduce the informational imbalance between consumer and seller/manufacturer, as well as whether guarantees could make it easier for consumers to obtain redress.

It has often been suggested that manufacturers could provide a better indication of product quality through the use of guarantees:

> [Guarantees] seem like an incredibly useful device for getting around asymmetric information about product quality. There are many products sold with [guarantees], but I find it surprising that they are not used even more often (Grossman, 1981, p.479).

Guarantees could therefore be used to reduce the informational imbalance. This will be analysed in depth in chapter 3. The contention that guarantees reflect product quality has been very influential, and it is readily assumed that there is a link between a guarantee and the quality to be expected of the product it covers. Most legal frameworks for guarantees therefore try to promote this link in some way.

Yet, the main theme of this book is that the link between guarantees and product quality may have been overstated. Instead, it will be argued that guarantees may provide an informal redress mechanism for dealing with instances of faulty products. If this is so, then guarantees could be used to help consumers obtain a remedy if they have bought a product which has a quality defect.

Before these suggestions can be considered further, it is necessary to take a closer look at the form and legal status of manufacturers' guarantees and to examine the problems that have been identified. This will be done in the next chapter.

Notes

1 The term "manufacturer" is used to refer to the person who actually makes a particular consumer product. It is used interchangeably with the word "producer" in this book. Similarly, the words "seller" and "retailer" are used interchangeably to refer to the person who sells a product to a consumer. On occasion, the word "trader" is used when it is not important whether the consumer is dealing with a seller or manufacturer.

2 For present purposes, the term "consumer" is used primarily to refer to natural persons who acquire goods of any kind for personal use. The focus is therefore on private individuals rather than businesses. However, the argument developed in this book may also be relevant in the context of professionals who acquire consumer goods which will be used as part of their business activity (such as a computer used by a law lecturer).

3 Early research by Udell and Anderson (1968) indicated that guarantees were used more frequently for more expensive and complex products, and more for products for which the duration of the replacement cycle is longer. They also discovered that guarantees were used more by firms with lower market shares. This would suggest that guarantees are most effective when the price is high, the product is of a type which is purchased infrequently and regarded as complex by consumers, and the market share is small. This is no longer the case today.

4 Although in the case of second-hand cars, consumers often have to purchase a guarantee.

5 Oughton and Lowry (2000) and Howells and Weatherill (1995) provide an overview of all the relevant legal aspects, and summarise various reform proposals put forward in the past (OFT, 1986; NCC, 1989; DTI, 1992). Leder and Shears (1996) only devote a few lines to this topic. Harvey and Parry (2000) are also rather brief, limiting their discussion to the context of the Unfair Contract Terms Act 1977. Miller, Harvey and Parry (1998) devote slightly more space to this topic, and refer the reader to relevant cases in this area. Lowe and Woodroffe (1999) equally limit their discussion to the few legislative provisions which apply, and to the various reform proposals.

6 See chapter 2 at 2.1.4.

7 Published at (1999) O.J. L 177/12.

8 See chapter 6.

9 All the above will be referred to, where appropriate, in the main body of this book.

10 This is the most recent year for which detailed figures are available.

11 Unfortunately, the OFT did not specify the instances of defective goods only.

12 Following Jarmin's terminology.

13 This distinction is crucial for the discussion of guarantees as signals of product quality in chapter 3.

14 A third factor which may be relevant is that of safety. A consumer will assume that a product he buys is safe and does not pose an unexpected danger. The regulation of product safety falls outside the scope of this book and this point will not be considered further. See Howells (1998a) for a detailed discussion.

15 This discussion does not consider defects which are the result of consumers using the product in an abnormal fashion. The present focus is on defects that occurred before the consumer has made a purchase.

16 Although a seller or manufacturer may say that a product is of a particular standard of quality, Akerlof's argument assumes that consumers are unable to verify the accuracy of such a statement.

17 A detailed consideration of English law can be found in any of the standard consumer law textbooks such as Oughton and Lowry (2000, ch.6) or Harvey and Parry (2001, ch.5). For an analysis of the Guarantees Directive, see Twigg-Flesner and Bradgate (2000).

18 "Consumer goods" under the Directive are "any tangible movable item, with the exception of goods sold by way of execution or otherwise by authority of law, water and gas where they are not put up for sale in a limited volume or set quantity and electricity"(Article 1(2)(b)). Member States are given the option to provide that second-hand goods sold at public auction are not covered by the Directive (Article 1(3)). The definition of "consumer goods" is therefore very broad.

19 Defined as any natural person "acting for purposes which are not related to his trade, business or profession" (Article 1(2)(a)).

20 The Directive treats contracts for goods to be manufactured as contracts of sale. In English law, such contracts would probably be treated as contracts for work and materials and would therefore fall under the Supply of Goods and Services Act 1982. For a detailed consideration of this point, see Twigg-Flesner and Bradgate (2000).

21 It may be possible to read this paragraph as applying only where the seller applies a description to the goods *and* provides a sample. This would produce the strange result that goods sold only by description or only by sample would not be covered by this presumption. The "and" between the two elements of this paragraph should therefore be read disjunctively as "The goods comply with the description of the goods *and/or* the qualities of the sample"(Twigg-Flesner and Bradgate, 2000).

22 It may be arguable that the seller can adopt the manufacturer's description, and therefore the description on the packaging would be given by the seller. However, this would introduce an unnecessary interpretative complexity.

23 This particular wording was already present in the first Draft of the Directive (COM (1995) 520 final), and attempts by the European Parliament to amend this provision to include descriptions given by the manufacturer (European Parliament, 1998) were rejected by the European Commission (COM (1998) 217 final). It was felt that this type of situation was covered by sub-paragraph (d). However, that paragraph only refers to statements made by the manufacturer in so far as these may be relevant in determining the quality and performance a consumer may be entitled to expect, and it seems that it would not cover all failures to comply with the description of the goods.

24 The European Parliament recognised this and proposed the addition of such an indicative list of criteria but this was rejected. An explanation for this failure may be that Parliament tried to introduce this list into sub-paragraph (b), rather than this paragraph (European Parliament, 1998, Amendment 22).

25 The Directive also provides (in Article 2(5)) that if goods are not installed properly, or if the installation instructions are inadequate if the consumer is to install the product himself, there will also be a lack of conformity.

26 See Twigg-Flesner (2003, forthcoming) for a detailed analysis of the remedial scheme.

27 The Directive grants permission to the Member States to provide in their implementing legislation that consumer and seller may agree that the seller's liability for non-conformity of the goods should be less than two-years, provided that it is not be less than one year (Article 7(1)).

28 However, if, under national legislation there is a limitation period, it needs to be a minimum of two years from the time of delivery (Article 5(1)).

29 The Article further requires that Member States notify the European Commission if they make use of this provision. The Commission had to publish a report by 7 January 2003 on the utilisation of the provision.

30 Defined in Article 1(2)(f) as "in the event of lack of conformity, bringing consumer goods into conformity with the contract of sale".

31 "Free of charge" is defined in Article 3(4) as referring to "to the necessary costs incurred to bring the goods into conformity, particularly the cost of postage, labour and materials".

32 The Directive provides no further guidance on this point.

33 There is a comprehensive body of literature on the price-quality relationship, which it is not necessary to consider further for present purposes.

34 Prior to the reforms which lead to the introduction of the satisfactory quality test, goods were deemed to have met the requisite quality standard ("merchantable quality") if they were fit for at least one of the purposes for which they were commonly supplied (see *Aswan Engineering Co. v Lupdine Ltd* (1987)).

35 See 1.2.1, above.

36 Contrast the earlier decision in *Millars of Falkirk v Turpie* (1976) where a leak to the power steering system of a new car did not render the car unmerchantable.

37 See 1.2.1, above.

38 A problem may arise if a seller refuses to provide a refund and instead insists to provide a replacement. Although not required to do so under SoGA, a consumer may nevertheless give in to such pressure from the seller.

39 See e.g. Bradgate (2000) at 12.3.3.

40 For a detailed examination of these arguments, see Bradgate and Twigg-Flesner (2002). See also Clark (1992).

41 This could be restricted through a term in the contract between seller and distributor: See Bradgate and Twigg-Flesner (2002).

42 See s.14(2C) SoGA and Article 2(3) of the Consumer Guarantees Directive respectively.

43 And the reference to 'freedom from minor defects' in particular.

44 See section 1.7 below.

45 However, factors other than strict legal rules may persuade the seller to accept the consumer's complaint nevertheless. Ramsay (1989, p.416) notes that sellers are more willing to provide a remedy if the consumer is likely to be a repeat purchaser.

46 It is not relevant for present purposes to consider ADR in detail. See e.g., Genn (1999) or Howells, James and Spiller (2001) for a useful discussion.

47 There are also now mechanisms in place to help cross-border consumers. There is no evidence as to their effectiveness available at present, and these are not discussed further in this book.

48 See chapters 3 and 4.

49 The different problems were combined under the headings "consumer problems", "money", "landlord problems", "employment problem", "neighbour problem", "Social Security/Education", "Divorce", "Accident at Work" and "Owning Property".

50 "Justiciable Events" were defined as "a matter experienced by a respondent which raised legal issues, whether or not it was recognised by the respondent as being 'legal' and whether or not any action taken by the respondent to deal with the event involved the use of any part of the civil justice system" (p.12).

51 "Consumer Problems" includes a range of problems which consumers may face, and is therefore broader than the narrower issue of faulty products, which is the primary focus of this book. Nevertheless, the findings are valuable because they reflect the general attitude of consumers to dealing with legal problems. Genn does not report any noticeable variation in the types of action pursued by consumers for faulty goods, and it is therefore assumed that these general findings are equally applicable to the more specific case of faulty goods.

52 The Office of Fair Trading reports significantly higher figures (85.8 million - see OFT (2000)). The problems in the study described here were limited to those which were 'justiciable' and not trivial, whereas the OFT research focused on all causes of complaint consumers have had, regardless of whether these would have given rise to specific legal action.

53 In most other categories, the number of those seeking advice was at least twice is high, and almost three times as high for those with a divorce problem.

54 Unfortunately, the report does not go into further detail on these figures, and it is not clear how many of those advised to utilise alternative dispute resolution mechanism were advised to use an arbitration scheme operated by a Trade Association.

55 Wilhelm Consulting (1997) reported that in the UK, out of 24 million transactions, Dixons Group had no more than 200 claims against them in court; Similarly, the John Lewis Partnership indicated that they had had 40 cases out of 10 million transactions. Although these figures were provided by the companies themselves, they are nevertheless indicative of the insignificance of formal court procedures to resolve quality disputes.

56 Again, a comparison with other types of problems suggests that this figure is at least 20% higher.

57 The report only comments that "only a very small minority took the complaint even further" (DTI, 2001a, p.11).

58 These were also the conclusions of the influential study carried out by Best and Andreasen (1977) in the United States in 1975.

Chapter 2

The Characteristics of Consumer Guarantees

2.0 Introduction

This chapter will explore the characteristics of consumer guarantees, in particular those given by manufacturers. This may help to identify the function of a guarantee, i.e., whether it may be used to provide information to consumer about product quality, or whether it is capable of constituting a redress mechanism. As noted in the previous chapter, the argument in this book is that the latter is more likely.

There are many statements directed at consumers which are called "guarantees", but not all of these could be described as manufacturers' guarantees in the sense of this book. There will therefore be a brief discussion of other types of guarantees[1] commonly found in the context of consumer transactions in order to explain the differences between manufacturers' guarantees and such other types of guarantee.

2.1 The characteristics of a guarantee

Guarantees vary considerably from product to product and brand to brand. However, it is possible to identify features that are common to all guarantees. Each guarantee is made up of three basic elements: (a) the guarantee promise; (b) the remedies that are to be provided if that promise is not fulfilled and (c) the terms and conditions on which the guarantee is provided. These will now be examined in more detail. Satisfaction guarantees and extended warranties will be considered in the final section of this chapter.

2.1.1 The guarantee promise

Every guarantee will promise something to the consumer. In most cases, the promise is that the product covered by the guarantee is free from defects in workmanship and material. The product should therefore operate as intended for a specific minimum period, provided it is used in accordance with the operating instructions and maintained in the way envisaged in the maintenance instructions.

This promise is limited in its duration. In some cases, it is fixed at one year, but recent years have seen an increase in the number of guarantees lasting for longer periods, sometimes extending to twenty years (e.g., for bed frames).[2] It is still the case that the guarantees are given for a period which is shorter than the average life expectancy of the relevant product.

Eddy (1977, p.844) presents a plausible explanation why many guarantees tend to be of limited duration. He argues that the longer the guarantee period, the greater the danger that factors other than shortcomings during the manufacturing process will be the cause of the defect. The longer the consumer has used the goods, the greater the danger that there will have been some misuse (i.e., lack of sufficient care to prevent malfunctioning or defects) by the consumer. When a product is returned under guarantee, it is often very difficult to establish what caused the defect. A guarantor may therefore "overfulfill" his obligations under the guarantee and provide a remedy in cases where there may be some doubt as to whether the defect in question was present at the time of sale or whether it was caused by a lack of care by the consumer.[3] In addition, Emons (1989) suggests that the duration of guarantees may be limited because consumers do not use products in a uniform manner. Some consumers will use a product infrequently whereas others may use it regularly; some take a lot of care when they use the product whereas others will be less careful. If the likelihood of product breakdown depends to a significant extent on the way consumers use the product, then guarantees may be of a shorter duration in order to minimise claims under the guarantee that are the result of high-intensity or careless use.

As mentioned previously, there are now products that are covered by significantly longer guarantees.[4] This may be because these are products that consumers will buy on a very infrequent basis or because they require very little maintenance. With such products, the opportunities for misuse by the consumer are limited. Other products (such as cars) may be covered by longer term guarantees on condition that the consumer ensures that regular maintenance is carried out in accordance with the manufacturer's requirements.[5]

A study carried out for the European Commission before the adoption of the Guarantees Directive (Wilhelm Consulting, 1997) observed that competition between guarantors may be partly responsible for the introduction of such longer-term guarantees (at p.24/25). It is suggested that manufacturers will offer guarantees for a period during which the potential cost of providing the guarantee will be less than the potential additional profits expected from an increase in sales. Extended warranties[6] may be offered where the likely profit margin would be very narrow.

2.1.2 Remedies for non-fulfilment

A promise on its own would be of little value if the guarantor did not also specify what he will do, should the product in question fail to meet the promises made in the guarantee. In most cases, the guarantor will promise either to repair the product or to replace it. However, it will also be subject to the guarantor's discretion which of these remedies will be provided.[7]

2.1.3 Terms and conditions

Finally, the guarantee will specify the conditions on which the guarantee is provided. These include conditions that have to be fulfilled before the consumer can benefit from the guarantee, such as the return of a registration card. Other terms may set out limitations to the availability of the guarantee. The following is a list of terms commonly found in manufacturers' guarantees. It should be noted that some of these terms may be regarded as unfair and therefore not binding on a consumer, or be ineffective for another reason. However, all these terms were found in guarantees on goods supplied to consumers in the United Kingdom in 2002.[8]

Conditions to be complied with to obtain the benefit of the guarantee: In order to benefit from a guarantee, a consumer is often required to complete and return a registration card. In some cases, the guarantee does not become effective unless this is returned within a specified time period. In other cases, the registration is optional and need not be complied with if the consumer has retained another form of proof of purchase.

For example, contrast this:

> The Guarantee becomes effective only if the Registration Card is duly completed and despatched to the company within **THIRTY DAYS OF PURCHASE.**[9]

with this:

> The conditions of the guarantee only apply if either the Guarantee Card (cut out of the box) with date of purchase, dealer's stamp and signature, or the receipt, is sent to the appropriate Service Station together with the appliance.

Moreover, some guarantors require that the seller stamps a guarantee card to provide evidence that the product was obtained from an authorised retailer.

Duration of the guarantee: All guarantees will state the period during which they are available.[10] Some will also specify whether the guarantee period will be extended if the product is repaired under the guarantee, or if parts are replaced.

> If replacement parts are fitted to any appliance, this will not extend the period under this Guarantee.

> Any replacement or repairs will be guaranteed for the unexpired portion of the [guarantee period].

Procedure for making a claim: A guarantee should provide sufficient information to the consumer on how to make a claim under the guarantee. This may include details of the person against whom the consumer may claim, and the procedure the consumer should follow. It will be seen below[11] that there are a number of different procedures for dealing with consumer claims under guarantees. There is no uniform approach that is used by all guarantors. This is evident from these examples:

> If any defect should occur during the [guarantee] period, please telephone the consumer Helpline given below. You will be asked to return the product in a postage paid package which will be sent to you. You could send the fault product with proof of purchase to the address given below.

> Under the terms of this guarantee any part or component which becomes defective in normal use will be repaired or at the company's sole discretion replaced free of charge if returned carriage paid, but will be subject to a handling charge.

> This [guarantee] service is available, on production of proof of purchase, from any ... service facility in any of the countries listed below in accordance with the [guarantee conditions] prescribed in each country.

Extent of parts coverage: Details may be given of which parts of a product are covered by a guarantee, and how long for. It may be the case that certain components of a particular product are covered for longer than other parts of the same product. Such variations are particularly common with guarantees on cars (so-called "guarantee menus").

Moreover, some parts may be excluded from a guarantee altogether. These will often be generic consumables such as light-bulbs or batteries, or other parts which may need to be changed on a frequent basis, such as an air filter in a vacuum cleaner.

Allocation of charges for work carried out under a guarantee: Some guarantees will not impose any charges on the consumer. Other guarantees may require the consumer to pay a call-out charge, or some other fee, when claiming under the guarantee.

> The guarantee covers the cost of all parts and labour used in the repair or replacement of any parts which are shown to be defective due to faulty materials or workmanship within 2 years of purchase.

> This guarantee covers none of the following: ... transport costs, home service transport cost and all risks of transport relating directly or indirectly to the guarantee of the product.

Work not covered by guarantee: Some guarantees include a provision that when a claim is made under the guarantee which does not relate to faulty materials or workmanship, the guarantor may charge the consumer for any repairs carried out:

> If a claim is made under this guarantee, and the defect is not due to faulty materials or manufacture, [the guarantor] reserves the right to charge the customer at the current hourly rate and list prices in respect of any service engineers' time or replacement parts.

Various use and repair exclusions: Guarantees may become void if the consumer uses the product for a particular purpose which would make the product more liable to break down. In such cases, the guarantor may decide to withdraw the benefit of the guarantee. Similarly, some guarantees will become void if a consumer attempts to carry out repair of the product himself. The justification advanced for such an exclusion is that the consumer may inadvertently do further damage to a product which has broken down if he attempts to repair it - but such damage is not something the producer of the product could prevent. This may also happen if important product information is tampered with:

> This guarantee will not apply if the type or serial number on the product has been altered, deleted, removed or made illegible.

Finally, some guarantees require that the product is only maintained and repaired by an authorised repairer. Ostensibly, this ensures that the product has been maintained to the standards required by the guarantor. However, it may also give the guarantor a competitive advantage in the repair market by tying consumers who wish to benefit from the guarantee to a limited number of repairers.[12]

Limitation to Original Buyer: A guarantee may be limited to the consumer who actually bought the product, and not be available to other users and subsequent owners. Not all guarantees are restricted in this way and some are available to any owner during the guarantee period. Guarantors may try to justify the use of such exclusions on the basis that subsequent owners are unaware of the way previous owners have used the product, and also do not know if previous owners have failed to comply with the conditions of the guarantee and thereby invalidated it. However, particularly in the case of products covered by long-term guarantees, consumers may lose out if they are unable to pass on the benefit of the guarantee when they sell the product.[13]

E.g.:

> This [guarantee] is personal to the original purchaser and is not transferable.

> This [guarantee] is offered to any person who has legally obtained possession of the product within the [guarantee] period.

Commercial use exclusion: Some products are provided for consumers, as well as for businesses, e.g., certain electric tools. Guarantees which accompany such products may limit the availability of the guarantee to consumer buyers only. An explanation for such a term is that a business user is likely to use the product more frequently and in a greater variety of situations, which makes it more likely that the product will break down:

> This [guarantee] does not cover any product which is used in any trade or business or for industrial or commercial purposes.

Some guarantees do not exclude commercial use outright, but instead limit the duration of the guarantee:

> [The guarantor will provide a remedy if the product is] defective due to faulty materials or workmanship within 12 months from the date of purchase (or 6 months where domestic appliance have in [the guarantor's] opinion been used for commercial purposes.

Geographical Scope: Some guarantees are available in more than one country[14] and the guarantee document may provide details of the guarantee's geographical scope:

> This guarantee is valid only in the UK.

> This [guarantee] is only applicable to products purchased in one of the countries listed in this certificate. It remains applicable when, following such a purchase, the product is brought into any other country listed.[15]

Attempts to curtail the consumer's statutory rights: Guarantees could be used to attempt to limit or exclude a consumer's rights under Sale of Goods legislation.[16] A guarantee might be designed in a way so as to preclude a consumer from relying on his legal rights, once he has decided to invoke the guarantee. Both in the UK and the EC, legislation has now been put into place to deal with this problem.[17]

These are just the most common terms found in guarantees, and there may be terms that deal with other issues in a particular guarantee, as well. There is no uniformity, and although there are certain essential terms (e.g., duration, or remedies to be provided), there can be a significant degree of variation between guarantees, both between products and within the same product category. Priest (1981) sought to provide an explanation for this variation. He suggested that it was possible to predict the terms for a particular guarantee by applying his "Investment Theory".[18]

2.1.4 Priest's investment theory

Priest's theory is based on a number of assumptions. First, he assumes that consumers are perfectly informed about the likelihood of a product defect and the losses that will be suffered when a product becomes defective. Second, consumers are able to make their preferences regarding guarantee content known to the manufacturer. Third, guarantees are standardised only to reduce negotiation costs. Finally, all products are manufactured under conditions of perfect competition (p.1307). These factors describe the ideal-type model of perfect competition. Priest's suggestions therefore have to be treated with caution, because the ideal-type he assumes is an unattainable position in reality. There will always be impediments to the free flow of information, both from consumer to manufacturer and vice versa.

The Investment Theory is based solely on "the relative costs to the consumer and the manufacturer of investments to prolong productive capacity and to insure for product losses" (p.1307). These investments do not have to be monetary, but can also include preventative action and self-help remedies. Thus, some repairs may be easier and cheaper for a consumer to carry out than for the guarantor (the manufacturer), and a guarantee may be expected to determine the types of repairs which should be provided by the guarantor because these would be too burdensome on the consumer. A manufacturer would also be expected to improve product design to minimise the probability of the product needing repairs, which is also a form of investment to minimise the risk of product losses.

The guarantee divides responsibility for allocative investments and insurance between the consumer and the manufacturer. Allocative investments are actions taken either by the guarantor or the consumer to prevent the occurrence of a product defect. Whoever is allocated the responsibility for taking a particular action must be in the best position to do so - for example, it is an allocative investment for a consumer to take care to prevent his children from hanging from a refrigerator door. The manufacturer invests in product design until his marginal costs[19] equal his marginal benefits.[20] In other words, if he can ensure that the design has been subjected to sufficient quality control procedures, he will provide a guarantee which will cover the losses which could not be covered more cheaply by insurance or allocative investments by the consumer. There is no moral hazard[21] problem here, as the insurance contract, i.e., the guarantee, is defined *ex ante* according to the relative costs of allocative investment and insurance. This theory is based on the notion of the least-cost avoider (Oughton and Lowry, 2000, p.205) - the party in the best position to absorb responsibility for a particular problem should deal with it.

The terms of such guarantees would thus very clearly limit the responsibilities of the guarantor, depending on the actions taken by the guarantor while the product is under his control. They would exclude actions which could best be taken by the consumer, such as adequately cleaning the product, proper adjustment of controls etc.

Whitford (1982) criticised Priest (1981) for ignoring other factors that may be relevant.[22] Although it was clear that Priest's investment theory offered a partial explanation regarding the content of a guarantee, there were other significant considerations. Whitford referred to a number of these: first, he noted that there may be market imperfections on the side of the buyer. By this, he referred to consumer ignorance and lack of sophistication. He speculated (but conceded that empirical evidence was required) that guarantees may vary between different socio-economic classes, if not in form, than at least in application ("the [guarantee]-in-action", p. 1381). Second, a fear of government regulation may influence the substance of guarantees. The content of guarantees is not regulated by law in all jurisdictions. Guarantors may be influenced by a desire to maintain this status by drafting guarantees less restrictively than would be possible under market conditions. In other words, even though certain limitations and exclusions could be included, a guarantor may choose not to do so in order to avoid potential legislative intervention. Third, consumers may tend to overdiscount long-term risks in favour of short term gratification. Consumers may delay considering the potential consequences of a product breakdown when faced with two similar products, one with full guarantee coverage, and another with little guarantee coverage, but significantly cheaper. This may affect the content of guarantees as consumers may prefer a less extensive content than suggested under the investment theory.

Whitford also referred to the organisational structure of the guarantor - e.g., a large corporation with its own legal department may include a number of technical and unlikely exclusions simply because a lawyer might have thought that there would be no harm in including the particular term in the guarantee.

Priest's theory is certainly not an exhaustive theory of the consumer guarantee. It provides a useful indicator as to why guarantees contain certain terms and limitations, but it does not provide a conclusive answer. In many respects, the views expressed both by Priest and by Whitford are less pertinent in the context of English and E.C. law, because unlike the U.S. system, on which their discussion focuses, English law imposes a separate mandatory quality standard.[23]

2.1.5 Summary

So far, this chapter has provided a detailed explanation of the format of manufacturers' guarantees. It has also considered a number of explanations that have been put forward to explain why there are certain terms and conditions in guarantees.

The next section will focus on the provision of guarantees. It will explain how arrangements for dealing with claims under guarantees are made in two major consumer product sectors, domestic appliances and cars. It is necessary to appreciate the diversity in dealing with claims under a manufacturer's guarantee that exist when considering the extent to which there should be legislative intervention.

2.2 Dealing with claims under manufacturers' guarantees

The following paragraphs provide a summary of how claims under guarantees are handled in two major consumer product sectors, domestic appliances and cars. These descriptions are based on informal discussions with representatives from these sectors and offer an insight into the part that guarantees have to play today. Generally, guarantees are implemented in an efficient and unbureaucratic way, with very little paperwork for the consumer to deal with.[24]

2.2.1 Domestic appliances

This section will provide a general overview of how manufacturers' guarantees on domestic appliance are implemented. An initial distinction must be drawn between so-called "white" and "brown" goods. "White" goods are products such as washing machines, freezers and refrigerators, whereas "brown" goods are products such as televisions, hi-fi equipment and video-cassette recorders. The arrangements for handling claims under guarantees generally differ between these two categories.

In the case of white goods, a manufacturer will usually have his own repair network. A retailer will not deal with any claims under such a guarantee but refer the consumer to the manufacturer. The guarantee document will normally specify that the consumer should contact the manufacturer. This initial contact may also be handled by a third party on behalf of the manufacturer. The details of the consumer's complaint under the guarantee will be taken and arrangements made for the product to be repaired or, if necessary, replaced.

In the case of brown goods, most retailers traditionally used to do their own repairs, and many still do so today. The general position in this sector therefore is that manufacturers offer a guarantee, and service under the guarantee will be provided by the retailer. Not all retailers have the facilities to provide repairs. For those retailers, the manufacturer will provide a list of repairers that the retailer can contact in order to deal with a claim under a guarantee.

The retailer or repair service provider will need to apply for reimbursement of costs from the manufacturer. There are forms to be completed, most of which are now standardised. These record the type of repair which has been carried out and the parts that were used to effect the repair. The standardised format allows the manufacturer both to keep a record of the way in which the guarantees are implemented and to identify recurrent problems. The latter information can then be utilised as part of a quality assurance mechanism. This information is increasingly processed electronically, but not yet exclusively so.

The manufacturer will only re-imburse, or indemnify, the retailer (or repairer) for the expenses he has incurred in connection with the repair provided under the guarantee. This is generally done on a fixed rate reimbursement basis (know as a "Claim-back contribution"). This rate varies depending on brand and particular model. It may also vary according to the category of retailer, and particular account is taken of the size and quality of the repair facilities. This fixed rate is intended to offer a strong incentive for the retailer to ensure that proper service is provided under the guarantee. If a product has not been repaired properly the first time and the consumer has to take it back to have it repaired a second time, the retailer/repairer is very unlikely to be reimbursed for this second repair service, because there is a presumption that the initial repair was not carried out satisfactorily. The fixed rate system is also designed to ensure that the retailer carries out the repair as swiftly as possible - there is no benefit for the retailer to take longer for repairs than necessary.

In the case of both white and brown goods, guarantees may have a discretionary element as to whether to offer repair or replacement. Thus, it would be for the guarantor to consider which remedy would be more appropriate, given the nature of the particular fault. There are no universal guidelines that can help retailers in exercising this discretion. There may be individual sets of rules in place by brand or class of product. Thus, some products are not repaired, they are simply replaced. Other products should be repaired; if in the repairer's opinion the product is beyond economic repair, then approval has to be sought from the guarantor to write-off the product and to provide a replacement instead. Whether a particular product is beyond economic repair depends on the nature of the particular fault. Frequently, support is offered to the retailers and the repair network by technical liaison officers. These visit the retailers and repairers to ensure that staff there are trained and able to deal with the products. They also ensure that repairs are carried out correctly and that the information provided by the retailers is accurate.

There are exceptions to the system just described. Sometimes, a retailer may "buy out" the manufacturers' guarantee. Thus, although the retailer would normally provide a guarantee service on behalf of the manufacturer, in this type of situation the manufacturer will not be invoiced for repairs carried out under the manufacturers' guarantee. Instead, the retailer will have negotiated a lower trade price for the product and implement the guarantee himself without consulting the manufacturer. This arrangement is more common with some brands than with others, and some brands refuse this kind of arrangement outright, primarily because of quality assurance issues and customer feedback on product performance. Those manufacturers that do agree do not regard this as a permanent arrangement, it might vary from season to season.

2.2.2 Cars

Guarantees (or "warranties", as they are usually called in the context of cars[25]), are an important aspect of the customer service provided by motor manufacturers.[26] Most manufacturers have a dedicated guarantee department or at least a guarantee manager.

If a car requires repair under the guarantee, the retailers will normally provide this.[27] Consumers who have encountered a problem with their car will therefore contact the retailer, rather than the manufacturer. In the case of cars, it will be possible for a consumer to contact any retailer who is a member of the manufacturer's distribution network - there is no need to return to the retailer who sold the car to the consumer in order to obtain a service under the manufacturer's guarantee.[28] The retailer will investigate the problem and will effect a repair as necessary. For most of these repairs, the retailer will simply remedy the problem he has identified. If in doubt, he may refer to the terms and conditions of the guarantee in order to establish if a particular problem is covered by the guarantee.

If major repairs are necessary, the retailer will be required to apply to the manufacturer's guarantee department for authorisation before the work is carried out. The guarantee department will consider the information provided by the retailer and may then authorise the work under the guarantee, or decide that the guarantee does not cover the problem in question.

There will inevitably be instances where it is not clear whether the problem complained about is due to a manufacturing defect, or simply the result of normal wear and tear. The retailer who investigates the problem may decide that the problem is not covered by the guarantee. A consumer who does not accept such a decision could then contact customer relations to register his dissatisfaction. This is not an appeals procedure and there is generally no discretion to ignore the limitations of the guarantee, but it may then be possible to provide a solution that would satisfy the consumer. However, this will inevitably depend on the circumstances of the particular case, and the retailer's and customer-service department's perception of the particular consumer - if they feel that the consumer may be unreasonably trying to claim under the guarantee, then they may be less inclined to find a solution that would be satisfactory. Moreover, if the consumer is a long-standing customer, there will be an incentive to provide a solution that would keep the consumer happy.

2.2.3 Some final observations

This section provided a useful analysis of how consumer claims under a manufacturers' guarantee are dealt with. There is no uniformity in the procedures for dealing with such claims, and different consumer product sectors have different procedures. These findings are important, because they demonstrate that individual sectors have designed a system for providing redress which works best for them. This diversity of approaches therefore needs to be taken into account in creating a legal framework for manufacturers' guarantees. It will be seen in chapter 4 that this diversity is an important part of the informal redress function of manufacturers' guarantees.

2.3 Problems with guarantees

So far, this chapter has provided a detailed explanation of the elements of a guarantee, and has outlined how claims under guarantees are dealt with. It is now appropriate to identify the problems that may arise with guarantees. It has already been seen that there is considerable variety in the terms on which guarantees are provided. The greatest problem is that the terms and conditions in guarantees may, in some cases, be unfair to consumers, because they offer very little of benefit to consumers and make what little they do offer subject to onerous conditions and limitations. Although it would be too bleak a picture to paint if it were suggested that all guarantees are like this, there are nevertheless frequent instances of guarantees not being quite what they seem. This particular problem has been referred to as exploitation theory, although it may be more appropriate to call this a problem of unfair surprise. The following section will consider this in more detail.

2.3.1 Exploitation theory and unfair surprise

The origin of exploitation theory lies in the notion of inequality of bargaining power.[29] In the classical model of contracting contract is the result of a free bargain between two parties of more or less equal bargaining power (see Brownsword, 2000, ch.2). However, in today's markets, contracting parties are rarely of equal standing, and frequently, one party will have greater economic strength than the other. This stronger position may enable this party to impose its terms on the weaker party, rather than to negotiate and compromise. In modern-day contracting, this has resulted in the use of standard-form contracts. Perhaps the most obvious benefit of using such contracts is the reduction in bargaining costs - it will take less time and expense to conclude a contract. Yet, a major problem with such contracts is that the party whose standard form is being used is able to utilise its position to maximise its benefit and minimise its liabilities. Clauses that limit or exclude that party's liability are a common feature of these contracts. The weaker party has no choice but to accept the terms put forward by the stronger one. Such "contracts of adhesion" are the consequence of the evolution of large-scale enterprises, which deal with a large number of customers (Kessler, 1943). This problem is particularly significant in the consumer context. There can be little doubt that in the vast majority of consumer contracts, the consumer will be in a weaker position than the trader. The trader will impose his standard terms and conditions, and the consumer will have to accept these or seek to make his purchase elsewhere.

Beale (1995) believes that bargaining power is less relevant and that there is no obvious link between market power and the use of exclusion clauses. Instead, he argues that exclusion clauses are used because the information costs for consumers to read the 'small print' in a contract is high. It is therefore rare for a consumer to make the effort to read all the terms of a contract, because this would be too time consuming. Instead, consumers look at the main elements of a contract, and a seller or manufacturer will be generous in that respect in order to remain competitive, but then shift more risk onto the consumer in the "small print". Beale (1995) regards this not so much as an instance of exploitation, but rather as one of unfair surprise (at p.233).

Exploitation theory, or "unfair surprise theory", is of relevance in two ways in the context of guarantees. First, a common problem is the use of exclusion and limitation clauses by which a guarantor would seek to limit his liability to the circumstances set down in the guarantee and either limit to very strictly defined circumstances or exclude outright his obligations under other relevant legal provisions, such as the SoGA. A guarantee might contain a term which expressly excludes implied terms as to quality. As consumers are often ignorant of the scope of protection they enjoy under the law, they may not be concerned about such terms in a guarantee.

This problem has been mentioned on numerous occasions. It was, for example, put forward as a dominant justification for legislation on manufacturers' guarantees by Trebilcock (1972). However, in contrast, Rothschild (1976) has argued that the implied terms are meaningless to consumers and to guarantors alike, because their scope is vague and it is difficult to define the extent of the guarantor's liability (if any) under the statutory rights.[30] In Rothschild's view, terms excluding the statutory rights would therefore be justified if this gave the consumer a clear written guarantee that is an exhaustive statement of the consumer's rights. Furthermore, it would help the guarantor in that it would become easier for him to assess the likely costs under the guarantee.

Second, the guarantor may use subordinate terms in the guarantee to limit the extent of his exposure under the guarantee, e.g., by making it very burdensome for the consumer to bring a claim under the guarantee. The exploitative aspect and the element of unfair surprise of guarantees were noted in this famous passage from one of Lord Denning's judgments:

> We all know what happens. Be it a motor car, a refrigerator, or a washing machine, the supplier will 'guarantee' it for two, three or five years, as the case may be. It sounds splendid. It looks fine. It is often headed in ornamental lettering 'Guarantee', sometimes with a seal attached, as if to show it is of great value. ... [The consumer] does not read it, of course. No one ever does. He takes it on trust that it is what the salesman says it is - a guarantee for those years. But when it comes to the pinch - when something goes wrong with the thing and he reads it - then he will discover that he would have done better without it. ... When a supplier says he gives a guarantee, he should be held to his word. He should not be allowed to limit it by clever clauses in small print - which in 99 cases out of 100, the customer never reads. Certainly he should not be allowed to cut it down by phrases of doubtful or ambiguous import. If he wishes to excuse himself from liability, he should say so plainly. Instead of heading it boldly 'Guarantee', he should head it 'Non-guarantee': for that is what it is (*Adams v Richardson & Starling* (1969), at 1648-9).

Lord Denning, in his inimitable style, criticised the potentially exploitative and unfair nature of guarantees. The consumer accepts the promise made in the guarantee and expects this to be honoured should he ever need to rely on the guarantee. When it does become necessary, he will discover that the many limitations and exclusions make the guarantee almost worthless.

Howells (1994; Howells and Weatherill, 1995, p.155) argues that these difficulties have now "largely been overcome" through the adoption of unfair contract terms legislation and other measures. The law may therefore have improved sufficiently to address both of these problems. However, such confidence cannot be shared unequivocally. There is still a tendency to use limitation and exclusion clauses in guarantees. The Office of Fair Trading (OFT) periodically publishes details of the terms it has challenged successfully under the Unfair Contract Terms Regulations 1999 in its *Unfair Contract Terms Bulletins*. These

Bulletins provide many examples of guarantees that contain exclusion and limitation clauses as well as other terms that are regarded as unfair.[31] Furthermore, the fact that such clauses are prohibited by legislation may only be of limited use. Eddy (1977) recognised that:

> The presence of such clauses buried away in a contract may allow sellers to force abandonment of claims by disappointed purchases who, though angered by this tactic, have no idea that the law would support them in their indignation (p.856).

Thus, the fact that many consumers are unaware of the level of protection they enjoy under consumer protection laws means that guarantors can in practice still rely on limitation and exclusion clauses in their guarantees.

Furthermore, there may continue to be problems with guarantees that appear to be free from such clauses. *Which?* has reported that there are recurring instances of retailers denying consumers a remedy to which they would be entitled in law (under SoGA) on the basis that the product in question is covered by a manufacturer's guarantee and the complaint should therefore be taken up with that manufacturer. A variation on this is to claim that nothing can be done because the manufacturer's guarantee has expired already.

This seems to suggest that the adoption of legislation to combat exploitative and unfair terms in guarantees necessitates two things to ensure that the legislation achieves its objective. First, it is necessary to increase public awareness of consumer rights and of the fact that it is not possible for a guarantor to restrict these rights through a guarantee. This might help to reduce instances where retailers refuse to acknowledge their liability under SoGA by claiming that the consumer should take up his complaint with the manufacturer under the guarantee instead. Second, the enforcement of such legislation is crucial. It is important that the assessment and challenge to unfair and exploitative terms is not limited to the realms of the private law suit, but instead opened up to public and private bodies involved in consumer protection. These will be in a better position to challenge such terms because they represent the broad consumer interest.[32]

2.3.2 Other problems

Leaving aside the concerns about the potentially unfair nature of particular terms and conditions in some guarantees, there has been very little research into the problems that arise with guarantees. The most recent detailed study that was produced in the UK is an OFT paper from the mid-1980s (OFT, 1986). The findings in that study are now somewhat dated; yet, it is nevertheless instructive to examine the problems that were identified. In 1986, the OFT suggested that there were around 12.5 million claims under guarantees, with around 2.5 million leaving the consumer dissatisfied. More recent figures (OFT, 1997c) suggest that about 8% of all claims made under a guarantee did not produce an outcome that was satisfactory for the consumer. The vast majority of claims therefore resolve the problem complained about.

A common cause for dissatisfaction was that the guarantee covered less than the consumer expected. Thus, some guarantees excluded labour costs, whereas others only covered some parts of the products, but not others. This relates back to the discussion in the previous section about unfair surprise - sometimes, consumers may simply not appreciate the extent of the guarantee's scope. However, this may not always be due to obscure terms and conditions, but simply the result of the consumer's misapprehension about the guarantee (see para 6.13, OFT, 1986). A further concern was that a small number of guarantors tried to evade their responsibilities under their guarantees completely. Other problems were delays in providing a remedy and the recurrence of faults after an initial repair under the guarantee (OFT, 1997c).

Trebilcock (1972) noted instances of manufacturers not living up to the terms of their guarantees. Although perhaps more wide-spread in the 1970s and 1980s, this is a problem which still occurs today, albeit in small numbers. Guarantees are given, but when it comes to dealing with consumer claims under such a guarantee, the guarantor may refuse to honour the claim.

Problems may also arise in the context of product advertising which mentions the guarantee. Consumers may often discover some of the details of a guarantee through newspaper or television advertising.[33] There are instances where statements made about a guarantee in advertising were unclear or even misleading. Thus, one motor manufacturer has recently advertised his cars with a three-year guarantee. However, only the first year guarantee is provided by the manufacturer, whereas the remaining two years are provided by the retailer who sold the car to the consumer. A consumer who buys a car and then moves to a different part of the country may therefore have some difficulty in obtaining a service under the guarantee after its first year because he would have to return to the retailer where he bought the car. This lack of clarity may be detrimental to consumers.

2.3.3 The European perspective

The European Commission examined guarantees in detail in its Green Paper (Commission, 1993).[34] It noted the diversity between guarantees offered in the various Member States. Such differences were found in respect of the defects covered under the guarantee, the parties providing and honouring the guarantee, consumers' rights with regard to claiming under the guarantee and the duration and formal conditions for invoking the guarantee. The relationship between statutory rights and guarantees was often not made clear.

This diversity was identified as a real problem in a cross-border context.[35] There was no general legal framework dealing with guarantees in place at the European level at the time. At the time of the Green Paper, several Member States (including the UK) had considered the introduction of a legal framework. In order to reduce the burden on business, a minimum standard of harmonised rules should be introduced in order to encourage consumers to utilise the Single Market.[36] The Commission made a number of proposals. First, consumers should be given correct information about guarantees offered. Second, it was essential to ensure that consumers were made aware of their statutory rights. Finally, it was proposed to establish a legal framework for guarantees, which at the very least required that certain minimum information be provided in the guarantee documents.

The Commission suggested two sets of rules. First, it proposed to create a framework to deal with the legal status of guarantees, their presentation and advertising, and consumer information. Second, it proposed the introduction of a voluntary "European" Guarantee. One of its hallmarks would have been that it could be relied on in all the Member States, regardless of the country of purchase. It would have been a standardised guarantee, with uniform conditions applying in all the Member States. As far as the relationship between guarantee and statutory rights was concerned, the Commission favoured an approach under which both would complement one another, and that reliance on a guarantee should not deprive a consumer of his rights under statute.

The need for such action was not accepted by all commentators. Cranston noted that:

> the European-wide manufacturer or distributor is not likely to face great difficulty in coping with different national laws relating to the commercial guarantee (1995, p.114).[37]

Accordingly, there was no real need for the EC to legislate in this area. This may be so, but it could be beneficial for the common market if a pan-European guarantee existed, because it could promote consumer confidence in the internal market.

2.3.4 Distance selling and electronic commerce

The problems identified by the European Commission for the Internal Market also exist in similar form in the context of distance selling and electronic commerce. Consumers have been able to buy goods by mail order for a considerable time. A consumer selects the goods he wants from a catalogue and sends his order to the catalogue company, which will then deliver the goods to the consumer. If something is wrong with the goods, the consumer who bought goods from a catalogue will find it more difficult to resolve this problem. The consumer may have to pack up the goods, take them to the nearest post office, possibly pay for postage and wait for at least a few days before he gets a response. Obtaining redress can therefore be difficult.

This is exacerbated in the case of electronic commerce. Electronic commerce usually involves the use of the internet. Rather than selecting goods from a catalogue, consumers can choose goods from a website and add these to an electronic shopping basket. Although the website may provide address details and contact telephone numbers, the consumer does not know where the retailer is actually located. It may therefore be even more difficult to obtain redress. Furthermore, claiming under a guarantee can also be problematic, particularly if the guarantee requires that the consumer contact the retailer rather than the guarantor to obtain the benefit of the guarantee.

2.3.5 Summary

The purpose of the preceding part of this chapter has been to analyse in depth the elements that make up a guarantee and to identify the main problems associated with the provision of a guarantee. It has been seen that concern has primarily been caused by the nature of some terms in a guarantee, although there are other potential areas of difficulty. The final part of this chapter will focus on other types of consumer guarantee, and satisfaction guarantees and extended warranties in particular.

2.4 Satisfaction guarantees

Manufacturers' guarantees are given against defects in workmanship or material which become apparent during a specified period after purchase. In addition to such guarantees, two further types of guarantee are very common, "satisfaction guarantees" and "extended warranties". Neither are going to be considered in any depth in this book; however, it is necessary to examine their characteristics in order to distinguish these from manufacturers' guarantees.

2.4.1 What are satisfaction guarantees?

It is now common practice for consumers to be given "satisfaction guarantees". These may be given by both the seller and the manufacturer. A satisfaction guarantee is provided free-of-charge, and is generally of short duration. A common period is 28 days, e.g., a "twenty-eight day no quibble money back guarantee" if the consumer is not satisfied with his purchase. These guarantees are provided to deal with a consumer's subjective dissatisfaction (Shieh, 1996), rather than with problems in material and workmanship.[38] Such guarantees may be useful when a buyer is unable to examine a product[39] prior to purchase. This may be particular important where the purchase is made by mail-order or via the Internet (Moorthy and Srinivason, 1995). Under a satisfaction guarantee, a consumer will get a full refund if he does not like the product and invokes the guarantee. In contrast to manufacturers' guarantees, there is no need to show that there is a problem with the product and to allow the guarantor to attempt to deal with this problem. The consumer simply has to inform the guarantor that he wishes to take up the offer to return the product.

The risk with a satisfaction guarantee is that a consumer may use a product for the duration of the guarantee period, and then invoke the guarantee - in which case, the guarantor may incur significant costs. Beale and Howells (1996) observe that some of these 'no quibble money-back guarantees' have lead to many goods being returned to suppliers and have thus proved to be rather costly, because returned goods cannot be sold as "new" products. Tom Pallister, Director of Marketing for the Ford Motor Company, explained the scheme operated by Ford in 1995:

> [L]ast year we had a programme where within 30 days of purchase you could replace the vehicle without a quibble for any reason, so if you did not like the colour, did not like the seat fabric, whatever, we would replace it ... last year we did just over 12,000 vehicles (Oral Evidence, Minutes of Evidence, p.88).

A product may be sold with both a satisfaction and a manufacturer's guarantee. The satisfaction guarantee may encourage a consumer to buy a particular product, and, should he decide to keep it, the manufacturers' guarantee may provide reassurance to the consumer that a remedy is available if there is a problem for some time after the purchase.

A further type of guarantee is the extended guarantee, or extended warranty. These are sold separately to consumers and a consumer has to pay to benefit from such a warranty. In the following section, the salient issues relating to extended warranties will be discussed. The objective is to explain what these warranties are and the difficulties encountered with extended warranties. A detailed consideration of the legal issues of extended warranties is not needed, although a basic understanding of extended warranties is important for the discussion in this book.

2.5 Extended warranties[40]

Consumers who buy an electrical domestic appliance are usually offered an extended warranty. Essentially, this is a form of breakdown protection (often sold as an insurance policy, although not always) which provides protection against product failure for a specific period after purchase. Coverage usually goes beyond defects which are the result of defective materials or poor workmanship and frequently includes breakdowns caused by accidental damage or by wear and tear. In this respect, extended warranties offer additional protection for those consumers who opt to buy one.

Crucially, extended warranties have to be paid for. In the UK, there has been considerable concern over the selling techniques adopted by retailers, in particular, and also over the pricing level of such warranties (see generally OFT, 2002b).

A retailer who tries to sell an extended warranty to a consumer is sending out conflicting signals. A consumer may regard the availability of a warranty as a reflection of the retailer's commitment to after-sales support (Kelley, Conant and Brown, 1988). However, at the same time, the retailer might create the impression that a product may have a high risk of breaking down and that the consumer should obtain additional protection. Consequently, some consumers may lose confidence in the product they have chosen (Voss and Ahmed, 1992).

2.5.1 Three types of risk

Extended warranties can reduce three types of risk. The first is the performance risk, i.e., the question of whether the product will actually work as intended. Some consumers might not expect a high standard of reliability and may therefore be tempted to reduce the perceived risk of product failure by taking out an extended warranty (OFT, 1994). The second type of risk is the financial risk of having to pay for repair or replacement if the product does break down. Although it may be possible to identify an average cost of repair for a particular product, a consumer cannot establish in advance how much it will cost to have things put right in their particular case. An extended warranty can help to quantify this risk, because consumers will only pay for the extended warranties and will then not have to worry about the actual cost of repairing a faulty product. Finally, there is the effort it may take to have a product repaired when it has broken down. An extended warranty may be of use because the warranty provider is likely to have a network of repairers who can effect a repair efficiently and quickly. The consumer avoids the uncertainty of whether he will be able to obtain affordable assistance.

2.5.2 Do consumers need extended warranties?

It may be asked whether consumers really need to purchase extended warranties. It has already been seen that consumers enjoy a significant degree of protection under statute.[41] If a product breaks down soon after purchase, it seems likely that there was something wrong with it when the consumer bought it, and a remedy will usually be available under sales law. However, the longer the gap between sale and breakdown, the more difficult it will be for a consumer to prove that a product was faulty when he bought it. An extended warranty may then be useful because it would obviate the need for having to prove that the product in question did not comply with the statutory quality standard (Twigg-Flesner, 2002).

Moreover, free manufacturers' guarantees offer a further mechanism for dealing with faulty goods. These offer redress if goods are defective due to inadequate materials or workmanship. However, it has already been noted that most guarantees offer protection only for a relatively short period compared to the average life-span of the corresponding product.[42] According to Heal (1977), guarantees have an insurance function in that they protect consumers against product breakdowns which occur during the guarantee period and are the result of a defect which is a result of the manufacturing process. The longer a consumer has used a product, the greater the likelihood that a breakdown is the result of the way the consumer has used the product (Eddy, 1977, p.844) or of the intensity of use (Emons, 1989). Consequently, guarantees will only be made available for a relatively short period of time.

Priest's investment theory[43] offers a helpful explanation of how extended warranties fit in with consumers' legal rights and free manufacturers' guarantees. It will be recalled that Priest argues that a guarantee divides responsibility for investments to minimise the risk of product failure between guarantor and consumer (allocative investment). Market insurance would cover risks which could not be reduced by allocative investments. Manufacturers' guarantees are such a form of insurance, albeit limited to a period during which product breakdowns are more likely to be the result of a manufacturing defect. Once this has expired, the consumer bears the risk of a product ceasing to work. If further protection is required, it will have to be obtained through additional market insurance. Extended warranties provide this additional insurance.

This suggests that consumers who are high-risk consumers would be more likely to purchase an extended warranty. Consumers may have experienced a problem in the past and might expect a further product breakdown to occur in the future (Voss and Ahmed, 1992). Others may expect to use the product frequently and intensively, which would increase the likelihood of a product breakdown (Padmanabhan, 1995). Furthermore, a product which is used by several individuals might break down quicker. These types of consumers have the greatest incentive to buy an extended warranty because they are more likely to have to rely on it to deal with a product breakdown. This is a good example of "adverse selection" (Holdych and Mann, 1996, p.797). According to this principle, a person is more likely to take advantage of insurance if he expects to need protection against a particular risk.

In practice, however, this is not borne out. In fact, the OFT (2002b) discovered that it is generally low-income consumers, rather than high-risk consumers, who buy extended warranties (para 4.48). It seems rather improbable that all low-income consumers who buy an extended warranty are also high-risk consumers, nor indeed does it seem probable that all high-risk consumers are on low incomes. The OFT does not analyse this in any depth, although it suggests that a major problem may be the selling techniques for extended warranties employed by some retailers.

2.5.3 Selling techniques for extended warranties

The OFT discovered that few consumers intend to acquire an extended warranty when they purchase a new product. Generally, these are only taken out as an afterthought and often only after a retailer has mentioned their availability (OFT, 2002, para 4.1). Most extended warranties are sold by retailers - the OFT concluded that the retailers are in a very strong position to market their extended warranties, and often consumers are not aware that such warranties may also be obtained from other sources, such as manufacturers or independent providers (para 4.21).

In the past, concern had been expressed over the pressure selling techniques adopted by many retailers (Day and Fox, 1985; OFT, 1996). Many retailers do not provide accurate information about product reliability, nor do they mention alternative providers of extended warranties. Individual salespeople are often encouraged by their employers to try to sell extended warranties, and are paid a commission on such sales. In response to the OFT's second report (OFT, 1996), the British Retail Consortium put into place a code of practice on the sale of extended warranties. However, in 2001, it became apparent that compliance with this code was not as high as desired by the OFT, nor did there appear to be an appropriate monitoring mechanism in place (see Taylor Nelson Sofres, 2001; OFT, 2002b). It seems that many consumers still feel under at least some pressure to give in to salespersons who seek to sell them an extended warranty (OFT, 2002b, para 4.5).

2.5.4 The high cost of extended warranties

A further problem which has been considered repeatedly by the OFT (1994; 1996; 2002b) is the surprisingly high cost of extended warranties. The Consumers' Association reported in 1994 that the revenue from the sale of such warranties constituted the major source of profit for many retailers. In some cases, the profit margin on the sale of warranties can be as high as 80%. In addition, the claims ratio for extended warranties seems to be significantly lower than the average claims ratio for insurance generally (OFT 2002b, para 4.31).

Although the fact that extended warranties are, at least theoretically, more likely to be purchased by high risk consumers suggests that their price (or premium) may be higher than the average repair cost for a particular type of product, it seems that the actual cost cannot be explained on the basis of insurance principles (see Twigg-Flesner, 2002). The OFT has suggested that the high price may be due to a lack of competition in the provision of extended warranties, and has asked the Competition Commission to investigate the market for extended warranties. A report is to be published in July 2003.[44] If this reveals that there are significant competition problems, the UK government may introduce legislation to deal with this.

2.5.5 Insolvency and consumer protection

A final problem which has caused some concern, particularly in the UK, is the fact that not all extended warranties are insurance policies within the scope of the regulatory framework for financial services. On several occasions, warranty providers have become insolvent and subsequently gone out of business. The warranties sold by these providers were not underwritten by an authorised insurance company. Consequently, consumers were unable to recover the premiums they had paid and were left with worthless extended warranties.

Some warranties are insurance policies or, at least, underwritten by an authorised insurer. If a provider of such warranties becomes insolvent, the Financial Services Compensation scheme operated by the Financial Services Authority compensates consumers if an insurance company is unable to honour claims because of its insolvency (see OFT 2002b, para 4.59). Such consumers would at least receive back the premiums they paid for their warranties. It is therefore arguable, and perhaps even desirable, that all extended warranties are underwritten by an authorised insurance company and therefore brought within the scope of the regulatory framework for financial services (see Twigg-Flesner, 2002). However, it is far from clear that such a requirement will be introduced in the foreseeable future.

2.5.6 Extended warranties: Conclusion

This brief section sought to provide an overview of the issues that arise with extended warranties. It was seen that such warranties can have an important function in providing protection to consumers against the risks of product failure where these are not covered by manufacturers' guarantees or consumers' legal rights. However, there are problems with the way the market for extended warranties operates at present, and legislative intervention may be required in the medium term. For present purposes, it is only necessary to be aware of the broad issues that exist in relation to extended warranties.

2.6 Other guarantees

In addition to manufacturers' guarantees, satisfaction guarantees and extended warranties, there may be other promises given by manufacturers or retailers labelled as guarantees. The word "guarantee" may on occasion be used to express a manufacturer's sincerity about a particular statement, for example (e.g., "guaranteed improvement in performance compared to the previous model"). It is unlikely that the manufacturer will offer a remedy himself if the "guarantee" is not met. However, it was seen in chapter 1 that such statements may be relevant in determining whether the relevant product reaches the statutory quality standard. Both satisfaction guarantees and manufacturers' guarantees contain a promise and indicate the remedy that will be provided by the guarantor if the promise is broken. This will not be the case with other types of "guarantee". Such statements generally form part of the manufacturer's advertising strategy. The question of whether the use of terms such as "guarantee" in advertising should be subject to tighter controls is a matter that falls outside the scope of this book (but see Willett, 1991; 1992).

Finally, it must be noted that retailers often provided guarantees which are similar to manufacturers' guarantees. Indeed, many of the issues that arise with manufacturers' guarantees are of similar relevance to retailers' guarantees. However, this book focuses exclusively on manufacturers' guarantees.

2.7 Conclusions

The objective of this chapter has been to analyse the characteristics of consumer guarantees. It was seen that a guarantee consists of three elements: the guarantee promise that the relevant product is free from defects in materials and workmanship; the remedies that are available if the promise has not been kept, and the terms and conditions on which the guarantee and its remedies are provided. Crucially, some of these terms will explain what a consumer needs to do to obtain redress under the guarantee. The basic characteristics of a guarantee therefore suggest that each guarantee presents a self-contained redress mechanism which can be utilised if the product covered by the guarantee has a manufacturing defect. The potential for guarantees as a redress mechanism will be considered further in chapter 4, but it is important to note at this stage that the elements which make up a guarantee are also the key elements that would be required for a redress mechanism: the conditions of access (breach of the guarantee promise), a range of remedies and the procedure for obtaining a remedy.

It was also seen that there has been particular concern about the terms and conditions on which guarantees are provided, especially with regard to the relationship between a guarantee and the consumers' statutory rights, but also in respect of the conditions that need to be fulfilled to benefit from the guarantee. These problems will need to be taken into account in designing a legal framework for manufacturers' guarantees. The task for the following chapters is to examine the function of manufacturers guarantees. Once this has been done, the elements of a legal framework for guarantees will be considered.

Notes

1 With the exception of financial guarantees, which are wholly outside the scope of this book.

2 Sometimes, such longer guarantees are more like extended warranties in that they are backed up by insurance. However, extended warranties will also generally cover a product breakdown that is not the result of a defect in workmanship or materials. Also, the consumer does not have to pay for the long-term guarantee, whereas he will have to purchase an extended warranty.

3 Cf. Whitford (1968, p.1028) who identified a similar attitude for guarantees for cars.

4 Some products such as outdoor equipment even come with a "lifetime" guarantee, but it is not clear whose "lifetime" the guarantee is referring to - that of the product, or of the consumer.

5 Significantly shorter guarantee periods are also possible. One example is a guarantee for a child's toy which lasted for three months. The remaining terms of the guarantee seemed very generous with regard to the remedies and the procedure for making a claim under the guarantee. One suspects that the short duration could be explained on the basis that the target consumers (young children) are unlikely to take great care when using the product.

6 See below, section 2.5.

7 This may be contrasted with satisfaction guarantees, where the remedy will be a full refund to the consumer and the guarantor has usually no opportunity to reject the consumer's claim. Of course, if the consumer has damaged the product, he may no longer be able to rely on the satisfaction guarantee.

8 The examples used in this section are taken from guarantees offered with products sold in the UK. No reference is made to the brand or type of product, but all examples are from guarantees on consumer durables.

9 Emphasis supplied.

10 See the discussion of factors which may influence the duration of a guarantee in the previous section.

11 See section 2.2.

12 These provisions may, in certain circumstances, give rise to competition law problems, but these are not considered further here. It will be seen in chapter 8 that such terms may also fail to meet a test of fairness (under the Unfair Terms in Consumer Contracts Regulations 1999, which are used to control the fairness of terms in consumer contracts), and may therefore not be binding on consumers - see 8.9.1.

13 This issue is discussed in detail in chapter 5 at 5.4.

14 See 2.3.3, below.

15 In this particular case, 39 countries were listed in the certificate.

16 This was set out in chapter 1 at 1.4 and 1.5.

17 See chapter 8 at 8.9.2 and 8.9.3 for discussion, and also section 2.3.1, below for a criticism of such legislation.

18 This is sometimes also referred to as "Comparative Advantage" Theory - see Schwartz and Wilde (1983), p.1398.

19 This is the additional cost per unit of the product that would be incurred as a result of making the particular improvement.

20 This is the profit per unit of the product that could be obtained.

21 "Moral Hazard" is the term used to describe the consequences of over-insuring against a particular event, such as a product defect. The availability of insurance may encourage a consumer to take less care with the product covered by the insurance, and thereby the likelihood of the occurrence of the insured event is increased.

22 For a criticism of the accuracy of Priest's claims against the backdrop of economic theory, see Schwartz and Wilde (1983), p.1400.

23 Priest responded to Whitford's criticisms: see Priest (1982). What seemed to become an interesting debate between two influential American scholars unfortunately ebbed away after their initial exchange.

24 This may be contrasted with the observations made by Whitford (1968), who noted that in 1960s America, the provision of guarantees involved a lot of bureaucracy.

25 The term "guarantee" will continue to be used for the sake of uniformity.

26 Lowe (1986) provides a useful, if now somewhat dated, overview of the different types of guarantees offered in the industry.

27 This is now a common arrangement. However, this may partly be the result of the old framework for motor vehicle distribution at the European level. Such distribution agreements may be regarded as anti-competitive and are therefore caught by the prohibition in Article 81 of the EC Treaty on agreements with an anti-competitive object or effect. Article 81(3) exempts agreements from this prohibition in certain circumstances. Regulation 1475/95 exempted motor vehicles distribution agreements on conditions that the criteria set out in the Regulation were followed. Article 5(1)(a) required that all the authorised retailers should be responsible for the implementation of the manufacturers' guarantee. A new Block Exemption was adopted on 30 July 2002 (Regulation 1400/2002). There is no direct equivalent of Article 5(1)(a) now, but Recital 17 makes it clear that "[v]ertical agreements that do not oblige the authorised repairers within a supplier 's distribution system to honour warranties … in respect of any motor vehicle of the relevant make sold in the common market amount to an indirect restriction of sales and should not benefit from the exemption".

28 However, if the guarantee is provided by the retailer, then the consumer will have to return to that retailer. Recently, some motor manufacturers have advertised cars with a three-year guarantee. The first year is the manufacturer's guarantee, whereas the second and third years are covered by a retailer's guarantee. As a consequence, a fault that occurs during the first year can be dealt with by any retailer in the distribution network, whereas faults that occur after the first year can only be remedied by the original retailer.

29 The understanding of bargaining power which forms the basis of exploitation theory may be too simplistic by modern standards. It is now evident that market power is only one out of a number of factors which have an impact on bargaining power - see Hadfield, Howse and Trebilcock (1998).

30 Cf. the discussion in chapter 1, which highlighted the problems of the flexible standard of "satisfactory quality" (or "conformity with the contract").

[31] See chapter 8.

[32] In the UK, this has been implemented in the Unfair Contract Terms Regulations 1999 (S.I. 1999/2083) and, for a broader range of consumer problems, in the Stop Now Orders Regulations 2001 (S.I. 2001/1422). The latter will be replaced with Part 8 of the Enterprise Act 2002 when this comes into force in 2003. See also chapter 8.

[33] Indeed, the relevant provisions in the Consumer Guarantees Directive are based on the premise that advertising may be the *only* source of information about a guarantee that may be available to the consumer at the time he purchases a product. See chapter 7 at 7.1.

[34] See Tenreiro (1995) and Madsen (1995).

[35] It is not clear why diversity of guarantees was identified as a problem, and it was not made clear why this was particularly pertinent in a cross-border context. Indeed, the *Green Paper* (1993) is premised on the idea that it may be desirable to encourage competition on guarantees - in which case diversity would be beneficial.

[36] Similar observations were made with regard to after-sales services, although here, the main concern seemed to be with the availability of after-sales services in the Home Member State.

[37] Clear evidence of this is provided by many guarantee documents which accompany consumer products. The guarantee is often given in numerous different languages, and a closer inspection reveals that there are different terms for different countries.

[38] Satisfaction periods are similar to cooling-off periods, which allow a consumer to cancel a contract within a fixed period after signing.

[39] Or a demonstration product (sample) of the same type.

[40] This section presents an overview of the relevant issues. For a detailed discussion of these and for an analysis of the legal context, see Twigg-Flesner (2002).

[41] See chapter 1, sections 1.4/1.5.

[42] See 2.1.1.

[43] See 2.1.4, above.

[44] Readers can obtain up-to-date information at http://www.competition-commission.org.uk/inquiries/warranty.

Chapter 3

Manufacturers' Guarantees and Information about Product Quality

3.0 Introduction

In chapter 1, it was seen that one of the biggest problems for consumers is that it may often be difficult to ascertain the level of quality of a particular item. Furthermore, it may also not be easy to discern the overall level of quality that can be expected within a product category.

It was also noted that voluntary guarantees could be a means of reducing the impact of this problem. In essence, by offering a guarantee, a manufacturer is viewed as sending out a "signal" to consumers that the product is of a particular quality standard. The assumption is that the more generous the guarantee, the better the quality of the product. This is known as "signalling theory". This chapter will focus on the potential role of guarantees as a signal of product quality. There will first be a consideration of signalling theory in general. There will then follow a discussion of its application to guarantees. Chapter 6 will complement this with a case-study of a legal framework that is largely based on signalling theory, the United States Magnuson-Moss Warranty Act 1975. It will also be seen that signalling theory has been influential in the U.K., and at the European level. It will be considered if consumers really perceive guarantees as signals of product quality, by drawing on research published in the literature on economics and business studies.

3.1 Quality signals

3.1.1 Signalling theory explained

This section will first outline the general concept of signalling theory. This will be followed by an exploration of how guarantees could be signals. This will take into account empirical research carried out to ascertain whether this theory holds in practice.

The fundamental premise for signalling theory is that the information available to consumers in the market is imperfect (Boulding and Kirmani, 1993). Misinformation or inadequate knowledge about product quality, and therefore the probability of product failure, may result in consumers choosing a product of low quality. If a consumer cannot establish the level of quality before purchase, there may not be a sufficient incentive for a seller or the producer to communicate the quality standard of their products, because a consumer is unable to verify this. To get around this, a seller may try to signal quality to a consumer instead.

So what is meant by "signalling"?[1] A simple explanation is that:

> Market signalling occurs when information is communicated between economic agents using various alterable and observable characteristics (Gerner and Bryant, 1981, p.77).

In the context of the sale of consumer goods:

> A signal is a visible product feature that consumers use to evaluate invisible product features (Kelley 1988, p.73).

Thus, something visible and observable is used to relay information between the signal provider and the consumer about aspects of a product which cannot be ascertained by a mere examination of the product in question. Buyers may be unaware of the real quality of a product if this can only be ascertained through using the product. Most consumer products are experience goods, and their quality, such as durability or reliability, can only be assessed during consumption, and not before purchase.

Signals may be particularly important when a consumer intends to buy a new[2] product (Bearden and Shimp, 1982). Consumers are generally risk averse,[3] and the adoption of a new product is risky. Signals may have a risk-reducing function in that they may convey information which a consumer could not obtain elsewhere. Such non-physical product characteristics[4] (also known as "extrinsic cues")[5] could be used to provide consumers who cannot evaluate a product before purchase with some reassurance that the product meets a particular standard of quality.

The effectiveness of signals appears to depend on a number of factors. Generally, the market must be able to separate into different equilibria[6] in order to support a signal (Boulding and Kirmani, 1993). Signals have to be viewed in combination with the costs consumers face when attempting to interpret a market signal. A consumer thus has to distinguish between high and low quality products, which can be done by relying on signals. Provided that sellers are rational,[7] consumers will look for signals which are profitable for sellers of high-quality products, but unprofitable for sellers of low-quality products. If it is possible for sellers of high-quality products to send a signal to this effect to the consumer, a "separating equilibrium" results. In a separating equilibrium, the market leads the sellers of low and high quality products to adopt separate strategies (assuming markets exist for both sellers). It is an equilibrium because both types of seller have an incentive not to deflect from their strategies. These strategies provide a basis upon which buyers can distinguish between sellers of products of different levels of quality.

Where the market does not support different strategies, a "pooling equilibrium" occurs. In a pooling equilibrium, there is no cost advantage as a result of signalling (Agrawal et.al., 1996). Both types of seller will adopt the same strategy, and consumers can no longer distinguish between low and high quality products based on the sellers' marketing strategies. Thus, only where there is a separating equilibrium will a seller's strategy serve as a signal.

A second factor is that the signal needs to be credible. A signal only works where the information emitted by the signal to the consumer indicates that the seller would suffer financially if the signal were not true. A credible signal will have a bonding component, resulting in cost to the seller if the signal is false. A seller who emits a particular signal will incur some cost if the signal is inaccurate. Therefore, signals only work where the seller has a sufficient degree of "bond credibility".

So what is meant by "bond credibility"? The consumer has to be able to ascertain whether the signal is correct, i.e., whether the seller sending out a signal will incur costs should the signal prove to be false. Factors which are relevant in this context may include the cost of having to provide a remedy under a guarantee, loss of investment and brand reputation (Boulding and Kirmani, 1993). Boulding and Kirmani suggest that brand reputation is the most significant factor in bond credibility. An established seller with a good reputation and quality record is more likely to attract consumers than a new seller or a seller with a bad reputation. A new seller is unable to prove himself as a lasting player in the market - this can only be established after many years.[8]

In a pooling equilibrium, bond credibility will be low, i.e., consumers are unlikely to believe that any signals sent out by the sellers are true. Where sellers do not have high bond credibility, they are unable to send accurate signals regarding quality of their products. This state of pooling equilibrium may result in consumers believing a seller to be honest where he signals a product to be of low quality, whereas a signal of high quality may be viewed as a sign of dishonesty, and may result in a perception of lower quality. Alternatively, consumers could treat the bonding component as meaningless, and therefore not rely on the signal at all. Generally, signals of high quality will be ineffective where bond credibility (i.e., brand reputation) is low.

However, consumers may not always be able to assess the bond credibility of a particular seller. This may enable a seller of a low-quality product to signal (falsely) that he sells a high-quality product. Those consumers who are able to assess the seller's bond credibility will not respond to the signal. However, consumers who are unable to do so may believe the signal and may therefore be mislead.

Signals can be useful to the extent that consumer utilisation of the signal results in accurate discrimination between sellers of high-quality and low-quality products (Agrawal et.al., 1996). The accuracy of a signal seems to correspond to the costs which may be incurred by the seller by sending out that signal. If costs differ depending on whether the signal is correct, signalling is accurate. If costs do not differ, the signal is ineffective.

A number of factors may influence the extent to which a signal can be accurate. These are: first, the variation of reliability between different brands, the level of market penetration of the product[9] and product age.[10] The degree of signalling value is also likely to be influenced by consumer knowledge of brand reliability (experience value), incentives to signal reliability, and a seller's ability to distinguish himself from his competitors.

This brief general discussion of signalling theory therefore reveals that signals can only operate efficiently where consumers can clearly distinguish between different types of signal. Furthermore, consumers have to be able to ascertain whether the signal is accurate. If a seller does not have a sufficient degree of bond credibility, then any signal sent out by the seller will not be effective. The next step is to consider how guarantees may act as signals of product quality.

3.2 Application to guarantees

A first consideration is what exactly is meant by claiming that guarantee can signal product quality. In essence, there has to be a positive relationship between the level of protection against product defects given to consumers under the guarantee and the quality of the product itself. Some commentators have taken this as meaning that the guarantee signals the "durability" of the product (e.g., Priest, 1981), whereas others consider that it signals the "reliability" of the product (e.g., Agrawal *et. al.*, 1996). The difference between these two concepts has already been discussed.[11]

If a guarantee is a signal of "durability", it reflects the expected lifetime of a product. In this case, the duration of the guarantee could be expected to bear some relation to the expected lifetime of the product. However, if a guarantee is a signal of "reliability", it indicates the period of time during which a product can be expected to perform trouble-free. Most products will eventually develop some sort of problem, but this will not necessarily bring the product's lifetime to an end. In this case, the guarantee would signal that the product will operate without a failure of any kind for at least the duration of the guarantee. It seems more sensible therefore to suggest that guarantees could be a signal of reliability, rather than durability.[12]

Guarantees could be a means for manufacturers of communicating information about the quality of a product, which they could not do through other means, such as a statement in advertising that the product is of "superior quality" (Wiener, 1985). It seems unlikely that consumers would be persuaded by such assertions.

For something to act as a market signal, it requires a "bonding component", which causes the person sending the signal to incur costs if the signal turns out to be incorrect. If a guarantee is a signal, then the cost to the manufacturer of providing the guarantee is systematically related to product reliability (Spence, 1977). Reliability is correlated negatively with the cost of giving a guarantee

(Priest, 1981). A guarantor will incur the cost of having to provide a remedy under a guarantee when the signal fails. As the guarantor will be interested to keep this cost to a minimum, he will ensure that the guarantee does not signal a quality standard which is higher than the actual level of quality of the relevant product. If the signal does not tally with the standard of quality, more claims will be brought as the product is unlikely to be as reliable as signalled by the guarantee. Consequently, the guarantor will incur higher costs.

A difficulty with bond credibility is the identification of factors which consumers may take into account in establishing whether a signal will not only result in cost to the person sending the signal, but also that the cost will be met. The reputation of the guarantor is possibly the most significant factor which can influence the signalling value of a guarantee (Bearden and Shimp, 1982). If the guarantor has a bad reputation, it seems that a signal such as a guarantee will do little to suggest that the products covered by the guarantee are of a certain standard of quality.[13]

The function of guarantees as a signal has to be examined from three different perspectives: first, it is instructive to review if there is an objective link between product quality and guarantee coverage. In the preceding paragraphs, it was demonstrated that guarantees have the capacity to be signals, but it is also necessary to examine if this is borne out in the use of guarantees in the market place. Second, it needs to be asked if consumers actually perceive guarantees as signals of product quality. This requires a more detailed examination of the factors which may influence consumers' perceptions in this regard. Finally, it is necessary to establish if manufacturers intend to use guarantees to signal the quality of their products. Examining the function of guarantees from these different perspectives may offer useful insights into the extent to which signalling theory is accurate.

3.2.1 Are guarantees objectively acting as market signals?

In order to ascertain whether a guarantee can be a market signal on an *objective* assessment, it has to be established if a product covered by a guarantee with a wide scope reflects a higher degree of product quality when compared with a similar product which is covered by a guarantee with a more restricted scope, or where no guarantee is given at all. If this were generally the case, significant support would be provided for the claim that guarantees are signals of quality.

There have been several empirical studies of this aspect. The studies discussed here were carried out in the United States. This research has not come to conclusive results. Gerner and Bryant's (1981) study of guarantees offered with five types of products (washing machines, refrigerators, air conditioners, televisions and ranges) was based on the assumption that consumers would not consider the content of guarantees in detail, with the effect that most guarantees would be similar, and therefore not act as signals of quality. Their analysis of the terms of the guarantees which were offered with the products forming part of their study lead them to concluded that there is a "median" level of guarantee coverage, and that most guarantees were such median guarantees, with few guarantees offering marginally better coverage.[14]

Priest (1981) followed this with a similar study of a guarantees offered on a wider range of products (such as dryers, cookware and automobiles). He also claimed that for a guarantee to be a correct signal, it would have to be similar in its content to the guarantees offered by other guarantors. Guarantees were commonly offered for products purchased infrequently, and a consumer would derive little benefit from obtaining information about specific guarantees. He continued that if a guarantee were offered on terms other than the "standard" terms which a consumer should expect for a guarantee accompanying a product of a particular type, these terms should be more favourable to the consumer, rather than more restrictive. Consumers would expect at least the "average" guarantee - a guarantee falling below would incur an increase in the administrative and financial burden of guarantors, because consumers would bring claims under the guarantee which are not covered, expecting the guarantee to provide the "average" level of coverage. He then stated that the central provisions of the various guarantees would be similar, but there would be greater diversity in sub-ordinate provisions on exclusions and limitations. Priest claimed that signalling theory proposes that consumers rely on the signalling value of central terms of a guarantee rather than that of sub-ordinate terms, particularly because consumers paid less attention to these terms. This seems to ignore an important aspect of the signalling function of guarantees. Even similar products produced by different manufacturers will not necessarily be of similar quality - therefore, the guarantee terms should, on the basis of signalling theory as explained above, vary according to the standard of quality provided by each manufacturer. Signalling theory considers guarantees as a whole, and not merely selected provisions. Although it is likely that there will be similarities between guarantees in some regards, and differences to a varying degree in others, the whole of the guarantee has to be considered. Priest found that most guarantees were restricted to a twelve-month period, and were very similar in scope. He concluded that signalling theory was not supported by his findings.

Agrawal et.al. (1996) criticised both studies for failing to consider data on the reliability of the products examined therein. Priest merely considered the products' service life expectancy (durability), rather than the average period of trouble-free service (reliability).[15] Subsequent studies have taken a different approach. Wiener (1985) suggested that guarantees on the products examined in his study (air conditioners, televisions, washing machines and clothes dryers) were accurate signals of product reliability. He compared the guarantees in the various product categories to ascertain an 'average' guarantee, and found that some guarantees were definitely above this average. He then analysed data on the reliability of these products,[16] and came to the conclusion that products with above-average guarantees were more likely to have above-average reliability, and thus be of higher quality. Kelley's (1988) research complemented Wiener's (1985) study by analysing additional product categories (refrigerators, air conditioners and dishwashers). He also concluded that guarantees are signals of product reliability. These results support the suggestion that guarantees can be signals of product reliability, and therefore offer support to signalling theory, if interpreted in this way.[17]

Agrawal et.al. (1996) noted the inconclusive state of the empirical examination of the relationship between guarantee coverage and product quality. They suggested that the signalling function of a guarantee may depend on factors other than the guarantor's reputation (i.e., bond credibility). They considered the effect of three product market characteristics on the signalling value of guarantees: age (length of time of the product category being on the market), market penetration (percentage of consumer households owning a product from the particular category), and variation in reliability between brands. They concluded that there was no clear relationship between guarantees and quality, but that these three product market characteristics played a significant part in determining when guarantees can have a signalling function. Guarantees were more likely to be accurate signals of quality when they were given with established products with a high degree of market penetration. However, consumers are likely to place greater reliance on signals (such as guarantees) at a point in time when these are the least accurate reflection of product quality, i.e., when considering to buy product which is new on the market (see also Bearden and Shimp, 1982; Shimp and Bearden, 1982).

A further product market characteristic which may influence the signalling value of guarantees is the cost of establishing a network of sellers and repairers, and of providing a remedy under a guarantee (Douglas et.al., 1993). It seems that the signalling value is higher where such a network is in place,[18] because the guarantor has already invested in setting up this network.

Empirical research does not offer unequivocal support for the objective view of the signalling function of guarantees. It provides some support, and there are definite instances where it is very likely that guarantees *will* act as signals. The next section will consider if consumers perceive guarantees as signals of product quality, and if so, in what circumstances.

3.2.2 Do consumers perceive guarantees as signals of product quality?

With limited support for signalling theory from an objective perspective, it is necessary to consider if consumers nevertheless use guarantees (perhaps mistakenly) as quality signals and, if so, when. The analysis of the factors that need to be present for guarantees to act as signals revealed that there needs to be a bonding component, and that this bonding component is credible, i.e., the guarantor must incur a cost if the signal is false and is perceived by the consumer to be willing to assume this cost. It will therefore be interesting to examine the factors that may influence a consumer's perception of guarantees as signals of quality.

Boulding and Kirmani (1993) took account of the effect of bond credibility on the signalling value of a guarantee when they considered the consumer perspective in a laboratory experiment. They did so by manipulating a guarantor's reputation. They discovered that guarantees are positive signals of quality when bond credibility is high, i.e., when the guarantor is reputable. They also found that negative perceptions of the signalling value of a guarantee result from a high guarantee when bond credibility is low. Therefore, a guarantee offering a high level of coverage is a better strategy for a seller who has a reputation for high-quality products, but not for a seller of low-quality products. Guarantees would therefore be signals of quality only where the reputation of the guarantor corresponds with the level of quality indicated by the guarantee. However, the authors conceded that their conclusions had to be treated with some caution and that their results were not suitable for generalisation.

More recent research provides stronger evidence for the significance of reputation. Thus, Purohit and Srivastava (2001) found that reputation was a more important factor than the guarantee itself, but that the signalling value of a guarantee could benefit from the good reputation of the guarantor:

> ... perceptions of quality were not influenced by [a guarantee] when the reputation of the manufacturer was poor ... (p.133).

Similar conclusions were also reached by Price and Dawar (2002), who observe that the credibility of a particular signal may depend on the synergistic effects of multiple signals. They also concluded that the signalling function of a guarantee depends to a large extent on the brand reputation of the guarantor (p.186).

Srivastava and Mitra (1998) build on Boulding and Kirmani's work by introducing a further factor which may affect the extent to which guarantees could be perceived as signals of product quality. They suggest that consumers fall into two broad categories, "novices" and "experts". In their terminology, "novices" are consumers who have not previously bought a particular type of product, whereas "experts" have purchased a particular product at least once previously. Their study suggests that experts did not pay much attention to the reputation of the guarantor. The authors conceded that this might be the result of the experts' general awareness of the scope of the guarantees offered in a particular product market and in how far there is a link between product quality and guarantee coverage in that market. However, as far as novices were concerned, the study suggests that they would only use guarantees as a signal of quality if the perceived reputation of the guarantor is high. It therefore seems that the extent to which guarantees are used as signals of product quality may depend on the familiarity of a consumer with a particular product sector. A negative reputation of a guarantor may therefore inhibit the use of guarantees as a quality signal for novices, but less so for experts, who are able to draw on their general awareness of the market. The authors emphasise the need for further research to support their initial findings.

A further factor which may have an impact on bond credibility, and therefore the signalling value of guarantees, is information about the country where the product is manufactured (Tan, Lee and Lim, 1999; Tan and Leong, 1998). Research by Tan and Leong (1998) suggests that consumers are influenced in their quality perceptions by information about the country of manufacture, and it seems that the reputation of the guarantor (or brand) is unlikely to overcome potentially negative perceptions based on the country of manufacture. Furthermore, the same appears to hold true for information about the country where the product was designed. Thus, if a product was made or designed (or both) in a country which has a low reputation for manufacturing quality and/or design, a guarantee would not have a sufficiently strong signalling value to be an accurate indicator of product quality. Tan, Lee and Lim (1999) provide further research evidence that a high reputation and a generous guarantee is likely to be perceived as an effective signal of product quality. However, a generous guarantee given on a product which is designed or made in a country of lower reputation will not be treated as an accurate signal of product quality.

Consumers may also take the view that a guarantee which offers substantially more than guarantees on products within the same category is "too good to be true" (Shimp and Bearden, 1982).[19] As a consequence, consumers may not assume that this particular product is, in fact, of a better quality than similar products. This may depend on by how much this particular guarantee deviates from what the consumer may expect by comparing the various guarantees on products within the same category. If it is slightly more favourable to the consumer, it may be taken as an indicator of better quality, but if it is considerably more favourable, consumers may become suspicious, and not regard the guarantee as a signal of product quality.

There are factors other than those relating to bond credibility which may have an effect on whether consumers regard guarantees as signals of quality. It may be speculated that this may depend on whether consumers are protected by non-excludable statutory rights and the extent to which consumers are aware of this protection (cf. Price and Dawar, 2002, p.186). If consumers are familiar with their legal rights, and the relationship between their legal rights and the rights they may have under the guarantee, the guarantee may not be as strong a signal of quality. This is because consumers know that they will in any event be able to obtain a remedy if they have acquired a product which is of lower quality than required by statute. There is no empirical evidence available that has considered this point.

Moreover, Trebilcock (1972) observed that there might be two reasons why guarantees may not be accurate signals of product quality. First, consumers may find it difficulty, or even be unable, to comprehend the terms of a guarantee. These may be presented in complex language and include legal terms of art, which many consumers are unlikely to understand. Second, he noted that guarantees were rarely, if ever, considered during the process of making a purchasing decision. Guarantees are not usually available before purchase, because they are enclosed with the product, and consumers are therefore unable to compare guarantees offered with different products and use the guarantee as an indicator of product quality.[20]

Furthermore, it has been remarked repeatedly that consumers may not so much be interested in the detailed terms of the guarantee, but merely in the fact whether a guarantee is offered at all (Gerner and Bryant, 1981; Kelley, 1988). This may be because the mere existence of a guarantee may be an indicator of the manufacturer's confidence in his product (Willett, 1992). If consumers were only interested in the fact that a guarantee is given, but not interested in the specifics of it other than its duration (Trebilcock, 1972), a guarantor would gain nothing from choosing to signal the better quality of a product through a guarantee (Gerner and Bryant, 1981). However, it may equally be the case that consumers would draw adverse inferences of product quality if *no* guarantee were given at all.

Finally, empirical evidence largely suggests that few consumers take guarantees into account when deciding on a purchase.[21] In 1992, a survey in the United States appeared to suggest that around 50% of consumers use the information offered by guarantees to estimate the reliability of a product they are considering to buy (Agrawal et. al., 1996, p.422). However, Adler (1994) reported that only 10% of consumers examined a guarantee before purchase. In the United Kingdom, recent research suggests that 41% of all consumers looked for information about product quality before purchase, but only 18% of all consumers were interested in the existence of a guarantee (DTI, 2001a, p.7). However, this figure was higher for purchasers of domestic appliances (one quarter of all those who buy such appliances) and for cars (28% of car purchasers). These findings suggest that consumers in the United Kingdom generally rely on other sources to obtain information about product quality.

However, these statistics only suggest that consumers do not consider guarantees as part of their purchasing decision, but does not explain why they do not do so. An obvious explanation may be that there are better or more accessible alternative sources of information about product quality available. A different view may be that guarantees are not sufficiently clear to enable consumers to utilise them, but if they were drafted differently and available before purchase, then consumers might take them into account. It will be seen below that the latter argument is one of the basic reasons for legislative intervention in the provision of guarantees - the desire to promote the signalling function of guarantees and to encourage consumers to make greater use of guarantees to evaluate product quality. Yet, even such intervention may not have the desired effect if consumers still prefer alternative sources of information.

3.2.3 Do guarantors intend their guarantees to be market signals?

It may not be immediately obvious why this needs to be considered. However, the issue of the guarantor's *intent* could be crucial to the signalling value of a guarantee. Guarantors may simply chose to offer a guarantee as a promotional device, as an alternative to competition on price, or perhaps to gain a competitive advantage by offering additional 'rights' to a consumer in the form of an accessible complaints-handling mechanism (Kelley, 1988). In such instances, it would be difficult to argue that in offering a particular guarantee, a guarantor does so on the basis that the product covered by the guarantee is of a higher quality than similar products within the same category. A guarantor may choose to offer a guarantee simply because it is standard practice in his particular business sector to do so.

Signalling theory postulates that guarantors will seek to ensure that their guarantees are in some way related to the quality of the relevant product. This has sometimes been referred to as the "incentive effect" of guarantees (Heal, 1977). Guarantees have an incentive effect because a guarantor is given an incentive to improve quality in line with his guarantee signal. However, there may be factors which may influence a guarantor in limiting the scope of his guarantee to the extent that it signals a lower standard of quality than that actually attained by the relevant product.

The likelihood that a product breaks down depends not only on its quality, but also on the effort to maintain the product made by the consumer when using it. This has already been discussed in chapter 2.[22] First, it was seen that longer guarantee periods increase the likelihood of factors other than shortcomings during the manufacturing process causing a defect (Eddy, 1977, p.844). Second, consumers use products in different ways, and some consumers are more likely to cause a product to fail than others (Emons, 1989).

Furthermore, as the effort made by a consumer to maintain his product cannot be predetermined, moral hazard may also be a factor that is taken into account (Lutz, 1988).[23] Consumer moral hazard suggests that higher levels of guarantee protection decrease the incentive for product maintenance by the consumer. The relationship between quality and consumer effort is important. A consumer who is aware of higher quality may make a greater effort to maintain the product and keep guarantee costs low, but a consumer who thinks a product is of low quality will make less of an effort, even when there is a high guarantee. Moral hazard can therefore be an important element in limiting the signalling function of guarantees. Although a guarantor may be able to offer a more generous guarantee if purely based on the level of quality, the likelihood of increased claims under the guarantees may make the guarantor more cautious in respect of the breadth of coverage. On this basis, it may be advantageous for a guarantor not to use a guarantee as a quality signal.

In addition, Vandegrift (2001) suggests that the enforcement of guarantees, both in the courts[24] and through the market,[25] may affect the extent of coverage guarantors are willing to provide. This will inevitably affect the degree to which a guarantee can then be a signal of product quality. A guarantor may decide not to honour his guarantee and a consumer wishing to claim will seek to enforce this through court action. Alternatively, a consumer may try to force a guarantor to honour is guarantee in a situation where the quality defect is caused by the consumer, i.e., the consumer is trying to claim under a guarantee for something not covered by the guarantee. Vandegrift argues that guarantors may therefore offer less generous guarantees in order to reduce the risk of incorrect adverse judgments. If the courts are able to distinguish between instances where the guarantor is wrongfully refusing to honour his guarantee and instances of wrongful claims by consumers, this risk reduces and guarantors may offer more generous guarantees. The signalling value of guarantees may therefore depend on the perceived costs that may result from the enforcement of guarantees by a court.

Additionally, he suggests that if markets become more efficient in transmitting information about product quality between consumers, guarantees will become less relevant - in other words, if consumers can obtain information about product quality from other sources, there is no incentive for guarantors to offer a guarantee that reflects the level of quality of the corresponding product and therefore guarantees will lose their signalling function.

It may be correct to suggest that the potential cost of enforcing guarantees may be something that needs to be borne in mind in evaluating the signalling value of guarantees. However, this presupposes that court enforcement constitutes a significant concern for guarantors. This is unlikely to be the case - empirical evidence[26] suggests that only a very small number of consumers take legal action when faced with a quality problem. Vandegrift's observations would be of greater significance if there was a larger number of court cases involving guarantees, but the number of guarantees which form the subject of a court case will be but a negligible proportion of the overall number of guarantees.

A final reason why manufacturers may be less inclined to use their guarantees as signals of quality by offering long-term guarantees is that they would then restrict their opportunity for additional profit through the sale of extended warranties.[27] It was seen in chapter 2 that one of the main concerns with extended warranties is their high price in relation to the actual cost of repairing or replacing a product. This suggests that the profit margin on extended warranties is high. Encouraging consumers to purchase an extended warranty rather than offering a free guarantee has therefore clear financial benefits.

3.3 Guarantees and signalling theory: Some conclusions

What are the conclusions that can be drawn from this discussion? First, it was discovered that guarantees can only be an accurate signal of product quality if it is possible to identify a bonding component and if it can be shown that this is credible. A person giving a guarantee must incur a cost if the signal is not accurate (the product is not of the signalled quality and a remedy needs to be provided under the guarantee) and he must be perceived as willing to meet that cost.

Empirical testing of signalling theory has provided only limited support for the suggestion that guarantees can be signals of product quality. The research by Wiener (1985) and Kelley (1988) suggests that guarantees can accurately signal the reliability of products. However, there seem to be a number of variables such as age, market penetration and variation in reliability between brands which may affect the signalling value (Agrawal et. al., 1996). Furthermore, few consumers seem to take guarantees into account when making a purchasing decision (Adler, 1994; DTI, 2001a). For those that do, a number of variables will influence bond credibility and therefore the extent to which guarantees are taken as quality signals (Boulding and Kirmani, 1993). The familiarity of consumers with the particular product sector is also significant (Srivastava and Mitra, 1998). Finally, there are a number of factors which will limit the extent to which guarantors intend their guarantees to be quality signals, such as moral hazard (Lutz, 1998) and the likelihood of factors other than manufacturing problems causing a defect (Eddy, 1977; Emons, 1989).

In sum, the function of guarantees as signals of product quality is limited. Guarantees do "'not always' and 'certainly not consistently'" (Agrawal et. al., 1996, p.441) signal product quality. There are situations when guarantees have the capacity to reflect accurately the quality of a product, but there are also just as many, if not more, situations where they do not. The literature on signalling theory cannot support fully the proposition that guarantees are signals of product quality, and signalling theory is "not useful for policy purposes" (Schwartz and Wilde,

1983, p.1398). Yet, it will be seen in the following section that the fundamental assumption that guarantees are indicative of product quality has influenced the design of legislation on guarantees in the past, and continues to do so today.

3.4 Legal frameworks based on signalling theory

The basic proposition put forward by signalling theory seems attractive, but - as demonstrated in this chapter - there are significant limitations to the scope of guarantees as a quality signal. Nevertheless, this theory has influenced numerous proposals for legislative reform. It forms the roots of the U.S. Magnuson-Moss Warranty Act (see chapter 6), and has also been referred to in recent reform proposals both in the U.K. and the European Community.

3.4.1 Signalling theory remains influential

In spite of the limitations on the signalling function of guarantee identified in the previous section, the basic premise of signalling theory remains popular and influential. For example, Sheriff Principal Macleod in *Thain v Anniesland Trade Centre* (1997) noted *obiter* at 106:

> If one buys a new car, one can reasonably expect to use it for at least the guarantee period without experiencing the failure of an important component or system.

This could be taken more generally to mean that a consumer could reasonably expect to enjoy the use of a product without any failure at least during the guarantee period. Importantly, Macleod suggests that the guarantee is an indicator of reliability rather than durability,[28] because he assumes that the guarantee period reflects the period during which a consumer may expect trouble-free use. After the guarantee period has expired, the consumer may have to expect a product failure that will require a repair.

The European Commission's perception of the function of 'consumer guarantees' was very much influenced by signalling theory. The basic premise for the consideration of guarantees was that:

> Guarantees are steadily becoming a preferred method of competition between firms and one of the most widespread arguments used in advertising (*consumers look on guarantees as a quality label*)[29] (Green Paper, 1993).

To say that "consumers look on guarantees as a quality label" is to suggest that consumers regard the existence of a guarantee as evidence of better quality - it is thus assumed that consumers perceive guarantees as signals of quality.

The perception of guarantees as competitive devices is also reflected in the Directive which was ultimately adopted (see chapter 7). Recital 21 states that:

> Whereas, for certain categories of goods, it is current practice for sellers and producers to offer guarantees on goods against any defect which becomes apparent within a certain period; whereas *this practice can stimulate competition*; whereas, while such guarantees are legitimate marketing tools, they should not mislead the consumer; whereas, to ensure that consumers are not misled, guarantees should contain certain information, including a statement that the guarantee does not affect the consumer's legal rights.[30]

This, too, is an indication that the signalling function of guarantees was a dominating factor in the approach taken by the E.C. This is, perhaps, further re-inforced by the requirement in Article 6(3) of the Directive, according to which a guarantee has to be made "available in writing or feature in another durable medium available and accessible to [the consumer]" before purchase.

3.4.2 Characteristics of a framework based on signalling theory

It is therefore clear that the influence of signalling theory is strong, despite the fact that the research evidence only offers limited support for it. If signalling theory should form the basis of a legal framework for manufacturers' guarantees, what should be the main characteristics? A legal framework based on signalling theory has to deal with two challenges: first, it needs to encourage consumers to treat guarantees as a signal of product quality. In effect, it needs to encourage consumers to take guarantees into account as part of their purchasing decision. The evidence that is available suggests that few consumers do so at present. It would therefore be necessary to explain to consumers that they ought to have regard to guarantees as part of their decision-making process.

Second, it needs to ensure that consumers are able to process the information about product quality that is provided by a guarantee. Consumers need to be able to see the guarantee before purchase. However, it seems unlikely that many consumers would wish to read a detailed guarantee document whilst they are in a shop intending to make a purchase. Rather than to take into account all the available information, consumers will only use the information which they regard as sufficient to make a purchase (they "satisfice" - see Grether, Schwartz and Wilde, 1986). It would therefore be necessary to simplify the information sufficiently still to convey enough detail about the quality of the product whilst not taking more than a few moments to be understood by a consumer.

This would suggest that it would be necessary to reduce manufacturers' guarantees to one or two variables which consumers could easily take into account in deciding on a purchase. Trebilcock argued that consumers are most likely to be interested in the duration of a guarantee (1972, p.29). Furthermore, there are common assumptions among consumers with regard to the coverage of most guarantees (Madsen, 1995, p.149). A suitable approach would therefore be to standardise most aspects of a guarantee,[31] but leave it to the guarantor to determine the duration of the guarantee. Consumers would then only need to consider the length of the guarantee period and could take manufacturers' guarantees into account when shopping without having to read all of the guarantee in detail.

Additionally, such an approach could encourage improvements to the general level of product quality. If consumers are persuaded to utilise guarantees as part of their pre-purchase decision-making process, guarantors might seek to compete on the scope of their guarantees and attract consumers by offering more generous guarantees. However, as noted above, offering more generous guarantees may increase the guarantor's cost unless the number of claims during the guarantee period can be kept to a minimum. The obvious way of achieving this is through improvements to overall product quality. Therefore, promoting the use of guarantees as signals of product quality will not only provide greater transparency for consumers, but also lead to overall improvements to product quality.

Creating such a framework is not impossible, as the example of the Magnuson-Moss Act demonstrates. However, in light of the limitations to the signalling function of guarantees discussed in this chapter, it seems highly unlikely that a legal framework based on signalling theory will attain is objective of promoting competition on guarantees and increasing product quality.

3.5 Conclusions

Despite the problems that have been identified with regard to a signalling based approach to manufacturers' guarantees, the idea that there is a link between product quality and guarantee coverage remains popular. As a basic proposition, the link between guarantees and product quality seems attractive. However attractive it may be though, it does not withstand detailed scrutiny. There is now a well-established body of research evidence which clearly demonstrates that there is no consistent relationship between guarantees and product quality. Furthermore, it seems highly unlikely that manufacturers would seek to offer guarantees which reflected more accurately the quality of the relevant product, because there are a number of constraints, notably the moral hazard problem.

Moreover, most consumers do not take guarantees into account in deciding on a purchase. At best, they may be interested in the existence of a guarantee, but they are unlikely to use a guarantee to establish the level of product quality they could reasonably expect from the relevant product. In order fully to evaluate the level of quality signalled by a guarantee, a consumer would have to be aware of several additional factors, which are unlikely to be available at the time of making a purchase.

Signalling theory seems to be much less significant than commonly assumed. Guarantees are therefore unlikely to play a significant part in the pre-purchase context. Consumers are unlikely to take these into account when deciding on a purchase, nor do manufacturers generally intend to signal product quality with their guarantees. This suggests that guarantees may be of greater significance in the post-purchase context, once the consumer has used the product and the product has broken down because of a quality defect. The guarantee may then be useful as a means of obtaining redress. This will be examined in detail in the following chapter.

Notes

1 This section will refer to terminology from the field of economics. This book draws on economics literature only to the extent that this assists in the evaluation of signalling theory.

2 "New" can have two meanings in this case - it can either be used with reference to a product of a kind which the consumer has never previously used or possessed. It can also refer simply to the acquisition of a new product to replace an older product of the same kind.

3 i.e., consumers try to avoid risk wherever possible.

4 Such as guarantees, price and manufacturer reputation.

5 "Extrinsic Cues" are aspects which are related to the product. Price is such a cue because consumers may deduce from a high price that the product is of a higher quality than a cheaper product. Similarly, a product made by a manufacturer with a good reputation may appeal more to consumers than a product made by a manufacturer who is less highly regarded.

6 "Equilibrium" is the situation in the market where there is neither excessive supply nor excessive demand for a particular product, service or business strategy. A "separating equilibrium" exists where different companies adopt different strategies, but there is demand for both types of strategy. On the other hand, a "pooling equilibrium" exists when companies would not benefit from adopting different strategies, i.e., when consumers would not use a company's particular strategy as a guide when making a purchasing decision.

7 In the present context, "rational" refers to actions which are taken on the basis of logic and reason - in other words, a rational firm would act in such a way as is dictated by the market - and not take freak decisions.

8 Priest (1981) correctly observes that the bonding component is going to be of relevance whether or not guarantees are treated as signals of product quality. Whenever a manufacturer offers a guarantee, there will be an incentive to improve product quality to minimise the number of claims under the guarantee (at p.1309).

9 i.e., how many households have a product of that particular kind, which reflects consumer knowledge of reliability and promotes a market disciplined against sending misleading signals where penetration is high.

10 i.e., for how long the particular class of product has been marketed.

11 See chapter 1 section 1.2.1.

12 Empirical studies of signalling theory (discussed below) provide some support for guarantees as signals of reliability, but not for guarantees as signals of durability.

13 It is not clear to what extent signalling theory could apply to guarantees given by retailers. Often, a retailer will provide a guarantee on all products sold through his branches. The retailer cannot have intended to signal the quality of the products with this guarantee, as the same guarantee on the same terms will apply to all products which he has sold. There may still be competitive advantages which a retailer may derive from his guarantee policy.

14 Grossman (1981), takes a similar line by suggesting that guarantees should be uniform, as consumers would otherwise not accept a guarantors claim about product quality expressed through the guarantee.

15 This is surprising, because earlier in his paper, he states that signalling theory is an indicator of product reliability (p.1303).

[16] Wiener (1985), Kelley (1988) and Agrawal et. al. (1996) all used reliability data compiled by *Consumer Reports*, which can be described as the U.S. equivalent of *Which?*.

[17] Kelly also compared guarantees offered before and after the adoption of U.S. legislation on guarantees (the Magnuson-Moss Warranty Act 1975, discussed in chapter 6), and concluded that guarantees have had the capacity to act as signals prior to and after the legislation was enacted.

[18] In economics terminology, bond credibility would be high in such a case.

[19] This would mean that bond credibility is low.

[20] This might account for the similarities between guarantees - the fact that consumers usually do not consider guarantees inevitably means that guarantors do not compete on their guarantees, but instead try to compete on other product attributes.

[21] Cf. Lord Denning's observations in *Adams v Richardson & Starling* (1969), at 1648-9, reproduced in section 2.3.1.

[22] See 2.1.1.

[23] Moral Hazard is a concept commonly found in the context of insurance. Guarantees could have an insurance function to cover the risks of unreliability and product failure. As such, a guarantee will provide that if during the period of coverage the product becomes defective, the guarantor will provide compensation, which may take the form of repair, replacement or refund of the purchase price (Priest, 1981).

[24] i.e., a consumer taking court action to force a guarantor to honour his guarantee.

[25] i.e., a loss of sales consequent upon a failure to honour guarantees.

[26] See chapter 1, section 1.7.

[27] See chapter 2, section 2.5.

[28] For the distinction, see chapter 1 at 1.2.1.

[29] Emphasis added.

[30] Emphasis added.

[31] See chapter 5 for a discussion of these aspects.

Chapter 4

The Role of Guarantees as an Informal Redress Mechanism

4.0 Introduction

The previous chapter examined the significance of signalling theory in the context of manufacturers' guarantees. This revealed that guarantees may only be signals of product quality in certain circumstances. It is therefore reasonable to conclude that the role of guarantees in the pre-purchase context is less significant than often assumed. Therefore, guarantees can only be of limited assistance in providing a solution to the first problem identified in chapter 1, i.e., the difficulty for consumers to ascertain the level of quality to be expected from a particular product.

The main theme in this book is that guarantees are more likely to be of relevance in a post-purchase context, rather than in the pre-purchase context. The discussion so far has provided support for the argument that the pre-purchase role of guarantees is limited. This chapter seeks to demonstrate why guarantees are of greater use after purchase.

The second problem for consumers identified in chapter 1 was the difficulty of obtaining redress when a product is faulty, i.e., of insufficient quality. Recent research in the UK provides clear evidence that consumers predominantly resolve disputes informally by complaining directly to a retailer or manufacturer. Genn (1999) discovered that consumers rarely involve the courts for their disputes (only 3% of consumers in her study reported that they commenced court action). There have been focused attempts in recent years to improve access to the courts, particularly through the small claims jurisdiction. However, the impact on consumer disputes has not been significant. Genn further notes that even fewer consumers have used an ADR mechanism. These findings are supported by research carried out by the OFT (2000) and the DTI (2001a).

In order to show that guarantees are of greater use in a post-purchase context, it is necessary to examine if guarantees can be used to support consumers who seek redress by complaining informally. This chapter will proceed to do so in three stages: first, recent research in the field of consumer complaining behaviour will be discussed in order to explain how the process of bringing a complaint works. Second, the implications of this research for the use of guarantees in this process will be analysed. This will provide support to the argument that guarantees are of use in a post-purchase context. Finally, there will be a discussion of why it can be beneficial to support informal redress seeking rather than formalised enforcement of consumer rights.

The function of guarantees as an informal redress mechanism has not been subjected to major analysis. Indeed, this has only once previously been discussed, in the context of U.S. law, in a paper by Jean Braucher (1986), in which she argues that the statutory rights of consumers are too complex and at best of limited use to consumers, who generally complain informally about faulty products, rather than to seek legal advice. It is useful to summarise Braucher's argument for the light it sheds on the present discussion.

4.0.1 Braucher's "Informal Resolution Model"

Jean Braucher (1986) proposed a legal framework for guarantees to support her "Informal Resolution Model". This was based on her criticism that the plethora of federal[1] and state laws[2] which govern the sale of consumer goods and the provision of guarantees were far from clear, frequently too broad,[3] and required a considerable degree of knowledge of statute and case-law to be applied effectively. Consumers were unlikely to obtain legal advice, and even less likely to get legal representation for a court action, because the cost of paying a lawyer may be significantly more than the value of the consumer's claim. Additionally, lawyers appeared reluctant to get involved in pure quality disputes because of the limited financial benefit, even if the action succeeded.[4] Litigation was therefore not a viable option, and even less so because of the strain on the judicial system and on the taxpayer which such cases may produce (p.1446). Most consumers tended to complain directly to a seller about a faulty product, rather than to seek legal advice and go to court.

Braucher then argued that the legal framework in the United States did not adequately support consumers who seek to resolve disputes informally because it was based on a "legal rights model", i.e., almost exclusively geared towards the resolution of disputes in court, rather than through direct negotiation. She proposed a restructuring of the legal framework to promote the informal resolution of disputes over product quality. This would have had two objectives: first, it would have encouraged consumers to complain more frequently to retailers or manufacturers when faced with a faulty product. Second, by clarifying the obligations of the guarantor under the guarantee, and the requirements for invoking the guarantee, it would have become easier to complain informally.

Braucher suggested that there should be greater reliance on the "dynamics of business reputation", i.e., consumers' perceptions of a particular business with regard to its sincerity in honouring its claims about product quality. If a guarantor frequently failed to honour his guarantee, or denied consumer claims under his guarantee, his reputation would suffer.

Although Braucher takes a similar view to the arguments presented in this book, her approach is different. Her argument focuses exclusively on the difficulties for consumers in the United States to utilise their statutory rights and the fact that most consumers will be unable to do so because these are geared towards enforcement in the courts rather than through informal negotiation. The objective of this book is to develop a suitable legal framework for manufacturers' guarantees, and its starting point are the fundamental problems consumers have to deal with when faced with a faulty product. The overlap occurs in the recognition that consumers may require support in resolving such problems informally, but analysis and conclusions are different. Where relevant, Braucher's argument will be considered.

The following section will examine the theoretical framework on consumer complaining behaviour and identify the factors that may be of particular relevance to the use of manufacturers' guarantees as an informal redress mechanism.

4.1 What makes consumers complain?

In order to gain a better understand as to how the complaining process works, it is necessary to examine the literature on consumer complaining behaviour (CCB).[5] This provides useful insights into the general behaviour of consumers and may have important implications for the development of consumer protection measures generally. This section will analyse this research, and subsequent sections will draw on this to identify how manufacturers' guarantees could support the complaints process.

4.1.1 Identifying the problem

Before a consumer can bring a complaint, he needs to identify that something has happened which is a problem and for which redress may be available. Although this may seem to be stating the obvious, it is a fundamental step in the consumer complaining process (cf. Best and Andreasen, 1977, p.702). If a product does not work, the consumer will need to establish why it does not work. There may be a trivial reason for this, such as having forgotten to plug the product into the socket or connecting all the relevant leads to the appropriate slots in the product. Although these are problems which cause the product not to work, they can be dealt with by the consumer and there is no need to make available redress to the consumer for this.[6] However, if the consumer has set up the product according to its instructions and it still does not work, then it is likely to be defective in some way. It is at that point that the consumer will seek a solution for this problem (unless he decides not to take any action at all). The obvious response would be to contact the seller or manufacturer to complain that there is a fault with the product. However, it will be seen in the next section that there is a range of different responses and that a number of factors influence the consumer's decision whether and how to respond.

4.1.2 Deciding on a response

This section will examine how consumers respond to problems which they have encountered. There will first be an explanation of the different types of response, followed by an examination of the factors which influence a consumer's decision as to how to respond to a specific problem. The objective of this discussion is to gain an understanding of the complaining process. Once a clearer picture of what makes consumers complain has been obtained, it will be possible to consider the role that manufacturers' guarantees may be able to play in this context.

4.1.3 Types of response

In the CCB literature, consumer complaining behaviour is separated into three potential types of response (Morel et. al., 1997): the "no action - private action - public action" scheme.[7] "No action" simply refers to the type of situation where the consumer has experienced a problem, but does nothing further about it. Around one in twenty consumers will decide not to take any action (Genn, 1999).[8] This may be because the problem resolved itself, because the consumer felt there was nothing that could be done about the problem, or because the consumer made a conscious decision not to pursue the matter. Moreover, some consumers may feel insufficiently powerful to voice their dissatisfaction. They may feel uncomfortable communicating with a trader in order to complain. In CCB terms, their "coping potential" is not high enough to enable them to make a complaint (Stephens and Gwinner, 1998, p.185).

What, then, is meant by "private" and "public" action? "Private action" include the decision by a consumer to switch brands or suppliers, or to boycott the product or service that has given rise to a complaint. A personal boycott is the paradigm of private action. The consumer will not buy products of the same brand again, or not buy goods from the seller which was the cause of his dissatisfaction. A further type of private action is to warn other consumers such as friends or relatives about the problem. Private action therefore does not involve an attempt to resolve the particular problem, but rather a decision to avoid the source of the problem in the future. It seems that only a very small number of consumers would decide to switch brands or suppliers, and then only after a number of problems have been encountered (Blodgett and Anderson, 2001, p.335). It therefore seems that the number of "private action" responses will be small, and that most consumers will take action which falls within the third category of responses, "public action".

The term "public action" covers a number of different responses. The most common public action response involves seeking redress from the retailer or manufacturer. Other public action responses can include a complaint lodged with a consumers' association or public regulator, or a complaint to the media. Many newspapers now feature consumer columns, and there are also television programmes that seek to highlight different types of consumer problems. Finally, public action can also involve taking legal action in the courts (Broadbridge and Marshall, 1995).

The different types of "public" action can be broadly classified under two headings (Bearden and Mason, 1984). Firstly, there are *redress seeking* responses. These will be adopted by a consumer who does not merely wish to express his dissatisfaction with the product he has bought, but also seeks remedy, such as repair or replacement of the product. Redress may be sought directly from the retailer or manufacturer, or indirectly, e.g., through a lawyer, or with the assistance of a consumer organisation.

A second broad class of responses is referred to as *venting*: if the consumer does not want a specific remedy, he may simply make his dissatisfaction known. Such a response might be adopted where the product in question has a 'fault' which is so minor that the consumer does not want the cost of seeking a remedy.

These are thus the types of response we could expect from a consumer. It now needs to be considered which factors determine the kind of action the consumer will ultimately take (see generally, Bearden and Mason, 1984).

4.1.4 Factors which may influence the consumer's decision to respond

A consumer's response is likely to be influenced by his perception as to who is responsible for the product failure. This is known in the CCB literature as "attribution". In her seminal paper, Folkes (1984) identifies three dimensions which may have an impact on the consumer's attribution. The first factor is "stability". This considers whether the problem is a temporary problem or a fairly permanent one. Thus, a product may break down once and this may be the only such failure of which a consumer is aware, in which case the problem is likely to be regarded as temporary. Alternatively, a product may break down on a regular basis and the consumer may have heard of other consumers having similar experiences. This would make it a permanent problem.

The second dimension is "locus". This involves an enquiry into the cause of a defect. For example, a washing-machine may not work because the manufacturer made a defective product, because it was installed improperly by the seller or because the consumer has failed to use it according to the instructions. Indeed, it seems that consumers are more likely to complain if a defect can be clearly attributed to a manufacturer or seller. If there is potential for disagreement,[9] consumers may be less confident about complaining (Best and Andreasen, 1977, p.719).

The third dimension is "controllability". Once the cause of the problem has been identified, it may be possible to consider whether this could have been controlled and the problem avoided. For example, a consumer who fails to use a product in accordance with the usage instructions could control the problem by reading and following the instructions.

It seems obvious that if the consumer attributes the failure to the manufacturer or the seller, he will take action, and this is confirmed by Folkes. However, her research provides evidence that all three dimensions influence a consumer's decision whether to complain about a product defect.[10] Her findings indicate that the stability and controllability dimensions may both influence the remedy sought by a consumer and encourage the consumer to vent his anger, e.g., by complaining to a regulatory body or the media. Thus, if a defect was perceived as stable and within the control of the manufacturer of the relevant product, consumers were more likely to prefer a refund and felt a desire to "hurt the firm's business" (Folkes, 1984, p.400) than when the defect was not controllable by the manufacturer. However, Stephens and Gwinner (1998) observed that this was only relevant where it was possible for the consumer to discern clearly the source of the problem. If it is not possible to identify the source, then there can be no attribution.

So although the consumer's attribution can be relevant, Folkes conceded that:

> the ability of an attributional approach to predict whether consumer complaining behaviours will actually occur is limited. Clearly, there are additional determinants of complaining behaviour ... [and] a model of consumer complaining behaviour must include factors besides attributions (1984, p.409).

It is therefore necessary to identify such additional factors. These are known as "situational factors", and have been found also to influence consumer complaining behaviour. Situational factors include the price of a faulty product and its ordinary life-expectancy (Broadbridge and Marshall, 1995, p.15), the severity of the fault, the perceived inconvenience of a complaint mechanism which may be available (Best and Andreasen, 1977, p.720) and the perceived willingness a seller or manufacturer to provide a remedy (Richins and Bronislaw, 1985). For present purposes, the latter two factors are of particular relevance and will be examined in more depth now.

The consumer's perception of the retailer's or manufacturer's reputation for quality and of the retailer's or manufacturer's responsiveness to complaints are both crucial factors in determining a consumer's complaining behaviour. If a retailer is perceived by consumers to be responsive to complaints, consumers are more likely to seek redress in this way. Thus, if the perception of the retailer is that he will listen to the consumer's request and respond accordingly, consumers will perceive there to be a reasonable chance of success. "Consumers complain largely when they believe their efforts are likely to meet with success" (Bearden and Mason, 1984, p.491).

Yet, although a retailer or manufacturer may respond to consumer complaints, he may do so only reluctantly. This may have an impact on the complaining behaviour of a consumer. Thus, if the retailer or manufacturer not only appears responsive, but also *willing* to respond, consumers will be more likely to complain. In contrast, if the response to a complaint is likely to be only half-hearted or *pro forma*, then a consumer is less likely to proceed with his complaint.

Linked to this is the consumer's perception of how easy or difficult it is to complain. If effective complaints handling mechanisms have been put into place, a consumer will probably be more inclined to make a complaint, whereas the absence of such mechanisms will deter a consumer from voicing his grievance (see Nyer, 2000).

An aspect related to the perceived ease of complaining is the cost to the consumer of the time and other expenses, such as travel, associated with this. If the consumer thinks it would take up too much of his time to complain to the retailer and obtain the desired redress, he may chose not to complain at all. Similarly, although the consumer may be willing to sacrifice the time it takes to complain, there may be other costs, such as having to take a faulty product back to the retailer or posting it to the manufacturer (which would be financial costs), which may deter him from pursuing his complaint.

Bearden and Mason (1984) carried out a study in which they sought to adduce empirical evidence of the relevance of these factors. This was done by means of a questionnaire sent to consumers, in which they were asked whether they had a consumer complaint and what they did about this. Their results lead them to express some scepticism about the importance of the retailer's or manufacturer's responsiveness (at p.495), although they concede that this may vary significantly from product to product, and that there is some evidence to support the relationship between responsiveness and complaining behaviour.[11] In contrast, Richins and Bronislaw (1985) find stronger evidence for the importance of these factors. There does, therefore, appear to be a link between the situational factors outlined above and the decision by a consumer to complain, although stronger evidence may be required to support this.

Broadbridge and Marshall (1995, p.16) emphasise that it is important how businesses respond to consumer complaints:

> To decrease the impact of dissatisfaction [over faulty goods] that can occur, companies need to show, at the least, that they are responsive to legitimate complaints. The best way to show responsiveness is by prompt and courteous handling of dissatisfactions.

This was also the conclusion reached by Richins and Bronislaw (1985):

> Clearly, producers and sellers themselves are best equipped to influence these consumer perceptions [about responsiveness to complaints] ... firms can make the complaint handling mechanism physically convenient for consumers ... (p.39).

It is therefore reasonable to conclude that the fact that a retailer or manufacturer appears to be willing to deal with consumer complaints will encourage consumers to make a complaint. Conversely, if a consumer does not believe that his complaint will be received adequately, he may decide not to complain at all, or try to complain to somebody else, such as a regulatory body or the media.

In addition to the perceived responsiveness of the retailer or manufacturer, the fairness of the complaints mechanism is also of significance. In the consumer complaining context, Saxby, Tat and Johansen (2000, p.214) have identified the following factors which influence the perceived fairness of the mechanism: first, consumers will seek to ensure that their complaint is listened to. If they feel that they are not given an adequate opportunity to present their complaint, they may regard the complaints mechanism as insufficiently fair. Second, consumers are concerned that their complaint is handled with honesty and consistency. This does not necessarily mean that similar complaints are given similar treatment, but rather that the complaint is dealt with in accordance with the procedure that is advertised by the seller or manufacturer.

Finally, demographic factors may be crucial.[12] Consumers who adopt a "public action" approach tend to be younger, with better educational qualifications and higher income. This was also noted by Genn (1999), who observed that consumer disputes were special in that the demographics of those who took action were considerably different from other categories. Howells and Weatherill (1995) therefore suggest that individual complaints by consumers are of limited interest (p.574). They suggest that the high success rate of those who complain is primarily due to traders' goodwill in return for consumer loyalty and repeat-business - which would be less likely to be forthcoming from low-income consumers.

It seems that the reasons why those from lower socio-economic groups do not complain need closer attention, and potential solutions to improve this need to be considered.[13] The fact that there are divergences between socio-economic groups in their propensity to complain means that complaining should not be treated as the only means of obtaining redress to be promoted. However, it is nevertheless vital to appreciate the significant role of complaining as a response to specific consumer problems. It would be beneficial if it were possible to encourage direct complaints from consumers of all socio-economic classes, because this would inevitable reduce the number of consumers who take "no action". Those consumers who take no action because they mistakenly believe that there is nothing that could be done need to be convinced that their perception is not accurate. In the context of faulty products, consumers who think they cannot do anything about the problem need to be made aware of their options. It will be argued below that guarantees could have an important role to play in this respect.

4.1.5 Summary: key factors which influence a consumer's decision to complain

The preceding discussion has identified a number of factors which influence a consumer's decision whether to complain about a product quality problem. First, a consumer will take action if he attributes the problem to somebody other than himself, such as the seller or manufacturer. Second, the decision to complain will be influenced by the perceived willingness of the trader who will be the target of the complaint to respond to the consumer's problem. A related consideration is the ease with which the complaint mechanism itself can be accessed, and how fair the mechanism is. The likely cost of complaining will also have an impact on the consumer's decision. Finally, it seems that consumers from some backgrounds are more likely to complain about a problem than others.

These are the factors identified specifically in the context of consumer complaining behaviour. It is also important to appreciate the constraints upon consumers caused by the potential cost of a formal dispute and the fact that a business is likely to be better resourced to respond to court action (Tur, 1982, p.137).

The next step in this discussion is to consider the role of manufacturers' guarantees in the process of seeking redress informally.

4.2 The role of manufacturers' guarantees in the informal redress seeking process

It is now possible to consider the role which manufacturers' guarantees can play as part of the informal redress seeking process. Chapter 2 saw an analysis of the basic format of a guarantee.[14] There, it was explained that a guarantee consists of three main components: the guarantee promise, the remedies to be provided if the promise is not fulfilled, and the procedure for bringing a claim under the guarantee to obtain the relevant remedy. A guarantee therefore consists of all the relevant components of a redress mechanism. However, it is necessary to analyse further if guarantees could be used by consumers when they seek redress informally. This section will now turn to consider the application of the CCB principles discussed in the previous section to manufacturers' guarantees.

4.2.1 Identification

As noted above, the first stage is that the consumer has to identify that there is a problem for which redress is available. At this stage, guarantees are of limited assistance (cf. Braucher, 1986). This is because most consumers will only consult the guarantee once they have identified the problem. This may be because guarantees rarely explain how a product should perform, or what might go wrong. Instead, help in identifying the problem could, for example, be derived from a users' guide for the relevant product. Consumers therefore need to identify the problem by means other than the guarantee. A guarantee will therefore only become relevant once a consumer has identified a problem and is trying to find a way to resolve this (Trebilcock, 1972). It can then indicate to the consumer that a remedy may be available for the problem.

4.2.2 Attribution

Once consumers have identified the problem, they will attribute the fault to either the seller or the manufacturer. A guarantee can be of limited assistance in this respect. As explained in chapter 2, a manufacturer's guarantee promises a remedy if there is a fault in the design, materials or workmanship of the relevant product. If the problem identified by the consumer is likely to be the result of such a fault, the guarantee will assist in attributing the failure to the manufacturer.[15] Therefore, a guarantee may be of some, albeit limited, impact in respect of the "locus" dimension of the process of attribution.[16]

4.2.3 Perceived willingness to respond to consumer's complaint and ease of complaint

It has been demonstrated that the decision to complain will be influenced by the perceived willingness of the trader who will be the target of the complaint to respond to the consumer's problem. This includes a consideration of the ease of the complaint mechanism itself. The likely cost of complaining will also have an impact on the consumer's decision.

A guarantee indicates at least a basic willingness by the guarantor to deal with complaints. If a manufacturer chooses not to give a guarantee, a consumer may perceive this as an indicator that the guarantor is less likely to deal with a complaint in an adequate manner. Conversely, if a guarantee is given which promises a remedy if a product does not work and the guarantee contains few restrictions and is easy to invoke, then the consumer is likely to regard this as reflecting the guarantor's willingness to deal with complaints. If guarantees contain such information, then the conclusions reached by Halstead et. al. (1993) are significant:

> [Guarantees] are promises of complaint resolution and thus they often encourage dissatisfied consumers to complain (p.35).

Richins supports this (1983):

> They need to show their customers that they are responsive to legitimate complaints. Manufacturers may do this through detailed [guarantee] and complaint procedure information on labels or in package inserts ... (p.76).

In the CCB literature, there is some support for the fact that consumers are more likely to complain where they feel they will be successful, particularly where the retailer or manufacturer appears willing to deal with the complaint and has put into place a mechanism for this purpose. Guarantees may make it easier for those who are willing to complain to bring a more focused complaint that will lead to a faster provision of redress. Guarantees can help consumers voice a complaint, by stating how and to whom to complain. The easier it is to complain, the more likely it is to actually get consumers to complain. It could also help to reduce any negative feelings and thereby preserve consumer loyalty:

> Providing the consumer with a product [guarantee] is one means of providing immediate reassurance that the problem will be addressed and so may reduce negative feelings (Lassar *et. al.*, 1998, p.265).

A guarantee can therefore be an indicator of the guarantor's willingness to deal with consumer complaints.[17] The extent to which a guarantee could be utilised as an informal redress mechanism seems to depend on the ease with which the consumer can obtain the benefit of the guarantee. A guarantor who provides a guarantee which appears, at first sight, to be generous, but which contains many restrictions and requires the consumer to bear most of the costs associated with bringing a claim is unlikely to be regarded as receptive to consumer complaints, and a consumer may prefer a different avenue of redress.[18]

A guarantee which is equally generous but contains few or no restrictions and under which the guarantor assumes most of the costs of claiming under the guarantee is likely to indicate that the guarantor is willing to respond to consumer complaints. It has already been seen that there are significant variations in the procedures put into place by guarantors for dealing with claims.[19] This could therefore be a crucial factor in a consumer's decision to complain.

It may therefore be suggested that a guarantee can act as a signal of redress availability which operates *after* a consumer has made a purchase, rather than as a signal of product quality in the pre-purchase context. Bearden and Shimp (1982) noted that a guarantee can be a signal by which consumers are reassured that there is some form of redress available to them. Indeed, it has been noted that mechanisms which support the effective resolution of consumer complaints can provide the relevant trader with a competitive advantage (Estelami, 2000), which is what signals are intended to do.

The redress function of guarantees could therefore also be a signal, but of a different kind from the quality signalling function usually associated with the notion of guarantees as signals.[20] Signalling theory could have a role in so far as a guarantee could reassure consumers that there is a redress mechanism for the duration of the guarantee period which is immediately accessible, should a product fail to be of a particular quality standard. It is, perhaps, misleading to use the term "signal" in this context, and the parallel with the quality signal which forms the subject matter of signalling theory should not be drawn too readily. Of course, it may be that signalling theory could also encompass the "signal" that redress is available, but this is far from clear at present.

A guarantee could thus signal the guarantor's willingness to offer redress to consumers whose products develop a fault during the guarantee period. The question then arises whether this signal indicates to a consumer before purchase that redress is available, or whether it only operates after purchase once a problem has occurred. It seems plausible to suggest that the signal that redress is available may take effect in a pre-purchase context by convincing consumers that the relevant product might be worth having because if there is a problem, a remedy will be available. If this so, then similar problems regarding the effectiveness of the signal to those identified in the context of quality signals in chapter 3 could apply in the present context. There, it was seen that few consumers consider guarantees before purchase. Guarantees are not an important factor at this stage, be it as a signal of quality or of redress availability.

The better view seems to be that consumers will assume that the products they buy will work. The availability of redress would therefore not be a significant factor in the pre-purchase context. Instead, a consumer is likely to consider a guarantee only once a problem has arisen with the product and a remedy is required to deal with this. At that point, the signal that redress is available would operate.

This signal would therefore work in the post-purchase context when a consumer is looking exactly for the information provided by the guarantee, i.e., a means of obtaining redress. Unlike the quality signal, it would not relate to an unobservable product characteristic and may therefore be more easily interpreted by consumers.[21] If the procedure for bringing a claim under the guarantee is simple and favourable to a consumer, then the guarantor can be perceived as willing to respond to complaints and the guarantee may provide the easiest route to obtaining redress. This does, of course, presuppose the ability of a consumer to distinguish between favourable and unfavourable procedures, but it seems likely that most consumers would be able to make this distinction.

The discussion has so far focused on the accessibility of the claims procedure. However, it must be acknowledged that one factor which may make a complaint mechanism appear easily accessible is its physical proximity of the person to complain to in relation to the consumer. If the consumer can return to a shop in his local High Street, he may be more likely to complain than if he needs to write to the manufacturer's guarantee department to obtain a service. Thus, accessibility may not only refer to the structure of the mechanism itself, but may also be influenced by the geographical proximity of the mechanism to the consumer's home.

4.2.4 Overcoming demographic factors by encouraging more consumers to complain

A final factor identified in the previous section was that consumers who are better educated and have a higher income are more likely to complain. Guarantees may encourage consumers who would not otherwise take any form of "public action" to try to resolve the problem by claiming under a guarantee. One problem outlined above is that some consumers may simply take no action when they encounter a problem with a faulty product. A guarantee could be useful in that it may foster awareness among consumers that there *may* be something else they could do, such as taking up the complaint with the person who provided the guarantee. This may be particularly important for those consumers who do not feel powerful enough to bring a complaint, because a complaints procedure which is easily accessible may bring about a shift in the balance of power from the consumer's perspective, and may therefore encourage complaints (Stephens and Gwinner, 1998, p.185).

Furthermore, a guarantee may include a reference to the legal rights of consumers. Thus, a guarantee could be the first step towards empowering those consumers who would not normally take any action at all.

4.2.5 Guarantees can support informal complaints

It may be concluded from this discussion that guarantees can support the complaints process by making it easier for consumers to identify a target for their complaint, by "signalling" the willingness of that target to respond to a complaint and by providing a procedure within which a complaint can be brought.

In order to support further the argument that guarantees can be an informal redress mechanism, the next section will consider the advantages of using guarantees rather than the statutory right for informal complaints. It will then be necessary to consider the potential disadvantages for consumers of relying on guarantees as a redress mechanism. Finally, it will be considered to what extent informal redress seeking by consumers can and should be supported.

4.3 Advantages of guarantees over statutory rights for informal redress seeking

The discussion in this chapter has focused on the role that guarantees may play in helping consumers obtain redress informally for faulty goods. In chapter 1, it was observed that the flexible quality standard adopted under the SoGA and the Guarantees Directive is also useful in resolving disputes (and see Adams and Brownsword, 1988). It is therefore necessary to explain why guarantees are more suitable for the informal redress process than the statutory rights (which are more likely to be of use once a third party such as a judge has got involved in the dispute). The relevant issues to consider are: first, guarantees are more accessible than the statutory rights in the sense that consumers who are not sure about their rights need to make a greater effort to obtain information about these; second, guarantees are more focused than the statutory rights, which have to be available for a broad range of goods and third, consumers are unlikely to be sufficiently educated about their statutory rights. Although presented as separate issues, all three are inter-related, as this section will show.

It would be wrong to deny that there are clear advantages to the statutory rights. In contrast to guarantees, the statutory rights of consumers are mandatory and cannot be limited or excluded in any way. They provide an objective standard which cannot be deviated from by the seller. A seller will be responsible if products fail to meet the standard demanded by the law, and is obliged to offer the remedy stipulated by the law. Yet, it seems that consumers are more likely to look at the terms of a guarantee when something goes wrong than to consider the relevant law. An explanation for this can be found by considering the cost to the consumer of seeking redress when a product has become faulty.

The primary "cost" incurred in obtaining the remedy or remedies prescribed by law is the cost to the consumer of obtaining information about his legal rights, and about the different options to enforce these. The difficulty of ascertaining his legal rights and enforcement procedures may deter the consumer from pursuing his claim. Consumers may thus not be aware of the full extent of the rights, nor of the limitations. The DTI reported in 2001 that "consumers' knowledge of their rights is generally patchy, with some confusion over particular issues" (DTI, 2001a, p.13).

There will invariably be ambiguities as to the exact extent of the legal rights because of the inherently flexible nature of the statutory quality standard.[22] Furthermore, consumer and seller may disagree about the availability of a particular remedy.[23] A consumer may, for example, not be required to accept the seller's offer to repair a defective product and can instead demand his money back. Also, a seller may misinterpret the law, either deliberately or through ignorance.

In contrast, most guarantees are presented to the consumer in a document which accompanies the product. This document can state clearly what is offered to the consumer and how the consumer can claim this. Even though the broad gist of the legal rights could be summarised in a document which could be made available to all consumers, such a document would still not be able to take account of the details of the relevant law.

This leads on to the second advantage of guarantees over statutory rights - not only does a guarantee document ensure that consumers are immediately aware of what they could do, but the guarantee itself is likely to be more focused in the remedies that are made available. The statutory standard has to be flexible so as to be of use in as wide a range of different circumstances as possible. A guarantee, on the other hand, applies to a particular type of product only. Provided that the guarantee document is not written in complex legal language, a consumer can readily discern his 'rights' under the guarantee. This advantage of guarantees over statutory rights is explained by Clark and Davies thus:

> The implied warranty [the statutory rights], though often a powerful weapon, is to most consumers a shadowy, legalistic concept that inherently deters utilization. Even an informed consumer can face severe difficulties and considerable expense in carrying the implied warranty through the court test that its lawyerly nature encourages. [Guarantees], on the other hand, are right there in the box, the desk drawer, or the glove compartment, explicitly committing the [guarantor] to remedy specific defects without being dragged into court. Every buyer is his own lawyer for at least the first round; he is encourages to exercise his talents by both the distinctiveness of the assurance and the intentionally created impression that the [guarantor] must be eager to follow through on promises so widely and expensively touted (Clark and Davies, 1975, p.569).

This statement reflects the fact that the statutory rights offer a good level of protection to consumers, but that it is very difficult for consumers to enforce their rights, because their application requires some awareness of the overall legal context. Guarantees usually set out clearly when the guarantor will assume liability and what the redress he will provide to the consumer.

This view is also shared by Willett (1992), who noted that:

> If a dispute does arise, the consumer, being more informed, is in a stronger position to negotiate a satisfactory settlement. He is also more informed, and perhaps less daunted by the prospect of a formal dispute (p.102).[24]

If the guarantee provides a solution for the consumer's problem, it seems unnecessary to obtain information about the statutory rights. This acknowledges that consumers are not well educated about their rights (see DTI, 2001a; 2001b). Braucher (1986) argued that a clear express written guarantee is more useful than the statutory rights in negotiations between a consumer and a retailer, because most consumers are unaware of their legal rights (p.1421). Braucher is critical of rules which require the disclosure of the legal rights because these rights are very complex and difficult to summarise concisely without over-simplifying. Disclosure would therefore confuse consumers more than inform them (p.1422). However, following Willett's view, if the guarantee creates sufficient awareness among consumers that there is a remedy available, he may be encouraged to look for additional avenues of redress if he is unable to negotiate a satisfactory settlement.

If consumers were properly educated about their rights and retailers' obligations, more consumers might seek a remedy when something has gone wrong. There can be little doubt that better consumer education is indeed desirable. In fact, consumer education about their statutory rights would benefit informal complaining: if consumers were fully aware of the extent of their legal rights, and the relationship between these rights and any additional guarantees offered with a product, they may feel more confident about trying to claim under a guarantee first. They would be aware that if this failed to produce a satisfactory outcome, they could still enforce their statutory rights. It may therefore be speculated that greater general awareness of consumers' rights with regard to faulty goods would encourage guarantors to make a better effort to remedy a problem under a guarantee, because they will have set the perimeters for claiming under the guarantee. Once a consumer relies on his statutory rights, the guarantor has to comply with rules set by the law, rather than by himself.

4.4 Disadvantages of using guarantees as an informal redress mechanism

Although the preceding analysis suggests that guarantees could have a very useful role to play in the informal resolution of disputes over product quality, there are a number of potential difficulties. A fundamental problem is that a guarantee is drafted by the guarantor, and it will therefore be the guarantor who determines the extent of his liabilities under the guarantee. It is therefore subjective. This contrasts sharply with the statutory rights, which lay down an objective standard.

There is a danger in encouraging consumers to complain with reference to a guarantee, rather than the statutory rights. Whenever consumers encounter a faulty product, they would concentrate on what is offered in the guarantee, rather than what they would be entitled to under the law. The guarantee may assume undue prominence, and, as a consequence, the general level of awareness of the statutory rights, which already appears to be low, would be reduced even further. Furthermore, the guarantee may provide less protection for the consumer than the statutory standard, and the consumer may not obtain redress because he focuses on the guarantee when he would be able to obtain redress under the statutory rules.

These are not inevitable consequences. Although valid criticisms, they are not fatal. Rather, this problem needs to be taken into account in creating a legal framework for manufacturers' guarantees. A rule which requires a concise reference to the statutory rules may be enough to prevent such problems, and, in fact, may have the opposite effect of *raising* the level of awareness. This issue will be discussed further in chapter 5.

A related problems is this: if a consumer, having read the details in the guarantee about making a claim, decides that the guarantor does not seem willing to deal with his complaint, he may be left without redress altogether. Greater awareness of his statutory rights might at least encourage him to seek a remedy by other means. However, this will be more difficult because the consumer may not be able to ascertain how the party to whom he complains will react.[25]

A problem which may be of greater concern is the inherent discretion given to the guarantor in determining whether to provide a remedy under the guarantee.

This is a problem which is not specific to guarantees, but which arises in the context of informal complaining generally. Ramsay (1981) observed that in informal consumer-retailer dispute resolution discussions:

> many retailers perceived themselves as exercising a discretionary power, applying reasonable standards of the market place for the privilege of reasonable consumers ... onsumer's 'rights' at this level of two-party negotiation are therefore dependent on norms generated by sellers partly in response to market forces rather than in response to legal rules (p.129).[26]

This observation was made in the context of a study analysing the responses of sellers to complaints by consumers about the quality of products they had purchased. These complaints were not made on the basis of a guarantee, nor with particular reference to statutory rights. The study focused on how sellers respond to all types of complaint and revealed that the statutory rights had a negligible role to play. Although it is conceivable that the retailer may simply be mistaken as to the actual rights of the consumer under the law, it is more likely that the seller will be concerned about the reputation of his business. This is not unusual - Ramsay (1981) comments that research had shown that "consumers, retailers and industry representatives ... attached minor importance to the conventional sales law" (p.122).

This may be detrimental to consumers, but not invariably so. It is clear that this is a rather more subtle exclusion of the statutory rights of consumers, because there is no mention of these at all. Ramsay's observations are likely to be less significant in the context of complaints made with specific direct reference to a guarantee. The guarantee document will state when the guarantee can be invoked by the consumer, and what the guarantor will do if the guarantee is applicable. That reduces the scope of the "discretionary power" Ramsay refers to - at least with respect to the remedies which would be available to the consumer.

Yet, an attempt to invoke a guarantee may give rise to a dispute as to whether the problem identified by the consumer is, in fact, one which is covered by the guarantee. There is therefore a different "discretionary power" given to the guarantor - that of determining whether the guarantee applies to the problem, or not. Thus, the consumer would demand performance of the guarantee, whereas the guarantor claims that the guarantee does not apply. The guarantor may do so for two reasons: first, he may be acting in good faith, and there is a simple difference of opinion as to whether the problem the consumer complains about is covered by the guarantee (Best and Andreasen, 1977, p.717; Palfrey and Romer, 1983, p.98). In such a situation, the guarantor's view is final, unless the consumer is able to persuade the guarantor to allow the claim.

Second, the guarantor may refuse to perform his obligation under the guarantee in bad faith. Thus, even though the consumer would be entitled to claim under the guarantee, if considered objectively, the guarantor nevertheless declines to entertain his claim.[27]

Once the guarantor has accepted that the consumer's complaint is covered by the guarantee, its terms will fetter the discretion as to the remedy to be provided to the consumer. So, for example, if the guarantee clearly promises a replacement, the guarantor may have difficulties in forcing the consumer to accept repair of the product instead. However, many guarantees still give the guarantor discretion with regard to the remedies which will be made available to the consumer. But even here the guarantee document will indicate the remedies that will be available to the consumer and the guarantor's discretion will be limited to a choice between these remedies. The guarantor therefore lists the remedies he is willing to offer, but he does so before a specific complaint is made. This contrasts with the general situation referred to by Ramsay, where a decision on the remedy to be offered is made once the complaint has been received.

This built-in discretion would clearly need to be controlled by a legal framework for guarantees. However, there will be non-legal constraints on the ability of the guarantor to exercise his discretion arbitrarily. Braucher (1986) notes that concerns over business reputation will encourage guarantors to honour their guarantees. The fear of negative reputation will ensure that the guarantor sticks to his promises and will not seek to take advantage of the discretion given to him by the guarantee to refuse to perform his obligations. Her proposal is criticised by Macaulay *et. al.* Thus:

> Doesn't any proposal for mediation and settlement rest on power created by the chance of costly litigation? Why should manufacturers mediate seriously when there is no real threat of sanctions for not settling a dispute? Could Professor Braucher answer this objection? How? (1995, p.728).

Her response[28] to this is that the primary reason any seller accommodates customer complaints is that this will support the maintenance of a good relationship with the consumer and maintain its good reputation. If it is made clear to the consumer what he is entitled to, he may be persuaded to complain where he has grounds for doing so. The statutory rights of consumers, often phrased in legal language, do not encourage consumers to complain and may, in fact, result in them not obtaining any redress at all. She concludes that litigation needs to be available as a back-up to informal dispute resolution – but consumer protection law will not work if it only becomes accessible through the involvement of lawyers. Furthermore, Collins (1999) has demonstrated that strict legal entitlements are often insignificant, and the preservation of good business relations and trust may be much more important.

So far, this section has demonstrated that guarantees have advantages over the statutory rules when consumers seek redress informally through complaining. It has also identified the major problems that may arise in this context. The extent of the guarantor's obligations are determined by the guarantor himself, and he also has some discretion with regard to the availability of a guarantee for a particular problem. However, concerns about business reputation may provide a safeguard against the unfair exercise of this discretion. It is also a factor to be taken into account in creating an appropriate legal framework for guarantees.

Before it is possible to move on to consider the implications of this analysis for a legal framework, it is necessary to consider whether an informal redress mechanism based on individual complaints is desirable.

4.5 Is it desirable to promote informal redress seeking?

Thus far, the discussion in this chapter has proceeded on the basis that most consumers complain informally and that guarantees could be a mechanism which will support consumers in seeking redress informally. Although this is in line with empirical evidence (Genn, 1999; OFT, 2000; DTI, 2001), it may be begging the question. To argue for a legal framework that seeks to encourage informal resolution outside the legal system may seem strange to a lawyer. Indeed, much concern has been expressed about the lack of third-party involvement in the resolution of consumer disputes and the fact that many consumers give up if they are unable to resolve problems themselves (e.g. Genn, 1999).

The notion of "informal redress seeking" entails that there has to be an approximate equality of power between the consumer and guarantor - there can only be negotiation if both parties are able to argue for their position without feeling unduly pressured by the other party. In the case of consumer-retailer or consumer-manufacturer disputes, there is an obvious imbalance of power - and the consumer, who is normally the party which has experienced the problem, will be at an immediate disadvantage. Yet, it is exactly this imbalance of power which would be redressed if the legal framework for guarantees were designed to support informal negotiation.

The analysis of consumer complaining behaviour has revealed a number of restraints which operate on guarantors to prevent them from abusing their strong position. Even though an individual consumer can do little against a major retailer or manufacturer, if the perception of the guarantor amongst the body of consumers is that he is relying on his stronger position when dealing with consumers, the repercussions of consumer boycotts, adverse publicity and potential investigations by consumer protection agencies should act as a brake on any guarantor trying to abuse his position.

The alternative to the informal approach would be a mechanism which involved an independent third party. This would be a move away from informal two-party negotiations, and an objective outsider would become involved in the dispute to offer advice, guide the parties to a solution or even adjudicate on the matter. Ramsay (1981) observed that "few consumers made use of third-party mechanisms even if they were dissatisfied with the seller's response" (p.125). Genn (1999), the OFT (2000) and the DTI (2001) provide empirical support for this. This is despite the improvements that have been made within the court system in the UK to improve access to justice and also the promotion of alternative means of dispute resolution. Consumers therefore seem to prefer to resolve disputes themselves, rather than involving a third party.

There are problems with the systems which involve a third party, be it a mediator, ombudsman or judge. *Prima facie*, the involvement of an independent third party in a consumer dispute may seem desirable because it would limit the scope for a seller or manufacturer to pressure the consumer to accept a particular remedy. Yet, the mere fact that a third party is involved may give rise to more problems than it may solve. Niels Christie suggested that one of the fundamental problems of western legal systems is that parties to a conflict do not get to resolve this through their own involvement (Christie, 1977). Thus, once lawyers become involved in a dispute, they do not assist the parties, they take over the conflict. Lawyers obviously know what the law is, and which arguments have the best prospect of succeeding in court, but these arguments may appear strange to the parties, or even be arguments that the parties had rather not presented themselves:

> Many...have experienced the sad moments of truth when our lawyers tell us that our best arguments...are without any legal relevance whatsoever and that we for God's sake ought to keep quiet about them in court. Instead, they pick out arguments we might find irrelevant or even wrong to use (p.4)

Although Christie's focus is on the criminal trial, his suggestion that the involvement of lawyers (or indeed any other third party) which causes the conflict to be taken away from those who are directly affected by it, produces a feeling of alienation with the legal system, applies more generally.[29] A person who has suffered a wrong may suffer further by surrendering control over their claim to somebody who will almost certainly do things they do not understand, or even disagree with. A consumer who utilises a scheme which involves some sort of third party involvement may soon feel alienated, and even frustrated with the entire process. The process will take over, and eventually deprive the consumer of having his grievance dealt with. The final outcome may be something which he would never have wanted.

Should a consumer go to court, his case is likely to be dealt with under the small claims procedure, which is an informal procedure within the formal court system.[30] This procedure has some advantages: often, no lawyers are involved, the setting is less formal and the strict rules of court etiquette are relaxed. The consumer himself is given the opportunity to present his case.

There is evidence that this produces a feeling of empowerment, of "being in control" over the dispute. This experience is regarded more favourably than that of surrendering the handling of the dispute to a third party (although the outcome will still be determined by a third party, i.e., the judge). Baldwin (1997), for example, found surprising evidence that individuals who used the small claims procedure in the English county courts[31] generally felt a lot more satisfied than those who went through a full trial in which both parties are represented by lawyers. Yet, the lack of involvement of lawyers could also be problematic - crucial rights which the consumer might otherwise have been able to rely on may not be drawn to the court's attention, and the decision which is reached may fail to give effect to what the consumer may be entitled to get under the law.

It may be the case that the extent to which consumers utilise such third-party mechanisms might depend on the accessibility and responsiveness of the mechanism. It might therefore be possible to transfer the aspects identified as influencing a consumer's decision to complain not just to situations where a consumer complains directly to another party, but where this complaint is transferred to a third-party mechanism. Cautious support for this is provided by Hogarth, English and Sharma (2001, p.85). If this is correct, than it might be necessary to reconsider the current structures of existing third-party mechanisms.

This could be beneficial for consumers who are unable to resolve their dispute informally.

An altogether different problem is raised by Howells and Weatherill (1995) who argue (at p.574) that informal complaints may mask problems which continue to affect the sizeable number of consumers who take no action when confronted with a similar problem. Inevitably, no formal records are kept of problems that are resolved through direct complaints.[32] A court judgment which is reported in the press and the law reports, may be of greater general use than a number of informally resolved disputes, because it will provide an authoritative indication of the level of protection consumers are entitled to under the law. It may also highlight the unfair practices of a particular trader. However, this does not mean that informal complaints should be discouraged. If a sufficient number of consumers complain about the same or very similar problems, a retailer or manufacturer will have to deal with this in order to avoid such consequences as exposure of the problem in the media or an investigation by the relevant consumer protection agency. Thus, if it transpires that a product has an inherent fault which materialises within a certain period, and this happens over and over again, the manufacturer will invariably have to take steps to remedy the problem.

If a problem is of such a magnitude that it affects more than just a few consumers, then it will eventually become known, be it by word-of-mouth of the shared experience, or because consumer organisations are made aware of it. The problem may then be publicised through other channels, such as the media.

A final point to emphasise is that seeking redress informally would not prevent a consumer from taking further steps. If the initial informal complaint is successful, then the consumer is likely to be satisfied and no further action needs to be taken. If it is unsuccessful, then the consumer may still seek to adopt a more formal approach, e.g., by enforcing his legal rights through an alternative dispute resolution mechanism, or by going to court. Admittedly, the number of consumers who will do so is likely to be very small. Genn (1999) concluded that most consumers who were unable to resolve their disputes when trying to do so informally would need to make a major effort to obtain redress - which may deter consumers from taking further action if the informal approach fails. This, however, is an altogether different problem which the present book cannot deal with.

4.6 A *caveat*: lack of specific empirical evidence

Although consumer complaining behaviour itself is still a young discipline, the research carried out over the previous three decades provides important guidance on how consumers complain. Furthermore, empirical evidence reveals that consumers do get results when they take matters into their own hands, and they do feel satisfied with the outcome. Supporting informal redress seeking can be useful for resolving individual problems, although it would be inadequate as a method of setting general standards and of systematically policing business behaviour.

The research evidence that is available provides stronger support for the proposition that guarantees can help in informally dealing with quality problems than for the proposition that guarantees are signals of product quality. However, there is, as yet, no empirical evidence on the use of guarantees for informal redress seeking. Research is needed on the use of guarantees by consumers, and whether these are more likely to be of significance before or after purchase. The analysis of existing research (both in this and the previous chapter) points towards the conclusion that guarantees would be of greater relevance after purchase, once a problem has arisen. However, this would need to be confirmed by empirical research.

Moreover, although there is consistent evidence that consumers complain informally, it is not clear how they do so and what factors influence their decision to complain, and to whom. The survey by the DTI (2001a) indicated that most consumers who complained did so to the seller, rather than the manufacturer. Although this would suggest that consumers prefer to contact their original supplier, this does not mean that guarantees given by a manufacturer have no real role to play. There may be two reasons for this initial reaction: first, the seller may have his own generous returns policy of which the consumer may be aware and which he may prefer. Second, as noted in chapter 2,[33] many manufacturers' guarantees are implemented by the seller. The seller may therefore be the point of contact under the manufacturers' guarantee.

The statistics currently available do not identify the basis for the consumers' claims, and this question therefore remains to be addressed through more specific empirical research. A future research project that builds on the present analysis could test the conclusions of this chapter.

4.7 Conclusions

It may be useful to summarise the key findings of this chapter which will be relevant for the discussion in chapter 5 on the eventual format of a legal framework for guarantees.

It was seen that guarantees can be of use for consumers who wish to complain in two ways: first, a guarantee may aid the consumer's perception of the guarantor's willingness to deal with a complaint brought by the consumer. As a general proposition it can be stated that the more generous the guarantee with regard to remedies provided and allocation of costs for claiming under the guarantee, the more likely it will be that the consumer will perceive the guarantor as responsive. Second, a guarantee also reflects the ease with which a complaint can be brought. The research on consumer complaining behaviour suggests that consumers are more likely to complain if the complaint mechanism is accessible. A guarantee which clearly states the procedure for bringing a claim may therefore encourage a consumer to seek redress under the guarantee.

However, several problems have been identified, as well. First, guarantors have a degree of discretion both in respect of the scope of their guarantees generally and their application to a particular consumer problem. The existence of this discretion in itself is not problematic, but its exercise may be detrimental to consumers. Second, there is a danger that consumers will focus on guarantees and ignore their protection under the statutory rights. However, the latter may provide a greater level of protection. It is therefore important that consumers are kept aware of their statutory rights and that guarantees do not displace these altogether.

Notes

1 The Uniform Commercial Code (UCC) and the Magnuson-Moss Warranty Act 1975 (MMWA), discussed in chapter 6.

2 At that time, almost all states had enacted additional rules on consumer guarantees and the relationship with consumers' legal rights (the implied warranties), as well as the so-called "lemon laws", which deal with the sale of faulty automobiles in particular.

3 Article 2 of the UCC deals with all types of sales and therefore has to be sufficiently flexible to cover the smallest of consumer sales as well as large-scale inter-state transactions. The problem is, of course, similar in the United Kingdom, where the Sale of Goods Act 1979 covers all types of sales.

4 Braucher observes that rules which, in certain circumstances allow the consumer to recover his legal costs from the guarantor are problematic because the courts are given a broad discretion as to whether to allow this, and have, in fact, frequently refused to allow recovery.

5 For a useful overview of CCB research generally, see Dick, Hausknecht and Wilkie (1995), esp. pp.115/116.

6 Cf. Priest's Investment Theory, discussed in chapter 2.

7 It must be noted that this classification differs from that which a lawyer would adopt. The broad heading of "public action" includes responses which a lawyer would refer to as "informal", such as complaints addressed directly to the supplier, as well as "formal" responses, such as taking legal action. Furthermore, the terms "private" and "public" have a different meaning for a lawyer and refer to different sets of rules and their enforcement. In this chapter, where reference is made to "private" or "public" action, this should be understood in the sense explained in this section.

8 The DTI (2001a) survey puts this figure at one in ten, but it is not clear from the report how this figure was calculated.

9 e.g., as to whether the fault was inherent in the product or caused by the consumer.

10 Her research also seeks to identify when a consumer is likely to seek a replacement and when a refund. For present purposes, these aspects of her research are not relevant and are not discussed.

11 Morel et. al. (1997) are similarly cautious.

12 There is emerging research on cultural factors, as well, but this is not relevant for present purpose. See Liu and McClure (2001) for discussion.

13 It would "strain credulity" (Best and Andreasen, 1977, p.707) to suggest the low complaining rate in lower socio-economic groups by suggesting that this is because the products they buy perform better. The problem is rather that such consumers feel unable to make a complaint.

14 See chapter 2, section 2.1.

15 In contrast, if the product itself appears to be working fine, but fails to do what the *seller* promised it would, a consumer may attribute the problem to the seller rather than the manufacturer.

16 See above at 4.1.4.

17 It is significant to appreciate the "feedback" function of guarantees and the fact that complaints under guarantees can serve a valuable quality assurance function for the manufacturer. If complaints are made under a guarantee, it is possible for the manufacturer to identify recurring difficulties and to improve product quality to reduce the likelihood of such difficulties occurring in the future. Indeed, it may be the case that guarantors are encouraging complaints under their guarantees for just that purpose.

18 Or, potentially, not to take any action at all.

19 See 2.2.

20 See chapter 3.

21 See 3. It was explained there that a number of factors may affect the quality signal emitted by a guarantee.

22 See 1.6.

23 See chapter 1 for more detailed criticism of the flexible standard adopted for the statutory rights.

24 Willett argued that this could be achieved by disclosing the relevant information at the time of purchase:

> Access to justice can also be enhanced by requiring the disclosure of information at the stage of contracting, which makes the consumer more cognisant of the legal environment of the relationship. ... A more informed consumer is a more socially able consumer who is able to rationalise the issue which govern any dispute which arises; and more effectively obtain redress, perhaps even before informal or formal state systems come into play(p.99).

Although his views on the relevance of information to settling disputes are clearly correct, it seems unlikely that disclosure at the time of contracting would create the requisite awareness. Consumers are unlikely to be concerned about potential disputes at the time of purchase.

25 Of course, many retailers operate their own returns policies. These may similarly indicate to consumers that redress can be obtained easily.

26 See also Best and Andreasen (1977), who noted that:

> Sellers have a near perfect monopoly on complaint handling. They can feel free to impose their own standards for complaint resolution, confident that consumers will not make use of third-party mechanisms to review their actions (p.714).

27 There is the possibility of going to court, but it seems highly unlikely that a consumer would do so: see 1.7.

28 The author is grateful to Professor Braucher for drawing this criticism to his attention. Her response was given in an e-mail sent to the author in September 2000.

29 In the consumer context, this seems to be a mutual feeling - Ramsay (1993) observed that "many lawyers seemed to view consumer clients as aberrational characters with individual disputes who simply did not understand the issues" (p.80).

30 See Baldwin (1997) for a general discussion. The Small Claims procedure is now used for claims up to a value of £5,000. This will clearly include almost all claims made by consumers.

31 This is an informal procedure, very much like arbitration, in which the parties to the dispute are generally not represented (although there is no prohibition on legal representation). Frequently, a consumer will simply represent himself.

[32] Although sellers and manufacturers may keep internal documents for their own purposes. Furthermore, it is also important to appreciate the feedback function of guarantees, which will enable a guarantor to identify product problems and enable him to make improvements to reduce the likelihood of subsequent failures (Stephens and Gwinner, 1998, p.172).

[33] See 2.2.

Chapter 5

A Legal Framework for Guarantees

5.0 Introduction: Aspects of a legal framework for manufacturers' guarantees

The previous chapters investigated the nature and function of manufacturers' guarantees. The next step is to identify all the elements of a guarantee that may be subject to legal rules. This is the task for this chapter.

A framework for guarantees could be based on a *normative* or a *predictive* approach (Whitford, 1973, p.423). A *predictive* approach is one which seeks to support the actual behaviour of consumers in the marketplace (*ibid.*). It is therefore based on an analysis of how consumers act, or would act if particular rules were in place. In contrast, a *normative* approach focuses on how consumers ought to act. Such an approach may be based on the desire to encourage consumers to act in a particular way, e.g., by taking account of particular matters in their purchasing decision (*ibid.*), although there is no evidence that consumers would, in fact, act in the desired way.

Chapter 3 examined the function of guarantees as an indicator of product quality. The central theory in this respect is "signalling theory". A framework based on "signalling theory" would be largely normative, because it would seek to encourage consumers to compare guarantees before purchase and to take these into account in their overall purchasing decision. An alternative approach to dealing with guarantees is to focus on their usefulness in assisting consumers who wish to complain about a quality defect (see chapter 4). A framework based on this would predominantly be predictive, because it is largely based on the actual behaviour of consumers.

5.1 Key principles for the framework: Transparency and fairness

One of the key conclusions that can be drawn from the previous chapters is that the redress function of guarantees prevails over the quality signalling function. The following discussion is based on the assumption that the redress function is the primary purpose of a guarantee. It is now possible to develop a suitable legal framework for guarantees which can promote this function of guarantees as an informal redress mechanism. "Informal" in this context means that redress is sought through negotiation between consumer and guarantor without the involvement of a third-party nor through an external dispute resolution mechanism (such as arbitration or the court system).

Before this discussion can turn to the nuts and bolts of the framework, it is first necessary to identify its key principles. In order for guarantees to be used as a redress mechanism, consumers need to be able to ascertain, on the basis of the guarantee, whether the guarantor would be responsive to a complaint made by the consumer.[1] A consumer therefore needs to be able to identify what exactly the guarantee offers, and how its benefit can be obtained. This can be achieved through the introduction of transparency, or disclosure, rules. However, there may be problems with the use of guarantees as a redress mechanism, because the guarantor, in effect, sets out the conditions on which a remedy will be made available and also determines whether a remedy should, in fact, be provided. There is nothing inherently objectionable to such an arrangement, provided that it is operated in a fair and consistent manner.

The key principles to underpin this framework should therefore be *transparency* and *fairness*. First, it needs to be ensured that there is transparency through adequate disclosure of the key elements of the guarantee, i.e., the types of defects covered, the remedies to be provided and the procedure for bringing a claim. If this information is clearly stated in the guarantee, then it will be possible for the consumer to decide whether a claim under the guarantee is likely to lead to a successful resolution of his problem. A guarantee should be presented in clear and intelligible language, and that all its terms are made clear. In the past (cf. OFT, 1986), concern had been expressed over the use of technical language in guarantees which resulted in their being incomprehensible to many consumers. This made it largely impossible for consumers to ascertain what exactly they were offered in the guarantee. Furthermore, as noted previously,[2] guarantees used to contain (and some still do) clauses which would not only make it difficult to claim the benefit of the guarantee but often also excluded any rights a consumer may have had under statute.[3] Such clauses were often obscurely worded and presented in very small print. A transparency and clarity requirement may not prohibit such practices altogether, but could draw them clearly to the attention of a consumer in order to make it easier for the consumer to ascertain the extent of the benefits offered under the guarantee. Moreover, it may sometimes be necessary to comply with one or more conditions before a guarantee becomes available to a consumer, such as the return of a registration card. If a consumer is not made aware of these conditions at the time of purchase, he may be deprived of the benefit of the guarantee altogether. A transparency requirement could therefore ensure that a consumer's attention is drawn to any such conditions.[4] A general requirement on transparency and clarity could be combined with a disclosure rule to provide specific information about particular aspects of the guarantee, such as the name and address of the guarantor, the duration of the guarantee or instructions on how to bring a claim.

Second, to minimise the potential for unfair practices on the part of the guarantor, there needs to be a general criterion of fairness. Such a criterion would act to balance the freedom given to the guarantor in determining the substance of the guarantee. There are three different aspects of fairness that need to be considered. First, it is necessary to regulate fairness to ensure that consumers are not caught unawares by restrictive terms, which may only become apparent once a claim under the guarantee has been made. This requires what has been termed "procedural fairness" (cf. Beale, 1995). Consumers need to be made aware of the conditions on which a guarantee is provided, and, importantly, their attention needs to be drawn to terms which may limit the scope of the guarantee (such as maintenance requirements). To some extent, this may already be covered by the transparency requirement, but it also goes further in that it may require not just disclosure of the key terms, but also greater emphasis to be put on onerous conditions.[5] It is important that consumers are made aware of their obligations to secure the benefit of a guarantee.

However, procedural fairness may not be enough. It will also be necessary to provide for "substantive fairness" in the guarantee. In essence, this means that the guarantee should not contain terms which could be regarded as unfair in that they may be too burdensome for consumers. It follows from the discussion in chapter 4 that certain terms are important in ascertaining the guarantor's willingness to deal with a consumer complaint under the guarantee. Generally, these will be terms that relate to the remedies to be provided and the procedure for bringing a claim under the guarantee. These terms should not normally be subject to regulation with regard to their fairness, because such intervention may distort consumers' perceptions of the guarantor's responsiveness.[6] However, there may be other terms which have only an indirect bearing on these matters, but which could have the potential of depriving the consumer of the benefit of the guarantee altogether, or at least make it significantly more difficult to obtain this. Also, there may be terms which might seek to exclude the statutory rights of consumers.[7] It is therefore necessary to control the use of unfair terms.

It may be necessary to go further. A guarantor determines the extent of his obligations under a guarantee. He can reject a claim by a consumer for not falling within the guarantee, as well as exercise a discretion as to which remedy to grant. In order to control this power, it is necessary to subject the implementation of the guarantee, i.e., the way claims under a guarantee are handled, to a general standard of fairness to ensure that guarantors do not exercise their discretion under their guarantee in an unfair or arbitrary manner. As noted previously, a guarantee is not only drafted but also implemented by the guarantor. The guarantor is also the person who is responsible for the problem the consumer complains about,[8] i.e., a manufacturing defect. By introducing a fairness requirement to cover the performance of the guarantor's obligations under the guarantee, it would be possible to control the exercise of the guarantor's discretion (cf. Farnsworth, 1995).

The difficulty which may then arise is how fairness could be measured. The debate about general requirements of fairness, or good faith,[9] in various contexts has been ongoing for some time now, although a detailed review of all the various arguments is not required for present purposes.[10] Instead, the focus will be on the shape the fairness requirement would need to take in the context of manufacturers' guarantees. It will be recalled that by offering a guarantee, the guarantor provides, at the very least, an indication to the consumer that he is likely to be receptive to informal complaints. Thus, in this sense, the guarantee acts as a kind of "signal", albeit not in the sense commonly understood and referred to as signalling theory.[11] Rather, the guarantee signals that consumers who complain to the guarantor will be treated in a particular way. In other words, it creates an expectation that a consumer who complies with the terms of the guarantee and makes a claim following the correct procedure as set out in the guarantee will receive the remedy promised by the guarantor. A fairness criterion would therefore have to protect these expectations. Such an understanding of fairness is not dissimilar to the interpretation of "good faith" adopted by Willett (1999).[12] Willett focused on the regulation of contract terms which are deemed to be unfair, and the concept of good faith that is utilised under the Unfair Terms In Consumer Contracts Regulations 1999[13] in determining whether a particular term is unfair. He argued that such regulation is facilitated by focusing on the signals that are sent between the contracting parties. Generally, consumers receive a signal from a business that they will be treated fairly by that business (p.77). This may be influenced by extra-contractual signals such as past dealings or pre-contractual statements. Further signals may be emitted through advertising, which enhance the positive image of the business in the consumers' eyes. If there is a divergence between the formal terms of the contract and the signals which the business has sent out through its extra-contractual communications, then there is a case to be made that these signals should be taken into account in determining whether such terms are unfair.

How can this be applied in the particular context of manufacturers' guarantees? In a narrow sense, Willett's analysis is relevant in the context of the elimination of terms in a guarantee which are detrimental to consumers. However, there is a wider application of Willett's interpretation of the good faith concept in the context of guarantees. It is submitted that it is not just important to consider any extra-contractual signals, but also the signals that are sent out by the contract itself. Of course, to describe a guarantee as a "contract" may be problematic, because not only is the guarantee entirely pre-drafted by the guarantor, but also the consumer does not "agree" to the guarantee - he receives it with the corresponding product without choice. Yet, that is why it may be more relevant to focus on the guarantee itself, rather than any external signals. It was seen earlier that one of the hallmarks of the guarantee system is that the guarantor determines not only the extent of his liability through the guarantee promise, but also the remedies for the situation where the product fails to comply with the promise given by the guarantor and set down in the guarantee and the conditions on which these remedies will be made available. A consumer can read the guarantee and thereby perceive whether the guarantor will not only be receptive to a complaint regarding the particular problem, but also offer a suitable remedy to the consumer. Thus, the signal sent out by the guarantee is that the complaint will be dealt with provided that the conditions set down in the guarantee are complied with. It would, then, be contrary to good faith (in Willett's interpretation) for the guarantor to fail to deal adequately with the complaint or to refuse to honour the guarantee. Put differently, it would be a matter of fairness in the performance of his obligations under the guarantee for the guarantor to act in accordance with this signal (cf. Willett, 1999, p.87).

This, in effect, reflects the reasonable expectations of consumers (cf. Steyn, 1997), and, indeed, it has been noted that fairness (or good faith) in the performance of contractual obligations can be related to the expectations of the contracting parties (Adams and Brownsword, 1995, p.201). A consumer who decides to bring a claim under a guarantee can expect his claim to be dealt with in accordance with the guarantee and not to have his claim rejected for what may be an arbitrary reason. If a guarantor is required to act fairly in performing his obligations under the guarantee, then this should be sufficient to prevent an exercise of discretion that would be detrimental to consumers.[14]

The broad principles to underpin the framework are therefore transparency and fairness in procedure, substance and performance. The remainder of this chapter will focus on how these principles should be reflected in the various elements that make up a guarantee.

In the remainder of this chapter, the different aspects of a guarantee that could be regulated are analysed as to the various different options for regulation. It will then be considered which of these options would best implement the principles of fairness and transparency to promote the objective of utilising guarantees as an informal redress mechanism. First, though, it is appropriate to return briefly to the framework proposed by Braucher (1986).

5.1.1 Braucher's informal resolution model

The previous chapter examined Braucher's suggestion for an informal dispute resolution model for guarantees. In designing an appropriate legal framework, she re-classified the various legal rules into three categories: The first are "benign" rules. These are rules which do not support the informal resolution of a dispute, but equally do not impede this either. This includes rules which do not affect the content of guarantees. It also includes the implied terms - their existence itself does not hinder the informal resolution of disputes, but they are also not helpful for this process because consumers are often not sufficiently aware of their existence or their scope to make effective use of them.

Second, there are "helpful" rules. These are rules which would further the objective of informally resolving a dispute. These are generally rules which promote clarity and transparency. This includes rules requiring guarantees to be simple, certain and written in understandable, readable and useable form. It also includes rules which require the disclosure of who is covered, what is covered, what the guarantor will do and how long for, and how to bring a claim.

Finally, there may be 'harmful' rules. These make it more difficult to resolve a dispute about a product in an informal manner. Braucher is particularly concerned about rules which require the inclusion of legal terms of art, or complex standard phrases which are clear to a lawyer, but almost incomprehensible to the average consumer. A notable example is the all-too-familiar phrase "This does not affect your statutory rights", which is intended to draw attention to the implied terms, but does not really achieve this because it does not provide any detail about the content of these statutory rights.

Braucher argued that rules within the "benign" and "helpful" categories could be retained, because they did not affect the use of guarantees to resolve disputes informally in a negative way. However, provisions that were characterised as "harmful" would need to be amended or removed altogether because these rules made it more difficult to use guarantees for informal dispute resolution.

Braucher's focus is therefore on the specific legal rules on guarantees and the extent to which consumers could utilise these for informal complaint resolution. Although not vastly different from the argument developed in this book, her focus is on re-adjusting an existing legal framework to make it easier for consumers to complain, rather than to use the process of consumer complaining behaviour to inform the development from scratch of the framework. Of course, the critical examination of E.C. and English law in subsequent chapters will look at existing rules and assess these against the aspects of the framework developed here. The framework itself, however, does not emerge from the existing rules themselves.

5.2 Which aspects would a legal framework for guarantees have to cover?

To lay the foundations for this discussion, it is first necessary to consider which elements of a guarantee can be the subject of legal rules. In chapter 2, it was explained that guarantees consist of three components: the guarantee promise, the remedy if the promise is not met, and the conditions on which the promise is given.[15] For the purposes of the discussion that follows, a different categorisation of the elements of a guarantee will be adopted. A broad division of these elements into two categories can be made. The first category includes the "procedural" aspects of a guarantee. This encompasses all those elements that relate to the implementation of the guarantee, such as the procedure for bringing a claim and the question of who is liable under the guarantee. The second category covers the "substantive" elements of a guarantee. This focuses on the guarantee promise itself, and the terms and conditions on which this is provided. It must be noted that not all aspects of a guarantee fall squarely within one of these categories, but all have been placed under one heading only.

The options for regulation under these headings will be considered first. A further consideration will be the question of sanctions that would have to be made available if a guarantee failed to comply with the legal framework. In the remainder of this chapter the various options will be set out. It will then be considered which of these should be preferred.

5.3 Procedural aspects

There are four aspects to be considered in this category. The first is the question of who should be the beneficiary of the guarantee - should this be limited to the consumer who bought the product covered by the guarantee, or should this extend to subsequent owners during the guarantee period? This issue is classed as a procedural, rather than a substantive, aspect of the guarantee, on the basis that the guarantee promise itself and the terms on which it is provided is not directly affected by this matter.[16] Second, there is the issue of who should be liable to the consumer for the implementation of the guarantee. The third is whether there should be requirements as to transparency and clarity. Finally, it is necessary to consider what the consequences for the duration of the guarantee could be once a claim under the guarantee has been brought, and how the costs that may be incurred in making a claim should be allocated.

5.4 Who should be the beneficiary of the guarantee?

A question that has been raised many times in respect of guarantees is whether a guarantee should only be available to the original consumer who bought the product, or whether it should be transferable to subsequent owners, or even subsequent users. Of course, many guarantors will make the benefit of a guarantee available to subsequent owners voluntarily, without a specific rule requiring this.[17]

5.4.1 Limited to original consumer

The simplest option is to limit the benefit of the guarantee to the original purchaser. This would be based on the assumption that the guarantee is an undertaking given by the guarantor to the consumer who bought the product covered by the guarantee. The guarantee would be for the benefit of that consumer only. The treatment of guarantees as a contractual obligation supports the suggestion that it is only the consumer to whom the guarantee was "offered" originally who should be able to bring a claim under the guarantee.[18] Only the consumer and the guarantor are parties to this "guarantee contract", and only they should be bound by it.

5.4.2 Any owner during the guarantee period is covered

It may be preferable to extend the potential beneficiaries under a guarantee to anybody who owns the relevant product during the guarantee period (Howells, 1994). Trebilcock (1972) argues that a guarantee should be transferable between consumers for the duration of the guarantee period, because it does not matter who uses the product - the product should not break down during the guarantee period. This was similarly echoed by the European Commission:

> The legal concept of guarantee should correspond to its economic substance, i.e., a feature of the product itself. Hence any person in possession of the guarantee document and able to furnish evidence of initial purchase would have the right to invoke the guarantee (*Green Paper*, 1993, p.98).

The OFT mentioned that guarantors expressed concern when this question was raised as part of its research into guarantees in 1986. A point of concern was that the original consumer may have mistreated the product in question or invalidated the guarantee in some other way, but that a subsequent purchaser might not be aware of this, yet never gain the benefit of the guarantee. However, this would only affect a limited number of consumers. The OFT therefore took the view that the benefits of transferability outweighed the concerns expressed by guarantors. Moreover, many consumer goods are bought as gifts. Where a product is bought for someone else, without having been used by the consumer who purchased the product, it would seem non-sensical to deprive the recipient of the product of the benefit of the guarantee.

The OFT (2001c) has also suggested that to deny a subsequent owner during the guarantee period the benefit of the guarantee would be unfair:

> Guarantees, while they remain current, can add substantial value to the main subject matter of the contract [i.e., the product covered by the guarantee]. If consumers cannot sell something still under guarantee with the benefit of that guarantee, they are effectively deprived of what they have paid for (at para 18.4.2).

However, the OFT (1986) previously reported that some manufacturers were concerned about the potential administrative problems associated with the transfer of a guarantee to subsequent owners. Some guarantors require the completion of a registration card. If the product is sold or passed on to another consumer during the guarantee period, a subsequent owner may need to be registered as the new beneficiary of the guarantee. This could potentially create a significant administrative burden for the guarantor. It may be expected that this objection will have lost some force in view of the fact that the use of information technology and call centres for customer care has grown rapidly over the last decade or so. This may make the administration of guarantees easier.[19]

5.4.3 Which option should be preferred?

If the main objective of the framework is to support the use of guarantees as an informal redress mechanism, it may be asked whether there is any need to regulate this aspect at all. After all, it is perfectly arguable that in restricting a guarantee to the first purchaser, the guarantor could be perceived as being less responsive than he would be if the guarantee extended to subsequent owners. However, the framework developed here is based on a principle of substantive fairness. The question of whether only the original consumer should be entitled to benefit under the guarantee, or whether the guarantee should be transferable to subsequent owners, as well, needs to be addressed to ensure that the guarantee system remains fair.

If a consumer is unable to pass on the benefit of a guarantee, together with the corresponding goods, to a subsequent owner, then the consumer would be deprived of some of what he paid for when he bought the goods. This seems to be unfair. It may, of course, be that this is more significant for some products than it is for others. Clearly, for a car or double-glazing, for example, it is vital that the consumer is able to pass on the guarantee. These are expensive items and subsequent buyers may be unwilling to buy these product without the guarantee, or may only agree to do so at a lower price. This may be less so with items which are less expensive or less likely to be sold during the lifetime of a guarantee, such as small household items. Furthermore, a restriction to the original consumer may be justified on the basis that a subsequent owner may not know whether the product was used and maintained in accordance with the instructions given by the manufacturer.

These are nevertheless items that may be passed on by the original consumer, e.g., as gifts, and therefore the guarantee should be available to subsequent owners. Moreover, it would be difficult to draw a line between products which would justify a guarantee restricted to the original purchaser and those which do not. A manufacturer who is concerned about improper use or maintenance may be able to include a condition in the guarantee that the product has to be serviced to his specifications, and may also request the consumer (original or subsequent owner) to provide full details. This may be important, for instance, in the case of products which require installation, such as washing machines.

Therefore, in order to prevent potential unfairness in respect of the transferability of a guarantee, the legal framework should provide that guarantees are freely transferable during the guarantee period.

5.5 Who should be liable to the consumer under the guarantee?

A second question is that of who should be liable for the provision of the guarantee service to the consumer. It is beyond question that the person providing the guarantee should be responsible for its implementation, but should it be possible to go beyond this? Thus, should a retailer who sold the product covered by a manufacturers' guarantee be responsible for the implementation of the guarantee? And if so, should this obligation exist jointly and severally with that of the manufacturer? In other words, should there be the option for the consumer to choose who to ask for the performance of the service under the guarantee, or should the liability of parties other than the original guarantor be limited to situations where it would be impossible for the consumer to go to the guarantor to obtain performance of the guarantee? These questions will now be addressed in turn.

5.5.1 Exclusive guarantor responsibility

The simplest view is that only the guarantor himself should be responsible to honour the guarantee. This can be justified on the basis that the guarantee is an undertaking given by the guarantor, and that it is therefore only the guarantor who can be held responsible for the implementation of the guarantee.

5.5.2 Joint responsibility of guarantor and retailer

It has been proposed on more than one occasion that retailer and manufacturer should be jointly liable (e.g., Howells and Bryant, 1993; Howells, 1994). This is frequently justified on the basis that the retailer is more accessible than the manufacturer, and that the retailer benefits from the ability to offer a guarantee:

> Often retailers hold out the manufacturer's guarantee as an inducement to the consumer. Moreover, in many cases, the manufacturer may be located at a considerable distance from the point of sale, and may indeed export from another country. In either case, he will not be readily accessible to the consumer. Finally, there is an ineluctable and perfectly reasonable tendency on the part of the consumer to look to the much more tangible person who actually sold him the product ... (Trebilcock, 1972, p.41).[20]

The Department of Trade and Industry also proposed that there should be joint liability. The primary justification put forward by the DTI was also the fact that the retailer is likely to be more accessible and it would therefore be easier for the consumer to obtain redress (para.14). Furthermore, it might help to prevent the problem of a retailer seeking to evade his responsibilities under sales law:

> In practice [a consumer] may well turn to the retailer to make good any defects and the retailer will not be able to pass off the responsibility as being solely that of the manufacturer, as some retailers attempt to do in such circumstances at present (para.14).

This seems to be trying to crack a nut with a sledgehammer. There is clearly a problem with the behaviour of some retailers, but to introduce joint liability of retailer and guarantor to deal with this problem is rather too simplistic a response. Such practices are in breach of sale of goods legislation and should be controlled by other means, such as the enforcement powers given to many public bodies (in the UK, these are the powers now contained in Part 8 of the Enterprise Act 2002).

If a system of joint retailer and manufacturer liability were adopted, it would be important that a system of indemnifying the retailer for the work done under the guarantee is put in place at the same time. Otherwise, there could be a very real danger of leaving the retailer with serious financial losses. It is important that the *consumer* is able to obtain a remedy quickly, but that should not mean that the loss should fall on the retailer who has had to provide a remedy under the guarantee when the defect complained of falls within the responsibility of the manufacturer. In order to limit the possibility of adverse consequences for the retailer, it may be possible to provide that a retailer should only then be liable if there is no express disclaimer of this responsibility.[21]

5.5.3 Legal liability limited to those responsible for the performance of the guarantee

It was seen in chapter 2 that the claims under a guarantee are rarely dealt with exclusively by the guarantor. In many cases, the guarantor will rely on the sellers to provide a remedy under the guarantee. However, this is not the case for all types of products. For some classes of products, manufacturers have put into place a separate service network that will handle claims under the guarantee on their behalf. There are therefore different ways of handling guarantee claims. Legal responsibility for the performance of guarantee obligations could therefore be based on the actual arrangements put into place by the guarantor for dealing with claims under the guarantee.

In contrast to the option discussed above, a seller would only be liable under a manufacturer's guarantee if the seller was directly responsible for the provision of a remedy under the guarantee. White supported such an approach:

> In most consumer sales, manufacturers should be able to offer [guarantees] without creating liability on the part of retail sellers. On the other hand, where sellers have substantial performance responsibility, legal liability should ordinarily accompany de facto responsibility (White, 1986, p.1068).

And further:

> There is, however, one important class of consumer sales in which seller liability under manufacturer [guarantees] should be presumed. This class consists of transaction in which the seller is responsible for repairs under [the guarantee] (*ibid.*, p.1069).

On this analysis, a seller would only be liable under the guarantee if he were given the responsibility to provide a remedy to a consumer. The guarantee document will normally contain details of how to bring a claim under the guarantee and would therefore make it possible to identify those who should be legally liable for the performance of a particular guarantee.

Flechtner, however, rejected this proposition:

> Surely a dealership can agree with a manufacturer to be an authorised agent for [guarantee] repair - and can even inform its buyers of the fact - without taking on a legal obligation to beneficiaries of the [guarantee]. A different view leads to absurd results. For example, all buyers of new Fords would have a cause of action ... against any authorised Ford [guarantee] service centre that closed its doors (Flechtner, 1998, p.427).

This view suggests that any arrangements put in place by a manufacturer for the provision of a remedy to a consumer are between the manufacturer and the seller or repairer, but should not create an enforceable right for consumers against those who implement the guarantee on the manufacturers' behalf. Flechtner's main concern is that such a system may, in effect, result in the creation of network liability (discussed below), which does not seem to appeal to him. His view seems difficult to accept - in contrast to Flechtner's view, it would seem absurd if a retailer could advertise the availability of a guarantee, but then turn around and refuse to honour a consumer's claim. If a guarantee states that a retailer will deal with claims under a guarantee, surely the consumer can legitimately expect that this undertaking will be honoured, and that it will be possible to enforce such an undertaking if the retailer did not honour the guarantee.

To sum up, this option would only impose liability, in addition to the guarantor, on the parties mentioned expressly in the guarantee and would therefore produce different results depending on the arrangements put into place by a particular guarantor.

5.5.4 Joint responsibility of guarantor and members of guarantor's distribution network

It may be possible to go one step further. For this, it needs to be considered how many consumer products are sold today. These are often sold through selective or exclusive distribution networks. A number of qualitative criteria are set down which retailers who wish to join the distribution network have to comply with. For those products which are sold through such a distribution network, it may be possible to require all the network members to honour the guarantee given by the manufacturer. This possibility was recognised in the *Green Paper* (1993):

> But for ... distribution systems, one might consider going one step further - namely establishing the joint and several liability of all vendors belonging to a selective distribution system set up by the same manufacturer (p.97).

This was supported by Madsen (1995). He noted that the contract between manufacturer and retailer in a distribution system usually includes a provision that allocates responsibility for the implementation of the manufacturer's guarantee. The advantages for the consumer of such a system are not difficult to identify and are summarised by Madsen thus

> If ... we accept the idea of a joint liability of all the vendors, the consumer will be free to choose the nearest at hand... This is of course of practical importance in case the consumer wants to exchange the product or have it repaired (p.151).

Further support of this idea came from the European Consumer Law Group (ECLG, 1994) and the Consumers in Europe group (CEG, 1996). Thus, the idea of joint liability of all the members of a distribution system under the guarantee would mean that consumer could be encouraged to "shop around" for the best purchasing option, whilst not having the risk of higher costs should the product require service under the guarantee - this could still be obtained locally. In contrast, Flechtner's objections (1998, p.427) to this concept have already been noted.[22]

The primary justification of such an approach is that all network members are engaged in the common venture of promoting the manufacturer's brand identity. Network members are able to use the manufacturer's logo and other aspects of the brand image. The network is likely to be seen as an extension of the manufacturer and therefore network members should be liable under the guarantee, as well (cf. Bradgate and Twigg-Flesner, 2002).

This possibility was raised in the context of the Single Market.[23] There is no compelling reason to limit this idea to that specific context. If goods are sold through distribution networks which only have a national dimension, there could still be a case made in favour of this system of liability. For example, a consumer from Scotland may buy a product from a retailer in Cornwall whilst on holiday and require service under the guarantee on his return to Aberdeen. Network liability would enable him to obtain this from the local member of the distribution network.[24]

However, in order to ensure that some members of such a network would not have to suffer under a disproportionately high amount of guarantee claims compared to the products they sell, it would be essential to allow the network members to obtain an indemnity from the guarantor for any work carried out under the guarantee. The details of this could be left to be agreed between manufacturer and network member.

5.5.5 Which option should be preferred?

Consumers who seek to complain informally are more likely to follow a particular route for their complains if they perceive this as accessible and likely to lead to a satisfactory result.[25] One important consideration therefore is whether a claim can only be brought against the guarantor directly, or whether there are more accessible contacts, such as the original retailer or independent repairers. In view of the various methods for dealing with guarantee claims adopted by manufacturers,[26] the best option would be to impose an obligation to honour a guarantee only on those mentioned expressly in the guarantee document. This would preserve the opportunity to gauge the guarantor's responsiveness on the basis of the claims procedure put into place.

This may, of course, cause difficulties if the consumer has bought goods through distance selling means, or in another Member State of the European Union, for example. If there is nobody close by that could be contacted with a guarantee claim, the guarantee might be almost worthless to the consumer. It might therefore be tempting to impose an obligation to honour a guarantee on all the members of a distribution network, where this exists, to make it easier for a consumer to claim under a guarantee. Indeed, it could even be presented as an issue of fairness in that it might be unfair if a consumer could not obtain service under a guarantee near to his home. Such a consumer would still be entitled to rely on the guarantee against the guarantor, although it would be more difficult to do so. This could be taken as an indicator of the guarantor's willingness to deal with complaints, and on that basis, there is no need to impose an obligation on network members.[27]

5.6 How should claims under a guarantee be dealt with?

If a consumer claims under a guarantee, then a number of issues arise that will need to be addressed. The predominant question will undoubtedly be that of who is to bear the costs of implementing a guarantee. This will be addressed first. A second issue is what will happen to the guarantee period if a consumer invokes the guarantee and obtains either repair of the product or replacement.

5.6.1 Costs

Making a claim under a guarantee will inevitably result in costs. The two main sources are the parts that may have to be used to repair a product, and the labour costs for the person actually carrying out work under the guarantee. In addition to these, there may be further cost such as the cost of returning the product to the retailer or to the manufacturer, or a call-out charge if the guarantor's representative has to visit the consumer's home. In many cases, the guarantor will assume some, if not all, of these costs, but there are guarantees that require the consumer to share some of these.

The question that arises therefore is in how far guarantors should be allowed to impose such "implementation costs" on consumers. One option would be not to regulate and leave this for the discretion of the guarantor. A second option would be to intervene and regulate the allocation of costs in such a way that the guarantor will always absorb all of these expenses. This may be justifiable on the basis that it might be unfair to require a consumer to incur any costs in order to obtain the benefit of a guarantee. Alternatively, it may be possible to require the consumer to pay some of these costs. A possible justification for this alternative is that to share the cost would make it more likely that only genuine claims are made under a guarantee.

It seems that no specific rule is required here. The allocation of costs for claiming under a guarantee is one of the most significant factors a consumer can take into account in gauging the responsiveness and ease of accessibility of a guarantor. A clear complaints procedure which imposes few or no costs on a consumer is a strong indicator of a willingness to deal with a complaint.[28]

5.6.2 Impact on guarantee period

An important question from the consumer's perspective is this: if a product is replaced under a guarantee, does the guarantee period continue whilst the product is out of use, or is it suspended when the defect is notified and re-started when the replacement is received, or does it expire completely once a replacement is provided? A manufacturer may decide to replace a product under the guarantee. This may come with a new guarantee, or it may be a substitute for the product covered by the original guarantee. The distinction is crucial - the replacement product may come with a full guarantee, in which case the consumer gains substantially - he receives a new product without incurring any additional cost. Should the replacement break down before the new guarantee period has expired, the consumer may receive another replacement, and so on. A consumer could thus theoretically receive a replacement product without ever having to pay. This might be regarded as imposing a heavy cost burden on guarantors. However, if a number of units of a particular product regularly break down during the guarantee period, it seems logical to suggest that there is a more serious problem with the product, in which case the guarantor may need to be persuaded to invest more in product reliability and durability.

An alternative approach would be to regard the replacement as a mere substitute under the original guarantee, with the effect that the product is not covered by a full term guarantee.

Furthermore, what happens to the guarantee period if the product is returned for repair? Is the guarantee period suspended (if so, when exactly does suspension occur), or does it continue? A consumer may not have been able to use the product for days or weeks while it was being repaired. If the guarantee period is not suspended during that time, a consumer would, in effect, not benefit from the whole of the guarantee period. It is, however, not easy to determine when exactly the guarantee period should be suspended - this may occur as soon as the consumer notifies the guarantor of his claim, or once the product has been dispatched to the guarantor for repair. Suspension of the period may involve considerable administrative duties on guarantors, as well - records would have to be kept on the dates that the guarantee period was suspended or restarted, for example.

From the point of view of promoting the use of guarantees as an informal route to redress, no specific rule is required. This aspects should therefore be left for the guarantor to determine.

5.7 Substantive aspects

Here, the focus is on two aspects of a guarantee, the actual guarantee promise, and the conditions on which this is provided. These will be referred to as the "content" or "substance" of the guarantee. There is a range of possibilities for regulating the content of a guarantee. These can be ranked according to the degree to which they would regulate the content of the guarantee. Thus, at the very bottom, there would be no regulation of the content at all, whereas at the top, there would be total regulation of all guarantees. There are a number of inter-mediate categories. In the following paragraphs, all these different degrees of regulating the content of a guarantee will be considered.

5.8 Positive regulation

5.8.1 No regulation

First, there could be no regulation of the content of a guarantee at all. In this case, the law would not specify what a guarantee has to promise, nor which remedies would have to be provided if the promise was not met. It would give guarantors complete freedom to determine the scope of their guarantees.

5.8.2 Limited regulation: Disclosure by category

Second, it may be possible to provide for limited regulation of the guarantee content. This would not set out any specific requirements, but rather set out the categories about which details have to be given in the guarantee document. This would, in essence, be a disclosure-based approach. Thus, the framework would require express details of such aspects as guarantee coverage, duration and claims procedures. However, there would be no specific requirement as to the substance of these aspects.

The disclosure of the relevant details of a guarantee can be useful at two different stages. First, it may be that disclosure before the consumer buys the product covered by the guarantee will enable him to assess the guarantee, and possibly to compare guarantees offered by different manufacturers. It will be seen in chapter 6 that the use of disclosure rules in this sense has been particularly influential in the United States. However, disclosure of relevant details can also be crucial after purchase when a problem has arisen and the consumer is seeking to obtain redress for this problem.

Trebilcock (1972) was sceptical about disclosure rules. He noted that proposals to introduce disclosure rules are often justified on the basis that this would improve competition between guarantors on their guarantees. Thus, consumers are said to be able to make a better informed shopping decision by being able to consider the different guarantees which are offered with the type of product they are interested in and select the brand on the basis of, *inter alia*, the guarantee given. Trebilcock observed that few, if any, consumers actually go through the trouble of examining guarantees prior to purchase, and that those who might like to do so were likely to meet with resistance from retailers and manufacturers.[29] Even those consumers lucky enough to gain access to guarantee documents prior to making a purchase might discover that there is insufficient information, or that it is presented in complex language. Although this could be remedied with disclosure rules, he still concluded that:

> The fact remains that a comparative shopping decision in relation to guarantees accompanying competing products is, for the average consumer, still likely to be an incredibly difficult exercise (p.19).

This might suggest that disclosure rules alone are of limited use in a pre-purchase context. However, in a post-purchase situation, when a problem has arisen and the consumer is seeking to find a solution, clear disclosure of the relevant aspects of a guarantee may aid the consumer in taking appropriate steps to obtain a remedy. Thus, if the guarantor has a designated service network for guarantee claims, then the consumer would save time and effort if he contacted the nearest member of that network, rather than to argue with the retailer who may have no responsibilities under the guarantee.

5.8.3 Further regulation: Limited types of guarantee

Third, rules may be introduced that would require anybody offering a guarantee to comply with definite rules. It may be possible to create a number of different categories of guarantees, with different specifications set down for each of these categories. In that case, it would not be permissible to offer a guarantee which could not be classified with reference to one of the designated categories.

A primary justification for specifying the substance for different categories of guarantee is based on the argument that the word "guarantee" creates specific expectations among consumers. If a manufacturer decides to offer a guarantee, he should therefore be required to take account of such expectations. This is the approach taken by the Danish Consumer Ombudsman (Madsen, 1995, p.149) which was considered during the discussions on the European Commission's Green Paper on Consumer Guarantees and After-Sales Services (1993). The Danish approach is to require anybody who uses the term 'guarantee' to provide a particular level of service, which has to be in addition to the rights of a consumer under the law.

Trebilcock (1972) argued that competition on guarantees could be improved by reducing the factors that are left to the decision of guarantors to the minimum:

> Consumers generally do regard the provision of guarantee coverage as important when they shop ... however ... the prospect of consumers making detailed pre-purchase evaluations of guarantees accompanying competing products is slight. The one proposition that consumers are capable of fastening on to quickly and easily is the *duration* of the guarantee (p.29).[30]

Therefore, competition in the field of guarantees could exist mainly in respect of the duration of guarantee coverage. A consumer who is torn between two MP-3 players might therefore select Brand C which comes with a 3-year-guarantee, and reject Brands A and B which come with one and two year guarantees respectively.

Trebilcock also argued that if it is indicated that a product is covered by a guarantee, there will be certain common assumptions among consumers, such as that if anything goes wrong with the product, it will be fixed without charge during the guarantee period. So what the consumer really looks out for is for *how long* the guarantee will cover the product, rather than what exactly it is that the guarantee will do - he will simply assume that certain things will happen if he needs to invoke the guarantee (Trebilcock, 1972, p.29). There could then be problems if the consumer's expectations were not met by the guarantee. Rules could therefore be introduced that would reflect consumers' expectations as to the level of coverage to be expected from a guarantee.

A legal framework would pursue two objectives in this respect: first, consumers must be made aware of the duration of a guarantee when making a purchase, and secondly, whilst allowing differences in the duration of guarantees, a uniformity of coverage in line with general expectations of consumers should be encouraged. Whenever therefore a manufacturer decides to offer a guarantee, he will have to provide a specified service, although he can determine for how long this guarantee is to be available. The primary expectation of all consumers is that the guarantee will cover all defects in materials and workmanship (Trebilcock, 1972, p.26) and that they will be able to get a faulty product fixed at no cost to them. Therefore, the terms of a guarantee must, at least, allow for this. Trebilcock does not appear too enthusiastic about the system adopted in the Magnuson-Moss Act 1975[31] (then only a Senate bill) of classifying guarantees as either "full"[32] or "partial",[33] because he believes such labels could cause confusion because consumers might think that a 5-year-partial guarantee is better than a two-year-full guarantee (p.32). He suggested that all guarantees must offer full coverage for the duration of an initial guarantee period, following which it may be permissible to offer a partial guarantee. In contrast, Geraint Howells ((and Bryant), 1993; 1994) favoured a system akin to that adopted under the Magnuson-Moss Act. This could be enhanced by allowing a broader spectrum of guarantees, depending on the generosity of coverage. Of course, having too broad a spectrum would defeat the object of creating clearly defined categories in the first place.

If it is correct that consumers never consider the terms and scope of a guarantee, other than, perhaps, its duration, then there could be an argument in favour of standardising all guarantees to ensure that consumers are not mislead as to what is available to them when a product is sold as "guaranteed". The creation of a mandatory guarantee could eliminate all opportunities for imposing terms which might restrict consumers' rights. However, this would only be justified if the vast majority of consumers were using guarantees in this way. Empirical evidence on the use of guarantees by consumers would be required to support this.

5.8.4 Guarantees to meet at least the standard set by the statutory rights

It may be desirable to ensure that guarantees offer at least the level of protection that is given to consumers under the law on the sale of goods. This point is discussed further below.

5.8.5 Total regulation

Finally, there could be total regulation of the guarantee. This would clearly specify what a guarantee would have to provide and would leave the guarantor without any discretion on the substance of the guarantee. However, there could be disadvantages with adopting such an exclusive system. First, it might be impossible to draft a guarantee that could be used by all guarantors and be suitable for all types of products. Kutner (1977, p.763) observed that a guarantee that is suitable for a relatively expensive and technically complex product (e.g., a car) may not be appropriate for a smaller and simpler product (e.g., an alarm clock). There would therefore be difficulties in defining exactly what a guarantee would have to provide:

> Should manufacturers' guarantees be standardised? Should they be made mandatory? Who should they protect? Most important of all, *what* should they guarantee? That a washing machine will last 20 years, 10 years, 1 year, will wash

> clothes brighter than brand new, will retain its [sic] gleaming enamel finish, for how long? (Trebilcock, 1969, p.65).

Second, if there were total regulation of the guarantee, then there would, in effect, be a legal standard that would be very much akin to the statutory rights of consumers, as already discussed in chapter 1. There, it was seen that the statutory standard usually only binds the final seller and not the manufacturer. A suggestion to provide total regulation of guarantees may therefore be based on the desire to ensure that manufacturers are directly liable to a consumer for quality defects.[34]

5.8.6 No specific regulation, but default or standard guarantee

A combination of some of the previous suggestions would be to maintain as high a freedom of choice as possible, but to specify the categories of a guarantee for which a guarantee must make provision. Thus, it may be required that the guarantee clearly states who can benefit from the guarantee, who will honour the guarantee, which remedies are provided, who is to bear the costs and so on. Provided that a guarantor expressly states in his guarantee what the guarantee offers in all these categories, there would be no further substantive requirement.

However, if a guarantor failed to state what his guarantee offered in one or more of these categories, then a default position could apply. Thus, if the guarantor failed to specify how the costs of invoking the guarantee would be allocated, then the default position might be that all costs would have to be borne by the guarantor.

An argument against the introduction of a default guarantee is that this may create pressure on guarantors to offer a guarantee which meets at least the standard set by the default rules, although this might depend on how high that standard is. If the standard is set at a level which reflects the substance of the vast majority of manufacturers' guarantees, the introduction of default rules would probably be of minimal impact. However, if the default rules were to go beyond this level, guarantors may feel obliged to amend their guarantees accordingly.[35] There is a danger, therefore, that the introduction of default rules could be perceived as a form of "back-door" regulation in that guarantors would, in effect, be forced to amend the substance of their guarantees to reflect the default rules. However, this would not be an inevitable consequence, as the experience under the Magnuson-Moss Warranty Act 1975 in the United States shows.[36] There, manufacturers did not respond to the introduction of the two-tier system by increasing the scope of their guarantees to meet the requirements for "full" guarantees.

5.8.7 Which option should be preferred?

The utilisation of guarantees as an informal redress mechanism will not require a significant degree of substantive regulation. It was seen in chapter 4 that consumers can consider the terms of a guarantee in assessing whether it would be worth their while to try to resolve a product quality problem informally through complaining to the guarantor. It is therefore crucial that the consumer is not hindered in evaluating a guarantee for this purpose. This process is best supported through the introduction of disclosure rules that require the guarantor to specify how to bring a complaint, against whom the complaint can be brought, the range of remedies that may be considered by the guarantor and the allocation of costs for honouring the guarantee. With these details, it will be easier for the consumer to make a decision on how to resolve the quality problem that he has encountered with a particular product.

It is not necessary, and would be rather counter-productive, if more specific rules regarding the substance of a guarantee were adopted. There are two reasons for this: first, the framework aimed at promoting informal complaints does not envisage that consumers will compare guarantees given with different products before they make a purchase. Rather, it acknowledges that consumers are most likely to read a guarantee once they have encountered a problem. At that point, they are faced with the decision how to proceed and who to complain to. If, after reading the guarantee, the consumer feels that a satisfactory solution to the problem could not be obtained by complaining to the guarantor, he could then either decide to complain to somebody else (such as the retailer if the manufacturer is the guarantor), or on the basis of his statutory rights.

The second reason is that guarantors will not have uniform procedures for dealing with guarantee claims. It has already been explained that some deal with guarantee claims in-house, some through a repair network and others through the retailer. Smaller manufacturers may impose an initial cost on a consumer for the return of the product for inspection, whereas larger manufacturers are better placed to absorb such costs and do not require the consumer to bear such costs. This variety and relative freedom to determine how to handle claims under a guarantee is fundamental to giving consumers the opportunity to establish whether an informal complaint is likely to be met with a favourable response. If more uniform rules were introduced, consumers would be deprived of this opportunity, and they would no longer be able to rely on guarantees in deciding how best to solve a product quality problem. Thus, as far as the substantive regulation of guarantees is concerned, this should be limited to disclosure rules.[37]

It is important to appreciate that the information disclosed in accordance with this rule would be made available to a consumer at a time when he is more likely to be able to use it. During the purchasing process, a consumer is unlikely to pay a great deal of attention to the details of a guarantee. However, once he has bought the product and needs to familiarise himself with the guarantee, disclosure of the relevant information is likely to be beneficial for the consumer (cf. Whitford, 1973, p.463). First, the consumer is made aware of the conditions he needs to comply with in order to obtain the benefit of the guarantee. Second, the consumer is able to ascertain the steps he needs to follow to claim under the guarantee. Third, the information will be accessed by the consumer when he actually needs it, rather than at a point when some (particularly proponents of signalling theory) think consumers ought to use the information (Whitford, 1973, p.467). If a product has broken down and a consumer seeks a remedy, that is the point when the information in the guarantee about available remedies and how to claim them will be most relevant. Disclosure "[comes] closer in time to when the consumer actually needs the information" (*ibid.*). Finally, there is no need to be concerned about the detail of information a consumer has to process, nor about potential variations between different guarantees, because it is less likely to be regarded as too inconvenient or time-consuming to read the relevant information (Whitford, 1973, p.468). On that basis, there is no need to standardise aspects of manufacturers' guarantees in order to make it easier for consumers to assess the value of a particular guarantee, because he will not be pressed for time to make a decision.

It should also not be ignored that a literal application of Signalling Theory would require no more than the introduction of disclosure rules in order to ensure that consumers can identify exactly what each guarantee promises. However, it is widely assumed that most consumers would not be able to utilise the information provided in this way in a meaningful manner, which is why proponents of a signalling-based approach have suggested a broader substantive intervention by introducing rules for the categorisation of guarantees. Thus, the types of guarantees would be restricted to three or four specific categories, at least one of which would prescribe extensively the content of the guarantee and only leave its duration to the discretion of the guarantor. This, it is argued, would enable consumers better to compare the guarantees offered with competing products and allow them to identify higher quality products on the basis of guarantee coverage. Therefore, it would be necessary to introduce disclosure rules combined with a limitation to the types of guarantees that can be offered. This would, however, undermine the objective of supporting the use of guarantees as an informal redress mechanism for the reasons set out above.

From the Single Market perspective, only limited intervention in the substance of a guarantee would be required. The main concern in this context is to ensure that guarantees are not used to impede market integration. The focus of substantive intervention would therefore be on the clause in the guarantee that specifies its geographical extent,[38] and require that where products are sold in more than one Member State, the guarantee should be available throughout the Single Market.

It can therefore be concluded that the disclosure of information in specific categories would best serve the primary objective, subject to a requirement that products sold on an EC-wide basis are accompanied by a guarantee that is available throughout the EC. This would, however, not entail that where the corresponding goods are sold through a distribution network, the members of such a network should be obliged to honour the guarantee.

5.9 Negative regulation

As well as specifying what should be included in a guarantee, it may equally be possible to specify what should *not* be included in a guarantee. This is a form of "negative" regulation, because rules adopted under this approach would not require the guarantor to make specific promises, but rather set out aspects that should not be included in a guarantee. Thus, it may be desirable to prevent the use of a clause which seeks to exclude the statutory rights of consumers. Moreover, it may be necessary to render ineffective terms in a guarantee which would make it very difficult for the consumer to obtain the benefit of the guarantee. Negative regulation would therefore primarily be targeted at unfair terms.[39]

Negative regulation is one of the key elements of the fairness principle which underpins the entire framework developed in this chapter. A potential difficulty may arise in respect of terms dealing with the allocation of costs for guarantee claims. Imposing the bulk of such costs on a consumer may be regarded as unfair because it would make it very difficult for a consumer to obtain the benefit of the guarantee. However, for reasons given previously, this term should be removed from the scope of the fairness principle.

5.10 Substantive regulation - concluding comment

It is clear from the preceding overview that substantive intervention can take a variety of forms. A decision on the extent to which there ought to be intervention on the substance of a guarantee will depend on a balancing exercise between two contrasting, and possibly conflicting, objectives (Whitford, 1968, p.1094). On the one hand, the detailed regulation of the substance of a guarantee could reduce or even eliminate some of the problems with guarantees that have been identified. On the other hand, every rule in this sphere will inevitably impinge upon the freedom and, more crucially, the expertise of the guarantor to frame a guarantee policy that he is willing and able to provide. Moreover, it could make it significantly more difficult to assess the guarantor's responsiveness if too detailed a set of rules were adopted. Thus, it is vital to examine how far the guarantee created voluntarily by a guarantor benefits consumers without causing intolerable detriment in order to gauge the extent to which the commercial freedom of a guarantor should be curtailed.

5.11 The relationship between the consumer guarantee and the consumers' statutory rights

It was seen in chapter 1 that there are remedies available to a consumer who has bought a faulty product. This is done through a flexible standard which must be met by the product.[40] If it is not met, the law will require that a remedy is made available to the consumer. Thus, in some cases, it may be that the retailer will be allowed to attempt to repair the faulty product; in others, the consumer may be able to require the retailer to replace the product, or to take the product back and give the consumer a full refund. This section considers what the relationship should be between the statutory rights and the guarantee.

There are a number of different options for the relationship between the statutory rights and the consumer guarantee. First, the guarantee could be "additional" to the statutory rights and therefore have to provide benefits over and above the statutory rights. Second, guarantees could be "complementary" to the statutory rights. There would then be no need for the guarantee to provide a higher level of benefit. Third, the reverse perspective of how far the flexible statutory standard should take account of the availability of a guarantee should be considered.

5.11.1 Guarantee as an additional benefit over and above the statutory rights

One view is that guarantees are intended to place a consumer in a position more advantageous than under sale of goods legislation, i.e., the requirements under the Sale of Goods Act 1979 (SoGA), or the rules contained in the Guarantees Directive. Guarantees should provide something *in addition to* the rights enjoyed by the consumer under the law. What does this mean, though? A very simple way in which a guarantee could provide something extra is if this is provided by somebody who would not normally be directly responsible to the consumer for the provision of a remedy for faulty goods. Thus, if the exclusive responsibility under the statutory rules falls on the seller, the mere fact that the guarantee is provided by the manufacturer would be sufficient to satisfy the demand that the guarantee must put the consumer into a better position than under the law. On that basis, this requirement would be toothless, because it could inevitably be satisfied simply by the manufacturer providing a guarantee, even where this would offer the consumer fewer remedies than he has against the retailer under his statutory rights.

It could also mean that the guarantee, even though provided by somebody who has no direct legal responsibility to the consumer, must incorporate the standard of protection set by the statutory rights and improve on this level. This could place a significant burden on any guarantor. It would have a significant impact on the substance of a guarantee and reduce the degree of choice given to a guarantor in determining the scope of the guarantee.[41]

A beneficial aspect would be that it could all but eliminate the impact of terms in a guarantee which seek to exclude the statutory rights. If a guarantee had to meet at least the level of protection set by statute, then an exclusion of the statutory rights would have no practical effect on the overall level of protection given to consumers - it would simply be obtained through the guarantee rather than the statute.

5.11.2 Guarantee to complement the statutory rights

The alternative view is that guarantees are complementary to the statutory rights and that there is no requirement that the level of protection under a guarantee should be higher. Thus, guarantee and statutory rights would remain completely independent, at least as far as their substance is concerned. A guarantor would be completely free to choose which remedies he will provide, and under what circumstances.

A problem with such an approach is that consumers who are unaware of their statutory rights might regard a less generous guarantee as the full extent of their rights in case the product is defective. It was seen in chapter 2 that some guarantees contain clauses which limit the extent to which the guarantor assumes liability towards the consumer for quality defects.[42] If this approach were adopted, it may be necessary to ensure that consumers are made sufficiently aware of their statutory rights, e.g., by including an appropriately worded statement in the guarantee document.

5.11.3 Taking account of the guarantee to determine the statutory standard of quality

A third question is whether the existence of a guarantee should influence the application of the statutory rights of the consumer. Bridge has argued that the assessment of whether or not a product meets the standard of quality set by law should take into account the provision of a guarantee:

> Anyone concerned with the minimum acceptable quality of, say, motor cars should wish to go beyond the contractual relations of garage and buyer to see how the manufacturer's [guarantee] scheme is worked into the relationship. ... The doctrine of privity of contract insulates buyers and sellers from outside parties and is probably responsible for the (perhaps fragile) orthodoxy that the merchantable quality of a car at the date of delivery is not to be assessed by regard being paid to the manufacturer's [guarantee] programme and after-sales service (Bridge, 1990, p.57).[43]

Implicit in this statement is the suggestion that the quality of a product *should* be assessed with reference to the guarantee programme and after-sales service. In order to deal with this point, it is necessary to separate this suggestion into two aspects. Bridge treats guarantees and after-sales services in the same way, but the two are different. After-Sales services can take any of a variety of forms, including customer helplines, repair services and the provision of spare-parts facilities.

It is easy to see how the availability of an appropriate after-sales service could have an impact on the statutory quality standard. The availability of after-sales services will often determine the extent of the period after purchase during which the consumer will be able to use the product. This depends on the availability of spare parts and maintenance and repair facilities. Once these cease to be available, it will no longer be possible for the consumer to use the product if it breaks down. In English law, one of the aspects of quality is durability,[44] and is conceivable that after-sales services could be relevant to durability, because the product life-time could be prolonged by replacing worn-out components with spare parts.[45]

A guarantee is not concerned with regular maintenance and replacement of worn out parts. A guarantee is there to provide a remedy to consumer who has bought a product which has broken down because of a fault in materials or workmanship. It therefore addresses a different problem. However, it is nevertheless arguable that a guarantee could also be taken into account in determining whether a product is of satisfactory quality. It may therefore matter that a consumer had the protection of a guarantee when determining whether the product meets the statutory standard of quality. Thus, if a consumer has bought a product which is faulty, but the fault could be repaired relatively easily by relying on the guarantee, the consumer may not be allowed to reject the product.[46]

5.11.4 Total exclusion of statutory rights by guarantee

A final point that may be raised is whether a guarantor should be allowed to exclude the operation of the statutory rights altogether. Rothschild (1976) argued that there should be no restriction on the possibility to exclude the statutory rights, provided that the consumer received a clear written guarantee. Surprising though this view may be, it has been supported by others:

> If a [guarantor] is willing to agree to a lesser obligation and attempts to abide by it, this may be worth more to the buyer than his somewhat hypothetical rights under an implied [term] by which the seller has not indicated a willingness to abide. The remedies that are statutorily provided require, in usual circumstances, litigation to compel a recalcitrant warrantor; but court action has been a singularly ineffectual goad to warrantors in the past (Eddy, 1977, p.857).

There may therefore be a case to be made to allow a guarantor to exclude the operation of the statutory rights altogether.

It is interesting to note that the New Zealand Consumer Guarantees Act 1993 (CGA) requires a consumer to seek a remedy under the guarantee before he is able to rely on his statutory rights. S.27(2) CGA states that where the guarantee provides that the manufacturer will remedy a defect either by repairing or replacing the product, then the consumer must give the manufacturer the opportunity to remedy a failure under the guarantee before a claim can be brought under the statutory rights. Only where the manufacturer declines to remedy the failure under the guarantee, or where he fails to do so within a reasonable time, can a consumer claim for a breach of his statutory rights. Although this does not amount to a total exclusion of the statutory rights, it does severely limit them and reduces the option to choose between a voluntarily given guarantee and statutory rights to obtain a remedy.

5.11.5 What should be the relationship between guarantee and statutory rights?

At the outset, it can be noted that the framework developed here does not envisage that a guarantee would be the exclusive avenue of redress which is pursued by a consumer. It was seen in chapter 1 that consumers generally complain informally rather than to seek third-party advice or utilise formal complaints procedures. A guarantee is valuable for this because it sets out the position of the guarantor and indicates the guarantor's willingness to deal with the consumer's complaint.[47] This gives the guarantee an edge over the statutory rights: the latter are determined objectively and imposed on seller and consumer by law, whereas the guarantee is a subjective decision by the guarantor to offer specified remedies to the consumer if certain events occur. Furthermore, the guarantee is usually contained in a written document which the consumer will be able to refer to, whereas it would be considerably more difficult for him to establish whether or not his statutory rights cover the particular problem he has encountered.

Where a guarantee is given with a product, this process of complaining could be channelled better by enabling a consumer to consider whether a complaint based on the guarantee is likely to lead to a satisfactory outcome. Where this is not the case, either because the consumer feels that the guarantee does not suggest that the particular problem would be resolved satisfactorily, or because the consumer was incorrect in his assessment and the guarantor in fact fails to resolve the problem, the consumer must have an alternative course of action. This suggests that it is vital that there is a strong set of statutory rules in place which will offer a remedy to a consumer independent from any remedies offered to a consumer in a guarantee. Thus, the relationship between guarantee and statutory rights should be one of complete independence - the existence and reliance on a guarantee should have no impact on the availability of the statutory rights (unless, of course, relying on the guarantee produces a satisfactory outcome, in which case there will be no need to rely on the statute). Equally, the fact that a guarantee is available should not affect the possibility for a consumer to chose to rely on his statutory rights, be it for an informal complaint or for formal action. Moreover, guarantees should not influence the assessment of whether a product meets the statutory standard, because to do so would be to allow a guarantee to operate as a limitation clause. This would be detrimental for consumers.

Why is the existence of a high level of statutory protection important for the informal complaints framework? Does it not seem contradictory to say that the statutory rights are hardly ever enforced in court and that consumers prefer to resolve disputes informally because they rarely know about their statutory rights, whilst demanding that there are mandatory statutory rights that provide a good level of protection to consumers? First, although it is hardly disputable that the statutory rights can be difficult to enforce without the assistance of a lawyer, that does not mean that consumers are unsuccessful in relying on their rights in the informal context. It seems likely that consumers who complain informally will use a mixture of different arguments. Some consumers will point to a guarantee, some will refer to their statutory rights and argue that the goods have not met the relevant standard, and some may simply argue that the product does not do what it is supposed to do. The statutory rights are therefore likely to be relevant. Even though both consumer and retailer may be relatively ignorant as to the exact scope of the statutory rules and their application to the immediate problem, there may still be a common understanding of how these rights apply and it may be possible to come to a negotiated settlement on that basis.

Furthermore, the existence of the statutory rights may provide an indirect control mechanism over the substance of a guarantee. The statutory rights and remedies reflect the reasonable expectations of consumers generally as to what should happen if they have bought faulty goods. A guarantor may use this as a yardstick for determining the extent of the guarantee he chooses to give with his products. If the guarantee is significantly more restrictive than the statutory rights, it may be regarded as worthless and therefore the guarantor would not benefit from offering a guarantee at all.

Moreover, the statutory rights may be important if the guarantor is unable to provide a remedy under the guarantee within a time that is acceptable to a consumer. In such a situation, a consumer may obtain a solution more quickly by relying on his statutory rights against the seller.

To ensure fairness, a guarantee should in no way limit or exclude the protection that a consumer enjoys under statute. Any attempt to do so should be thwarted. This does not suggest that the guarantee itself should provide something over and above what is granted to a consumer under statute, as long as the guarantee does not seek to take away this level of protection. This perspective therefore requires intervention to prevent terms in guarantees that may have the effect of depriving consumers of their protection under statute.[48]

The statutory rights should therefore never be displaced by the guarantee. Instead, the guarantee is but one form of using an informal approach to dispute settlement, but where this approach is likely to be fruitless, a consumer must be able to have another avenue of redress.

5.12 Enforcement

Finally, some thought needs to be given to the enforcement of the rules which would constitute a specific legal framework for guarantees. It is also necessary to consider what, if any, sanctions should be available.

5.12.1 Would a specific enforcement mechanism be necessary?

The question of sanctions is a difficult one to address. It seems that the extent to which a specific enforcement mechanism and specific sanctions are required might depend on the extent to which there is regulation of guarantees. Thus, the more rules are imposed by law, the stronger the case will be for introducing a range of sanctions for failing to comply with these. However, it may be sufficient to apply general regulatory consumer protection mechanisms in the context of manufacturers' guarantees.

5.12.2 Public or private enforcement?

Even if it is accepted that there needs to be an enforcement mechanism and that there should be sanctions for failing to follow the rules that may be introduced, it will further need to be considered whether these should be limited to private law sanctions (e.g., akin to breach of contract), or whether public law sanctions should be available, as well. These could include the use of injunctions to prevent continuing infringements, or even criminal sanctions.[49]

5.12.3 Regulatory enforcement: Criminal sanctions[50]

One option is to use a regulatory enforcement mechanism and create a criminal offence for a failure to honour a guarantee or to comply with the rules on manufacturers' guarantees set down in legislation. As a consequence, such failures would be met with prosecution by a relevant public authority and may result in the imposition of fines. Criminal sanctions are used in respect of numerous aspects of consumer protection (see Cartwright, 2001). Their existence may have a deterrent effect to prevent traders from acting in a way that would be detrimental to consumers - it communicates societal disapproval of such conduct (*ibid.*, p.86). However, the efficiency of the deterrence effect depends on the punishment for the wrong that has been done. Sanctions therefore have to be proportionate to the offence. A further difficulty is whether a criminal offence in the context of consumer protection should require a *mens rea* element, i.e., evidence of an intention to commit the act, or whether these should be offences of strict liability[51] subject to a defence that all reasonable steps have been taken to avoid committing the offence[52] (*ibid*, ch.5). An offence which requires *mens rea* may be difficult to prove in the case of large businesses, where it may be difficult to identify that the requisite intention was present. Strict liability offences may therefore be more appropriate in this context.[53]

It may therefore be possible to devise a criminal offence for a failure to comply with the legal rules on manufacturers' guarantees and for a failure to honour a guarantee. A failure to comply with the legal framework could be a strict liability offence. However, it seems that a *mens rea* element would be more appropriate for a failure to honour a guarantee because the problem such an offence would seek to address involves an active decision by a guarantor to reject the consumer's claim.

Intuitively, it seems that a criminal sanction may go too far. An observation made by Paul Salvidge (then Director of the Consumer Affairs and Competition Policy Directorate at the Department of Trade and Industry) when giving evidence to the House of Lords European Communities Select Committee, illustrates this problem in relation to the requirement imposed by the Directive that a guarantee must be available for inspection by a consumer prior to purchase of the goods:[54]

> There will presumably be a provision ... saying that the retailer shall, on request, make available copies of guarantees which are contained in boxes. Then we have to scratch our heads and say, 'If they do not do so, what is the sanction?'. Damages do not look particularly inviting so we are sort of getting driven, if we are not careful, to a criminal offence and the thought that this provision gives rise to a criminal offence does seem a bit strange (Oral Evidence, Minutes of Evidence, para 426).

This statement illustrates the difficulties that the introduction of criminal sanctions would create - a criminal offence for a failure to comply with a fairly basic legal framework seems to be going too far. Furthermore, a point emphasised by Trebilcock (1972) was that even if there were criminal sanctions available for a failure to comply with legal rules on manufacturers' guarantees, it seems very likely that there would not be effective enforcement. He dismissed the use of criminal sanctions in the context of guarantees. The criminal system has limited resources and there may therefore be few, if any, resources available to police the guarantee system. Furthermore, criminal law provisions are construed narrowly out of fairness to potential defendants. Finally, the criminal law has no compensatory effect - a consumer may not obtain any compensation through criminal sanctions imposed on a guarantor.[55] Therefore, criminal sanctions can, at best, support other types of rules, but not be used exclusively (p.13).

Trebilcock highlights a number of difficulties with the adoption of a criminal-law based enforcement mechanism. The greatest problem is the definition of a suitable criminal offence. Certainty demands that the acts which would fall within the scope of a criminal offence are clearly defined, and it may be very difficult to describe the acts that should be covered by a criminal offence.

Of course, there may be no need to devise a specific criminal sanction for a failure to comply with the framework on guarantees. Instead, it may be possible to treat a failure to comply with a legal framework for guarantees or to honour a guarantee as an infringement of consumer protection legislation generally and apply general criminal sanctions that may be available under regulatory rules. Many countries (including the UK - see the Trade Descriptions Act 1968) have legislative provisions to provide criminal sanctions that can cover many different trading practices which are detrimental to consumers.

A criminal sanction would therefore not seem to be sensible. Instead, it would make more sense to give a power to the relevant regulatory authority (such as the Office of Fair Trading) to warn and ultimately obtain an injunction against guarantors who persistently failed to comply with this legal framework. If this approach were adopted, then it may not even be necessary to introduce a specific enforcement mechanism if there are already general enforcement mechanisms in place.[56]

5.12.4 Regulatory enforcement - injunctions and undertakings

An alternative to an enforcement mechanism that would seek to apply criminal sanctions against a guarantor would be one that would focus on non-criminal regulatory sanctions instead. Thus, public bodies and consumer organisations could be provided with a power to seek undertakings or injunctions to stop a guarantor from continuing to ignore the rules on guarantees or failing to honour his guarantees. This would stop short of imposing punitive measures for a failure to comply with the relevant law. It could encourage traders to comply with the law and to honour their promises.

A good example of this type of regulatory enforcement is provided by the Unfair Contract Terms Regulations 1999, discussed in chapter 8. These give powers to the Office of Fair Trading, Trading Standards Departments and other public bodies with an interest in consumer protection to approach traders who use terms which may be unfair and persuade them to amend these. If unsuccessful, they may apply to the court for an injunction to prevent the use of such unfair terms.[57] No specific criminal penalties are available for the use of unfair contract terms,[58] except for a term in a guarantee which seeks to limit or exclude the statutory rights of consumers.[59]

Further consideration is required of an appropriate enforcement mechanism to deal with failure to act in accordance with the terms of a guarantee. The central objective of the legal framework developed in this thesis is that guarantees can be used most effectively when a consumer has encountered a problem with a product and is trying to resolve this informally. It was seen above that the requirement of fairness in the performance of the guarantee and Willett's conception of fairness (or "good faith") is very relevant. If a fairness criterion along the lines set out above were adopted, then this could be combined with an administrative enforcement mechanism to stop guarantors from persistently failing to act in accordance with their guarantees. Such a mechanism would not have to be specific to guarantees. Rather, a failure to honour a guarantee, i.e., a failure to act in accordance with the signal sent out to consumers, would be a failure to act in good faith more generally, for which a suitable sanction could be made available. Indeed, Willett 's ideas are developed in the context of unfair contract terms, but it seems that a good faith principle understood in this sense can be of wider application in the context of consumer protection law. For present purposes, a suitable sanction should be available if a guarantor had not acted in good faith in performing his assumed obligations under the guarantee.

This may, theoretically, be enforced by a consumer in a private claim. However, one of the findings on which this thesis is based is the fact that consumers will rarely invoke the formal legal process. It would, therefore, be a paradox to limit the policing of a framework which facilitates informal complaint resolution to individual consumers who have encountered difficulties when seeking to utilise a guarantee for that purpose. Therefore, public supervision and enforcement would be necessary. A consumer who has not been able to resolve a problem because of the guarantor's failure to act in accordance with the signal he has sent out via the guarantee is unlikely to persist, but may register his unsuccessful attempt to rely on the guarantee with a public body such as the Office of Fair Trading or a Trading Standards Department. If this body receives a number of complaints about the same guarantor, it may then decide to investigate that guarantor's practices and if it finds that there has been behaviour that is contrary to the idea of good faith, it may order the guarantor either to change his practices or, at least, to withdraw the guarantee. The nuts and bolts of such an enforcement mechanism need not be discussed here. The preceding paragraphs have sought to give a broad idea of the type of mechanism that seems most appropriate for the framework for guarantees developed in this thesis. It seems also clear that criminal sanctions would not be necessary. However, if there were evidence that a significant number of guarantors failed to comply with the framework or to honour their guarantees, further thought might need to be given to the introduction of criminal sanctions. The evidence that is currently available[60] suggests that this is unlikely to be the case.[61]

5.12.5 Private enforcement

In addition to a regulatory enforcement mechanism which is handled by an administrative or regulatory body, it would also be possible to rely on individual consumers to bring a court action against a guarantor who failed to honour his guarantee. If guarantees are treated as a particular type of contract, then a consumer could bring a claim for breach of contract and obtain a remedy. Such an action, if successful, would only help the particular consumer who took the trouble of going to court. It has already been noted that consumer cases rarely come to court,[62] and it seems unlikely that many consumers would seek to enforce a guarantee through court action. Furthermore, because a court case only resolves the dispute between the parties involved, it would not stop the guarantor from refusing to honour his guarantee in other cases. There are therefore drawbacks to a private enforcement mechanism, because it would only provide redress for those consumers who actually took action.

5.13 General implementation

A final consideration is the extent to which there should be mandatory rules for manufacturers' guarantees. When the European Commission (1993) considered the options for dealing with guarantees at the European level, it faced a similar question. Three broad approaches were identified: "regulatory and unitary", "mixed", and "voluntarist". Although these alternatives were presented in the context of the discussion that was taking place at the European level at the time, they are of general applicability.

5.13.1 The regulatory and unitary option

The first option would be to draw up a mandatory legal scheme which would apply to all consumer guarantees. Thus, all guarantees offered to consumers would need to comply with a definite set of rules, and there would be no scope to compete on the terms of a guarantee. This would therefore be an exclusively mandatory framework.

In the context of the European Community, this would have required the creation of a single "Euroguarantee", available throughout the common market and binding on any one who would want to offer a guarantee. The Commission did not support this option because it felt that full regulation would impose too heavy a burden on business.

5.13.2 The mixed option

This option would require the creation of a mandatory legal framework that would apply to all guarantees. This would not interfere with the voluntary nature of the guarantee itself, nor would it have any impact on the substance of the guarantee.

Rather, it would require the disclosure of certain aspects of the guarantee in order to ensure that consumers are better informed about what is available. Thus, it would have to be made clear what the conditions of operation for the guarantee would be, what is covered, who will be responsible for providing a service under the guarantee and who can rely on the guarantee.

There are two further strands to this option: first, the Commission suggested that a set of default rules should be put into place where a guarantee fails to specify certain aspects. Thus, a guarantee may, for example, be silent as to its duration, or whether or not it is transferable from one consumer to a subsequent owner. Second, there should also be a voluntary standard guarantee,[63] supported by a "quality label" or specific designation, as in the regulatory option. This could be at least of some use where a guarantor simply advertises or sells a product as being "fully guaranteed", without specifying anything further. It may be that such a guarantor intends to provide a guarantee service in line with what is generally considered a basic standard for a guarantee. However, there would inevitably be different interpretations of what would be this general standard, and therefore a standard guarantee could be introduced. Guarantors who advertised their goods as "X years guarantee", would not have to provide any of the details about coverage and duration - this would be determined by reference to the standard guarantee. However, it would still be necessary to provide at least one contact for invoking the guarantee.

5.13.3 The voluntarist option

This option would abandon any attempt at regulating manufacturers' guarantees. The Green Paper (1993) suggested two variants: first, although no rules for guarantees would be prescribed, the option would be created whereby guarantors could design their guarantee by reference to specified criteria, in return for which they could obtain a "quality label" for their guarantee, or use a particular designation which would be reserved for guarantees which complied with these criteria. However, it would be entirely up to the guarantor to (a) follow the criteria and (b) to use the quality label or the special designation. There would be no obligation to use these even if the guarantee was in line with the criteria specified. Consumers could therefore not be sure that a guarantee which does use a particular designation is any more favourable than one which does not.

A simpler form of the voluntarist approach would be to leave the regulation of guarantees entirely to the various trade associations and their respective Codes of Conduct.

Thus, the Commission considered options that required a varying degree of legislative intervention in the market. Inherent in its proposals is the recognition that consumers may have a general assumption as to what a guarantee should provide, but that there is a considerable degree of variation among the guarantees that are available. This might explain its repeated suggestion that there be at least some form of recognised standard guarantee, be it an entirely voluntary one, a default one that would operate to fill in gaps, or a standard mandatory guarantee.

However, the extent to which self-regulation should be used in the sphere of consumer law has been examined extensively (see Ramsay, 1989, pp.90-92; Cartwright, 2001, pp. 53-60). It can now be assumed that the most significant role for self-regulation is to complement broad legislative standards (cf. Howells, 1998b; Scott and Black, 2000, p.66) and therefore the "mixed option" may offer the best way forward.

The framework developed in this chapter is relatively minimalist. It creates a basic framework within which manufacturers' guarantees can be provided, but it leaves a significant degree of choice to the guarantor with regard to the substance of the guarantee. This does not preclude the adoption of codes of practice which would seek to require those who subscribe to such a code to follow more detailed rules. A code may lay down more detailed rules on aspects such as the allocation of costs for implementing the guarantee, the remedies which are to be made available to a consumer and the conditions on which the guarantee is provided.

A good example of a Code of Practice on guarantees is the one used by the British Retail Consortium (annexed to Commission, 1993). This requires that guarantees are clear and unambiguous, do not restrict a consumer's statutory rights and are not subject to onerous conditions.[64] It also requires that the guarantee period is extended by the amount of time the consumer has been unable to use the goods whilst these were being repaired.

It would therefore seem sensible to limit the legislative framework to the broad structure developed in this chapter and allow guarantors to define more detailed obligations through self-regulation.[65]

5.14 Conclusion

This chapter has developed a legal framework that would best promote the objective of utilising guarantees as an informal redress mechanism. It will be helpful at this stage to summarise the elements of this framework. It is based on the principles of transparency and fairness. These are taken as the foundations, and are reflected in the specific elements of the framework.

First, it seems appropriate to require that guarantees do not restrict the potential beneficiaries under the guarantee to the original purchaser. Guarantees are part of the overall package purchased by the consumer, and to deprive a consumer of the possibility to pass on the remainder of that benefit if the sells the product within the guarantee period has the potential to be unfair.

Second, on the question of who should be responsible to honour the guarantee, it was concluded that the best option was to require those parties expressly mentioned in the guarantee document to be legally liable for the performance of the guarantee. It would be for the guarantor to decide who should be named. This would relate to the arrangements made by the particular guarantor for the provision of a remedy under the guarantee.[66]

Third, in order to make it easier for consumers to identify if the guarantor will deal with complaints informally, no specific rules should be adopted in respect of the allocation of costs for claiming under the guarantee and the impact of a claim on the guarantee period.

Fourth, there is a limited need for substantive regulation of guarantees. The overall objective of promoting informal complaints is best achieved through disclosure rules that require that clear information be given about the main aspects of the guarantee. There should also be a degree of negative regulation, i.e., the removal of terms which are clearly detrimental or unfair to consumers. In the single market context, guarantees for goods which are marketed on a Europe-wide basis should be made available throughout the European Union.

On the relationship between guarantee and statutory rights, the best way forward is to regard both as entirely separate avenues for a consumer to pursue. Therefore, a consumer's decision to try to claim under a guarantee should in no way prejudice his possibility of invoking his statutory rights. Similarly, a consumer should never be required to claim under a guarantee before seeking to rely on his statutory rights. Moreover, the existence of a guarantee should have no bearing on the scope of the statutory rights of consumers.

With regard to the question of enforcement, the most suitable approach would be to rely on a broad principle of fairness and to use this as a yardstick by which the guarantor's actions are measured. Regulatory enforcement using regulatory enforcement would be the appropriate means of ensuring that guarantors do not take advantage of what is essentially a non-interventionist framework for manufacturers' guarantees.

Notes

1 See chapter 4.

2 Chapter 2 at 2.3.1.

3 i.e., the Sale of Goods Act 1979.

4 This would not go as far as to render any such requirement ineffective. Howells and Weatherill (1995, p.195) argue that such a requirement should not be imposed on consumers where this would be disproportionate.

5 This could be done, for example, by printing these at the top of the guarantee document, in a larger font-size, and also perhaps by printing a warning on the product packaging. However, it is not suggested that detailed rules should be laid down in this respect.

6 Terms in a guarantee which impose costs on consumers may be unfair, but they also reflect the guarantor's willingness to deal with complaints.

7 See chapter 2, at 2.3.1, and see also chapter 8, at 8.9.2, for evidence that this is still a regular practice today.

8 This is assuming that the consumer is bringing a claim which falls within the guarantee.

9 Good Faith in the present context is used interchangeably with fairness and fair dealing.

10 See e.g., Brownsword (2000), ch.5, Beatson and Friedman (1995) and Brownsword, Hird and Howells (1999).

11 Signalling Theory postulates a link between product quality and scope of the guarantee - the wider the scope of the guarantee the higher the level of product quality. In the context of the present discussion, the "signal" does not relate to product quality, but rather to the guarantors willingness to deal with complaints informally: see chapter 3 for a general discussion of Signalling Theory.

12 It would also be akin to what Brownsword (1996; 2000) has described as a "good faith requirement", or Wightman's idea of "contextual good faith" (1999), which would give effect to the standards of fair dealing recognised in the context of consumer transactions. However, the approach adopted here would not preclude the adoption of a good faith regime, or objective good faith, which would be based on a morally defensible standard of fair dealing. See Brownsword (1996), in particular.

13 These are discussed at 8.9.1.

14 Furthermore, one should not underestimate the significance of business reputation to keep the guarantor to the terms of his guarantee (Braucher, 1986; Collins, 1999).

15 See chapter 2, section 2.2.

16 This is, admittedly, not a clear-cut situation. It will be seen in chapter 8 (at 8.9.7) that a term which restricts the benefit of a guarantee to the original purchaser may be regarded as unfair and could therefore be subject to "negative regulation" (see 5.9 below). However, for present purposes, this issue is dealt with more appropriately under this heading.

17 Cf. chapter 2, 2.2.3.

18 This is the traditional view of the law of contract, according to which only the parties to a contract are able to enforce it. In English law, this is no longer quite so clear-cut, following the Contracts (Rights of Third Parties) Act 1999. See chapter 8, section 8.5.2.

19 However, no statistical evidence is available to support this suggestion.

20 Both Trebilcock (1972) and Howells (1994) correctly point out that there will be many products that are imported from abroad and consequently, the manufacturer may not be represented in the country in which the consumer is based. Both therefore argue that the liability under a manufacturer's guarantee should extend to the importer of goods where the manufacturer is based outside the country where the consumer has bought the product.

21 Cf. the observations made in *Alexander v Comet Group* (1994).

22 See the previous section.

23 See chapter 2 at 2.3.3.

24 The same may be true of international transactions, such as a purchase in the United States of a product by a consumer from the UK.

25 See chapter 4.

26 See chapter 2, section 2.2.

27 This does not rule out the suggestion that network members should be liable under sales law for quality defects: see Bradgate and Twigg-Flesner (2002).

28 There is an opposing argument according to which it could be detrimental to consumers if they had to incur any costs for claiming under a guarantee, particularly because it is generally the case that their claims under sales law should not result in any costs to them. However, because of the central function that costs play in perceiving responsiveness, it should be left to the guarantor to determine costs. Consumers retain the option to claim on the basis of their legal rights instead.

29 This might have influenced the provision now contained in Article 6(3) of the Consumer Guarantees Directive, which allows a consumer to request to see a guarantee before purchase: see 7.3.2.

30 Emphasis supplied.

31 Discussed in chapter 6.

32 e.g., providing repair free of charge, including parts and labour, or a replacement.

33 e.g., covering parts or labour only.

[34] Micklitz and Howells (1999) report that some countries in Central and Eastern Europe have adopted this approach to manufacturers' guarantees. For example, Slovenian law has detailed rules for guarantees given with certain types of products, such as machinery and motor vehicles (*ibid*, p.108).

[35] Anecdotal evidence suggests that when the E.C. Consumer Guarantees Directive was adopted, it was widely assumed that this required the introduction of a two-year manufacturers' guarantee. However, the Directive only specifies that a seller should be liable for defects at the time of delivery which become apparent within two years of delivery. There is no requirement as to the duration of manufacturers' guarantees in the Directive.

[36] See chapter 6.

[37] Exploitation theory would not require any specific positive rules, going beyond disclosure of the terms of the guarantee, because it is primarily concerned with the avoidance of such terms as exclusion and limitation clauses. In order to prevent unfair surprise, it is also necessary to ensure that there was a degree of disclosure of the crucial terms of a guarantee.

[38] The Green Paper (1993) also suggested the creation of a voluntary "Euroguarantee". Rather than to make this mandatory, it would have been a model guarantee that could have been utilised by guarantors in creating a guarantee that would be available throughout the Internal Market. Such a "Euroguarantee" would provide details for much of the content of the guarantee in order to maintain a reasonable level of uniformity within the Internal Market, but it would be voluntary and operate merely as an adjunct to the general legal framework for guarantees.

[39] See 2.3.1 for the problems with unfair terms in guarantees.

[40] The "satisfactory quality" standard in s.14(2) of the Sale of Goods Act 1979 (see 1.5), and the "conformity with the contract" standard under the Consumer Guarantees Directive (see 1.4).

[41] Such a requirement could be more onerous for retailers than for manufacturers, because retailers are clearly bound by the statutory rights. For example, English Law, prior to the implementation of the E.C. Directive, did not recognise the remedies of repair and replacement. A simple improvement would therefore be the express provision of theses remedies, as indeed is the case under many guarantees. Following its implementation, consumers could be put into a better position by breaking with the hierarchy of remedies the Directive introduces and, for example, offer the consumer a partial refund (i.e., price reduction), or the choice to return the product for a full refund.

[42] See 2.2.3.

[43] Bridge (1990) refers to *Rogers v Parish* (1987) in the accompanying footnote (p.57, n.40).

[44] See chapter 1, section 1.5.

[45] Cf. the judgment in *L Gent & Sons v Eastman Machine Co Ltd.* (1985), which suggests that there is no legal obligation on the seller or supplier to maintain stocks or to provide servicing facilities. However, it had been argued in this case that there was a trade custom that spare parts should be kept, but the Court of Appeal was not persuaded of the existence of such a custom.

[46] One potential problem could arise with retailers' guarantees. A retailer may offer a guarantee on the products which are sold by him. This guarantee may offer free repair for a period of, say, two years from the date of purchase. If a consumer has bought a product from that retailer, and that product has turned out to be faulty, what would the options be? The consumer could either reject the goods by enforcing his statutory rights, or he could give the retailer the opportunity to repair the products under the consumer guarantee. There is a further problem for consumers: It is, of course, possible for the consumer to enforce his statutory rights by rejecting the product, but he is perfectly entitled to waive his entitlement to a full refund and could instead ask the retailer to repair the faulty product instead. In this case, there could be a real problem of analysis: the repair could have been effected by the consumer's reliance on the guarantee or by his enforcing his statutory rights. This could become a problem if the repair has turned out to be ineffective - would the consumer then be entitled to rely on his statutory rights yet again and reject the goods?

[47] See chapter 4.

[48] Signalling Theory does not make such demands. In fact, the existence of statutory rules is almost entirely irrelevant for the signalling perspective. It will be recalled that signalling theory sees a clear link between product quality and scope of a guarantee - thus, the more favourable the guarantee is for the consumer, the higher is the level of quality to be expected from the product. Guarantees which signal only a limited level of quality are therefore more likely to be shunned by consumers, who will instead be looking out for products of higher quality. It does not matter, therefore, whether the guarantee is more restrictive than the statutory rights or more favourable - either case would merely serve as a signal of lower or higher quality respectively.

[49] A brief word on the public/private distinction drawn here. "Private" sanctions are those that can be obtained by individual consumers taking action themselves. Injunctive relief and criminal sanctions are grouped together under the broad heading of "public sanctions" on the basis that these would normally be obtained or enforced by public bodies, rather than individual consumers.

[50] This part presents a brief overview of the key aspects. See Cartwright (2001) for a detailed and valuable study of the role of criminal law in the context of consumer protection.

[51] Strict liability only requires evidence that the act in question has, in fact, been committed - there is no investigation into the trader's intent.

[52] This is known as the "due diligence" defence.

[53] But see the critical examination of the application of strict liability offences by English courts in Cartwright (2001, pp.111-123).

[54] See chapter 7, section 7.3.2.

[55] However, courts in the UK have the power under s.130 of the Powers of Criminal Courts (Sentencing) Act 2000 to award compensation to consumers affected by acts which are treated as criminal. In such cases, the criminal law does have a compensatory effect.

[56] Notably Part III of the Fair Trading Act 1973, and the Stop-Now Orders Regulations 2001 (both to be replaced by Part 8 of the Enterprise Act 2002). See chapter 8.

[57] In *Director-General of Fair Trading v First National Bank* (2001), the OFT was ultimately unsuccessful in obtaining an injunction against First National Bank. See chapter 8, at 8.9.1.

[58] Although a failure to comply with an injunction would be treated as contempt of court.

[59] The Consumer Transactions (Restrictions on Statements) Order 1976. See chapter 8.

[60] See generally chapter 2, section 2.3.2.

61 However, the existence of regulatory enforcement mechanisms would not rule out the possibility of a private action to enforce a guarantee.

62 See chapter 1, section 1.7.

63 The Green Paper, which was obviously concerned with the Single Market as a whole, considered the introduction of a specific "Euro-guarantee", but this suggestion can be generalised to consider the introduction of a standard guarantee for the reasons given in the text above.

64 Such as a requirement to return the guarantee in original packaging, a return of goods to the guarantor which cannot reasonably be considered as transportable, or an insistence that the purchaser register the guarantee.

65 This would, of course, be subject to Competition law controls against anti-competitive collaboration.

66 There is, in theory, a possibility that a manufacturer may provide that a retailer will implement the guarantee without adequate arrangements having been put into place. From the consumer's point of view, this should not affect his ability to require the retailer to perform, although the retailer would then have a cause of action against the manufacturer.

Chapter 6

A Signalling Framework: The U.S. Magnuson-Moss Warranty Act 1975

6.0 Introduction

This chapter examines a legal framework for manufacturers' guarantees which is largely based on signalling theory. Nowhere is this thinking more evident than in the legislative framework for guarantees adopted in the United States. The Magnuson-Moss Warranty Act 1975 is the leading example of a statute that is influenced by signalling theory, and also by exploitation theory. The Act will be examined in detail in the following section (and see also Reitz, 1978). There are two objectives in doing this. First, an analysis of the Act provides an example of how the influence of signalling theory (and to some extent, exploitation theory[1]), is reflected in the nuts and bolts of a legal framework. Second, an analysis of the Act itself and of its impact will permit the drawing of some conclusions as to its effectiveness and therefore the extent to which a legal framework for guarantees could promote the use of guarantees as quality signals, and also bring about general improvements to product quality. Reference should be made to the conclusions reached in chapter 3 that signalling theory appears to be of limited value.

In 1975, the U.S. Congress passed the Magnuson-Moss Warranty Act (MMWA).[2] This Act seeks to provide a comprehensive legal framework for guarantees.[3] The MMWA sought to address the problems identified earlier and referred to as exploitation theory,[4] but is also heavily influenced by a policy approach based on signalling theory. The Act therefore contains two main provisions: one on disclosure of guarantee details, and another on guarantee designation. The objective was to make guarantees more intelligible, and at the same time to encourage competition between guarantors. This chapter will examine these aspects in detail and consider if a legal framework that is based on a combination of signalling and exploitation theory works.

6.1 Background to the MMWA

Research in the late 1960s found that consumers in the U.S. had considerable difficulties understanding the terms and conditions contained in the guarantees that accompanied the products they bought (Brickey, 1978, pp.74-75). These were often too complex and contained too much legal language (Wisdom, 1979, p.1119).

There were severe problems with exclusion and limitation clauses which were hardly comprehensible. The automobile sector, in particular, had come in for a lot of criticism - guarantees were often not honoured, or the service performed under guarantees was insufficient to resolve the quality defect. These complaints later extended to other sectors, including domestic appliances (Smith, 1977, p.393). Deception of consumers had also been identified as a major problem. In addition to the problem of exclusion clauses, a common occurrence was that guarantors would interpret their guarantee in such a way that it would not cover the particular defect the consumer complained about (Eddy, 1977, p.849).[5] A related problem that had been identified was that the general level of quality was often not particularly high, both within product categories in general, and with individual units of a particular product category (Eddy, 1977, p.849).

These problems were investigated by a number of governmental inquiries in the late 1960s and early 1970s. Each of these confirmed that guarantees were too complicated and confusing for consumers to understand and contained too many exclusion clauses. Attempts to persuade guarantors to change their practice voluntarily did not succeed (Smith, 1977, p.394).

6.1.1 Uniform Commercial Code: Quality terms[6]

Consumers are given some protection against quality defects under the Uniform Commercial Code (UCC). This is a model code that is adopted by all but one[7] of the constituent states of the U.S. and therefore provides protection for buyers under state law.[8] Article II of the Code deals with contracts for the sale of goods. As with the English Sale of Goods Act, the UCC applies to all types of sales transactions, and not just to consumer sales. There are, however, differences in their respective fields of application, which are not further dealt with here.

The UCC's framework is not particularly consumer-friendly, and this in itself was a cause of the problems that lead to the adoption of the MMWA. S.2-314 implies into a contract of sale a warranty that the goods sold are merchantable. The buyer will only have a claim against the direct seller; thus, a consumer is only able to bring a claim against the retailer who sold him the product in question. It must be noted that s.2-318 contains provisions enabling a person other than the consumer-buyer to bring a claim.[9] S.2-315 also implies a warranty that goods must be fit for a particular purpose if this is made know to the seller. Under the Code, it is possible to exclude the implied warranties, provided that this exclusion is not unconscionable. There is no outright prohibition on the exclusion of the implied terms in consumer transactions. However, many states have now adopted additional rules that introduce such a prohibition.

Remedies under the Code are generally limited to damages, or, in limited instances, rescission of the contract. However, under s.2-719, it may be permissible to restrict by agreement the rights of a buyer, e.g., to return of the goods and repayment of the price, or to repair/replacement of a non-conforming part.

Consequential damages may only be limited or excluded if this is not unconscionable.

6.1.2 Signalling theory is evident in the objectives of the MMWA

Smith (1977) summarised the four objectives pursued by the Act:

> (1) the need for consumer understanding; (2) the need for minimum [guarantee] protection for consumers; (3) the need for assurance of [guarantee] performance; and (4) the need for better product reliability (p.396).

The first objective was to be achieved through the introduction of suitable disclosure rules. Realising the second objective depended on improvements to the level of competition between guarantors. Thus, by specifying the minimum requirements for "full" guarantees,[10] and by promoting competition on the basis of guarantees, it was hoped guarantors would end up offering "full" rather than "limited" guarantees. The requirements for "full" guarantees are fairly extensive, and the increase in "full" guarantees offered with products would therefore increase the overall level of protection (Wisdom, 1979, p.1121).[11] Improved performance of the obligations under a guarantee was to be achieved through rules which made it easier to bring court actions, e.g., by allowing a winning consumer to recover the costs of his legal representation in court.[12]

Finally, better product reliability was also to be achieved through detailed disclosure requirements:

> Clarity will promote comparison; comparison will increase competition in [guarantees]; competition in [guarantees] will lead to more extensive [guarantees] and, in turn, to greater product reliability. (Eddy, 1977, p.858)

This confirms the strong influence of signalling theory on the MMWA. It will be recalled that the effectiveness of a signal is linked to the costs that the person sending the signal would incur if the signal was not correct.[13] Thus, in the context of guarantees, if the guarantee signals that a product is of a specific level of quality, then the guarantor will incur the cost of having to meet claims under the guarantee if the product is of lower quality.

The thinking stated by Eddy explains how this can be linked to greater product quality. If consumers are able to compare guarantees, they are more likely to select a product that is covered by a guarantee that signals higher quality. Guarantors will therefore have to improve their guarantee coverage if they are to be able to compete. However, if guarantors do improve the scope of their guarantee, then they will have to invest in improvements to the quality of their products in order to avoid an increase in costs for dealing with claims under the guarantee. Therefore, disclosure that promotes competition will also lead to improvements in product quality.

This inevitably leads to the question of why guarantors had not sought to compete on guarantees in the past. Eddy (1977, p.859) commented that manufacturers sought to compete on product features and price, but rarely on guarantees. He concluded that the reason that there had been no competition on guarantees in the past was because manufacturers regarded this as insufficiently useful to improving sales. The lack of clarity therefore was a result of a lack of competition in this area, rather than its cause. Introducing greater clarity would enable consumers to ascertain what was covered and what not, but it did not entail that there would be an improvement to the scope of guarantees as a result. The hope of the legislator that competitive pressures would increase guarantee coverage:

> may be overly optimistic. The continued existence of the abuses which ultimately prompted congressional action may well indicate that competitive forces are not particularly active in this aspect of retail marketing (Denicola, 1975, p.280).

If this analysis is correct, then the Act is based on a misconception, namely that competition in guarantees can be improved by requiring disclosure. This may be because there had been no systematic analysis of the role of guarantees in consumer sales. There had been no analysis of the proportion of consumers who considered guarantees before sale, nor whether this proportion would increase if access to guarantee documents were made easier (Feldman, 1976, p.47). If consumers paid little attention to guarantees, then manufacturers would be unlikely to invest a great deal of effort in promoting their guarantees, or competing on guarantees.

6.2 Scope of the MMWA

The Act adheres to the objective of promoting competition in that it does not make it a requirement that a written guarantee is given. If a manufacturer or retailer chooses not to give a guarantee, there will not be a breach of the Act.[14] The Act only applies where a guarantor offers a written guarantee for a consumer product. A consumer product is "any tangible personal property ... which is normally used for personal, family or household purposes ..." (s.101(1). "Written guarantee" is defined is s.101(6) as:

> (a) any written affirmation of fact or written promise made in connection with the sale of a consumer product by a supplier to a buyer which relates to the nature of the material or workmanship and affirms or promises that such material or workmanship is defect free or will meet a specified level of performance over a specified period of time; or
>
> (b) any undertaking in writing in connection with the sale by a supplier of a consumer product to refund, repair, replace, or take other remedial action with respect to such product in the event that such product fails to meet the specifications set forth in the undertaking,
> which written affirmation, promise or undertaking becomes part of the basis of the bargain between a supplier and a buyer for purposes other than resale of such product.

The term "supplier" is defined very broadly in s.101(4) as "any person engaged in the business of making a consumer product directly or indirectly available to consumers". This definition therefore covers not only the final seller (i.e., the retailer), but also the manufacturer and anybody else in the distribution chain.

The definition of "written guarantee" is further elaborated on in FTC rule 700.3 (§16 C.F.R. 700.3). There, it is made clear that satisfaction guarantees are not covered by the Act:

> For example, a seller of consumer products may give consumers an unconditional right to revoke acceptance of the goods within a certain number of days after delivery without regard to defects or failure to meet a specified level of performance ... such terms of sale alone are not written [guarantees] under the Act.[15]

Furthermore, under s.101(6) MMWA, the guarantee must become "part of the basis of the bargain" between seller and consumer. In essence, this means that the guarantee must be given to the consumer at the time that the contract of sale for the product covered by the guarantee is made. The consumer does not provide any additional consideration for the guarantee.[16]

The Act also does not apply to express statements about product characteristics (Brickey, 1978, p.85). Thus, an express warranty that does not refer to performance over a specified period of time, even if it is in writing, is not a written guarantee for the purposes of the MMWA (Saxe and Blejwas, 1976, p.6).

The definition of "written warranty" does not include statements made in general advertising material, no matter how precise these are in relation to product characteristics.[17]

6.2.1 Who can benefit under the guarantee?

"Consumer" is defined as a:

> buyer (other than for purposes of resale) of any consumer product, any person to whom such product is transferred during the duration of an implied [term] or written [guarantee] applicable to the product, and any other person who is entitled by the terms of such guarantee ... to enforce against the guarantor the obligations of the guarantee (s.101(3)).

Thus, the MMWA is based on the premise that guarantees are not just effective between purchasing consumer and guarantor, but are also effective for transferees. This in itself may be a reflection of the influence of signalling theory on the MMWA. According to the theory, the guarantee is a signal of the quality of the product it accompanies. The quality of the product does not usually depend on the person who buys or uses it, but rather on its design and assembly. There is therefore no reason to limit a guarantee to the original purchaser.[18]

6.2.2 Who is required to honour the guarantee?

It is also important to note that under s.110(f) MMWA, only the guarantor himself is legally liable for the performance of the guarantee. A manufacturer's guarantee can therefore only be enforced against the manufacturer, but not against the retailer (Kutner, 1977, p.759).

6.3 Procedural regulation: Pre-sale disclosure

The MMWA imposes two types of disclosure requirements. First, it specifies the categories of information that each guarantee must contain (discussed below). Second, it requires that guarantees are available before a consumer commits himself to a purchase.

6.3.1 Pre-sale availability

In order to promote competition between guarantors, consumers have to be able to examine guarantees before purchase and rules were put into place to facilitate this. The pre-sale availability of guarantee documents is governed by FTC Regulation 702.3 (§16 CFR 702.3). These rules are detailed and specify the obligations of the seller and the guarantor in this respect. Furthermore, there are specific rules for distance selling (catalogue sales) and door-step sales.[19]

Seller's duties: The seller has to make the text of the guarantee available for examination by a consumer before he commits himself to a particular purchase. One way of doing this is by displaying the guarantee document close to the product. Alternatively, this requirement can be complied with if the guarantee is produced on request by the consumer, provided that notices are displayed around the shop that attract the consumer's attention to this possibility.

Guarantor's duties: A guarantor is required to provide a seller with the materials that will enable the seller to comply with the pre-sale availability requirement. A number of options are given in the FTC rules. These are not exclusive, and guarantors are encouraged to implement more than just one of these. A guarantor can assist a seller by providing copies of guarantee documents; by providing labels that contain the full text of the guarantee; printing the text of the guarantee on the packaging of the product, provided that the packaging is normally used for display purposes; finally, by providing a notice that contains the full text of the guarantee.[20] A guarantor is also required to provide sellers who use distance or door-step selling methods with copies of the guarantee documents.

Distance selling: The FTC rules defined this widely as " any offer for sale, or any solicitation for an order for a consumer product ... which includes instructions for ordering the product which do not require a personal visit to the seller's establishment". This is wide enough to cover mail-order, catalogue and electronic commerce means of distance selling.

The catalogue must include, either on the same page, or on a page clearly indicated on the same page as the product covered by the guarantee, the full text of the guarantee. Alternatively, there can be a statement that the guarantee document can be obtained free of charge from a specified address. If the seller chooses the latter option, he will also be under an obligation to provide such guarantee documents promptly on receipt of the consumer's request.

Door-step selling: This is defined as "a sale ... in which the seller or his representative personally solicits the sale, including those in response to or following an invitation by a buyer, and the buyer's agreement to offer to purchase is made at a place other than the place of business of the seller". If it seems that the prospective consumer is interested in buying a product covered by a guarantee, the seller must inform the consumer that he has the guarantee document available for inspection before the sale is completed. This information must be given both orally and in any written material that is presented to the consumer.

6.3.2 Guarantee registration cards

It is common practice for guarantors to require the return of a registration card before the guarantee becomes effective. Under §16 CFR 701.4, it is therefore necessary that when a registration card is a condition precedent to guarantee performance, that this is disclosed in the guarantee document. There is also recognition of the fact that in practice, guarantors will honour their guarantees even if the registration card is not returned. If this is so, then this must also be disclosed in the guarantee document.

The MMWA goes further in respect of "full" guarantees. "Full" guarantees are those that meet the minimum standard set down in the Act.[21] There is an outright prohibition under section 104(b)(1) on the requirement to return a registration card in order to activate the guarantee. FTC Regulation 701.7 (§16 C.F.R. 700.7) confirms that this is deemed to be an unreasonable requirement. It is, however, permissible to offer the consumer to register his guarantee with the guarantor as a means of proving when the product covered by the guarantee was purchased, provided that this is not made mandatory.

6.4 Substantive regulation: Guarantee content

Under s.103 MMWA, only two types of guarantee can be offered to consumers, "full" and "limited" guarantees, and all guarantees must be designated as either. The guarantee document must therefore either be headed "Full (statement of duration) guarantee" or "Limited Guarantee". A guarantee will be a "full" guarantee if it meets all of the conditions laid down in s.104 MMWA.[22] If it fails to comply with any of the requirements listed there, it can only be called a "limited" guarantee. Both types of guarantee have to comply with the disclosure requirements discussed below.

These designations are intended to standardise the terminology used for guarantees to make this area more transparent and meaningful to consumers (Smith, 1977, p.397). Guarantors who decide to offer the minimum standard of protection are entitled to use the "full" label, which may convey to consumers that they are better protected in case something goes wrong with the product they have bought (Bourgoignie, 1979, p.269). If a guarantee is merely a "limited" guarantee, a consumer will not only be alerted to the restrictive coverage of the guarantee itself, but he may also infer that the guarantor's reluctance to offer the higher level of protection demanded by a "full" guarantee suggests that the guarantor lacks confidence in the performance of the product (Denicola, 1976, p.283). The influence of signalling theory is apparent. A guarantee which is less generous than another guarantee implies that the product covered by the former guarantee is of lower quality than that covered by the latter.

These designations are not mutually exclusive. It is possible to offer both a full *and* a limited guarantee on the same product (s.105 MMWA). This provision envisages that full guarantees may be given on crucial components of a complex product, whereas a limited guarantee is given for ancillary parts. For example, there may be a full guarantee for the tube inside a television, but only a limited guarantee for the television case. It is also possible for these guarantees to be consecutive, provided that the limited guarantee that follows the full guarantee does not seek to limit the duration of the implied terms in any way - once a full guarantee is given, there cannot be any limitation on the implied terms (cf. Kutner, 1977, p.748).[23]

6.4.1 Full guarantees

S.104 MMWA sets down the "Federal minimum standards" for full guarantees. The following requirements have to be met:

Non-compliance to be remedied: If a product does not correspond to the guarantee, the guarantor must *at least* promise to remedy the defect, malfunction or failure to conform with the guarantee within a reasonable time and without charge.[24]

No restrictions on implied terms: The guarantor cannot limit the duration of the statutory rights. S.108(b) MMWA permits a limitation of the duration of the implied terms to the duration of the guarantee. If a full guarantee is offered, no such limitation is allowed. The difficulty of "limiting" the duration of the implied terms is discussed below at 6.5.

Consequential damages: The guarantor is not permitted to exclude or limit consequential damages that arise from a breach of the guarantee or from a breach of the implied terms *unless* this exclusion or limitation is highlighted on the front page of the guarantee document. This is an important provision, because it permits limitation or exclusion clauses, provided that these are clearly identified as such in the guarantee document.

Failure to remedy defect after reasonable number of attempts: If the guarantor has made a reasonable number of attempts to remedy a defect or malfunction in a product, but has not been successful in doing so, then the guarantor must give the consumer the option of either a refund or a replacement of the product free of charge.

No conditions on coverage other than notification: S.104(b)(1) MMWA states that a full guarantee must not make coverage dependent upon the consumer being required to do anything other than to notify the guarantor of a defect and to make the product reasonably available to the guarantor. This may include returning a small electrical appliance to the retailer, for example. However, it would not cover the return of a piano to the factory at the cost of the consumer.[25]

A guarantor can specify all of the above requirements in his guarantee document and then use the designation "full guarantee". Alternatively, if the guarantor simply refers to his guarantee as a full guarantee, then it is presumed that the federal minimum standard set down in s.104 MMWA is met (s.104(e) MMWA).

6.5 Substantive regulation: Items to be disclosed

S.102(a) MMWA empowers the Federal Trade Commission to adopt a rule to specify the items that have to be disclosed fully in clear and intelligible language (§16 CFR 701.3). The disclosures that have to be made relate to two aspects of the guarantee: first, it must be made clear what the level of protection under the guarantee is; second, information has to be provided on how to obtain a remedy if the guarantee promise is not fulfilled.

Beneficiaries of the guarantee: It must be stated who is to benefit from the guarantee. As noted above, there is a presumption that anybody who owns the product during the guarantee period is an intended beneficiary. If there is a limitation to the original consumer purchaser, or some other limitation on who can benefit from the guarantee, this has to be stated expressly.[26]

Coverage of the guarantee: There has to be a clear statement of what is covered by the guarantee and, where relevant, any parts or components that are *not* covered.

Remedies to be provided: It must be stated clearly what the guarantor will do if the product covered by the guarantee is defective or fails to conform with the guarantee in some other way. It must be clearly ascertainable what the guarantor will provide or pay for in such a case. It may also be necessary to state expressly what the guarantor will not provide or pay for.

Date of commencement and duration: It has to be stated clearly in the guarantee document if the guarantee period begins to run from a date other than the date of purchase. There also has to be a clear statement of how long the guarantee will last.

Claims procedure: There has to be a step-by-step explanation of the procedure which the consumer should follow in order to get a remedy under the guarantee. Most importantly, the person or class of persons who have been authorised to perform under the guarantee must be given. This includes the name of the guarantor, as well as his postal address and the details of any other contact which consumers may use to obtain information about guarantee performance.

Dispute resolution mechanism: The MMWA encourages guarantors to put in place informal dispute resolution mechanisms that can be used in order to deal with any disputes that may arise in connection with the performance of the guarantee. There is a separate set of criteria that have to be met by such dispute resolution mechanisms for them to be effective under the Act. For present purposes, it suffices to note that these rules are so strict that there are only very few informal dispute resolution mechanisms in place today.

However, one important observation needs to be made. Recently, there have been concerns about the relationship between MMWA dispute resolution schemes, arbitration and the Federal Arbitration Act 1925 (FAA). The FAA was adopted to give effect to arbitration clauses agreed on by the parties to a contract. In effect, it is possible to exclude the jurisdiction of the courts and instead resolve all disputes through binding arbitration. An informal dispute resolution procedure under the MMWA is non-binding. Where one exists, a consumer needs to take his dispute through this procedure first before taking a claim to court. The question that has caused some debate is whether the MMWA excludes the operation of the FAA with the effect that arbitration clauses in a written guarantee are not binding on the consumer. Gunter (2001) argues that mandatory arbitration is prohibited under the MMWA because to allow the FAA to prevail would be contrary to congressional intent and the FTC's interpretation of the MMWA. Wiechens (2001), on the other hand, points out that nothing in the MMWA suggests that the FAA should not apply and that the FTC's interpretation should be disregarded. According to Wiechens, the MMWA only deals with informal dispute resolution mechanisms, which are different from arbitration, and the FTC cannot therefore adopt rules that exclude the FAA from the MMWA. An authoritative ruling by a higher court is required to resolve this problem. Lower courts have come to conflicting results (see Guerin, 2001; Gunter, 2001).

There are two aspects to this debate. The first issue is whether the MMWA excludes the FAA from its scope. The arguments presented by Wiechens (2001) are strong evidence that it does not. The second issue is whether it *ought* to do so. There are clear advantages to arbitration, such as the speed of the procedure; the lower cost compared to court action and its informality. However, arbitration is generally based on the idea that the parties have agreed to submit any disputes to arbitration. In the context of consumer transactions, including guarantees, the consumer will not have agreed to anything, but will have been presented with a standard form contract. This is therefore an issue which may have to be addressed by the US legislator.

Limitation of implied terms: In the case of "limited" guarantees, it is permissible to limit the duration of the implied terms (s.108(b) MMWA). This has to be stated clearly, and there also has to be a statement to inform consumers that this may not be permissible in some of the constituent states of the United States. It is interesting to examine this provision in a little more detail, because it suggests that there can be a very definite link between the degree of protection under statute and under the guarantee.

Some limited guarantees could, in effect, shorten the period of protection under statute. However, there is some uncertainty about the meaning of "duration of the implied terms".[27] As in English law, compliance with the implied terms is assessed at the time the contract is made. There is therefore no duration of the implied terms, because any subsequent instance of non-compliance has to be shown to have existed at the time the contract was made (cf. Bradgate, 2000, p.292). Reitz (1978, p.70) suggested that there was a "remote possibility" that "duration" could, in fact, mean that a defect would not have to be related back to the date of purchase. Thus, if a "one-year duration" were placed on an implied term, then it would not only have to comply with that term on the date of purchase, but for the entire year after purchase. Such an interpretation would be very unusual.

There are several more conceivable ways of interpreting this particular provision (Brickey, 1978). One view would be that the limitation period for bringing a claim for breach of the implied terms is reduced to the duration of the guarantee (Saxe and Blejwas, 1973, p.21; Smith, 1977, p.409).[28] This seems unlikely. On this analysis, a breach of the guarantee itself would give rise to an action for breach of contract, which would be subject to the full limitation period, whereas a breach of the implied term would be limited to the duration of the guarantee.

An alternative approach is suggested by the idea of "prospective breach" (Brickey, 1978). In the case of a latent defect, it is arguable that the limitation period should not begin to run until the defect has been discovered or ought reasonably to have been discovered, rather than from the time of sale. The duration of the guarantee would be the same as the period within which the defect should be discovered. However, compliance with express terms in the contract of sale regarding product quality would still be assessed at the time of sale. This view would lead to different starting points for the limitation period.

Brickey (1978) suggests that the duration of the implied term can be explained under the "required manifestation" approach. The UCC provides that there is to be a reasonable time within which a defect has to be discovered. The parties can agree a time within which a defect has to be discovered, provided that such a time is not manifestly unreasonable. Thus, limiting the duration of the implied terms to the duration of the guarantee would therefore mean that the reasonable time within which the defect has to be discovered is during the guarantee period. The limitation period for bringing an action for breach of the implied terms would therefore still begin to run from the time of sale.[29]

Whatever its exact meaning, this provision does reflect the influence of signalling theory. The decision by a guarantor to offer a limited guarantee does not oblige him to limit the duration of the implied terms. If he chooses to do so, a consumer may interpret this as a signal that the product may not be of quite as high a standard of quality as a similar product that is covered by a guarantee that does not restrict the duration of the implied terms. However, as it continues to be "difficult to predict what will be the result of so foolish a provision" (Reitz, 1978, p.70), the real impact of this provision may never be explored fully.

Consequential losses: If consequential losses are excluded in the guarantee, this also has to be stated expressly. Again, there has to be statement to inform consumers that some states may not allow this.

Legal rights statement: Finally, there is a requirement that a specific statement about the legal nature of the guarantee is included. The following statement is specified by the FTC: "This warranty gives you specific legal rights, and you may also have other rights which vary from State to State".

It has been remarked that these disclosure requirements do not go far enough to enable consumers to evaluate if the guarantee truly provides useful coverage. Brickey (1978) comments that:

> In the absence of information regarding the anticipated level of product performance and cost of repair, consumers are unable to determine whether increased [guarantee] coverage is likely to provide benefits commensurate with the cost of the coverage.

Thus, in order to evaluate the usefulness of a guarantee as a signal of product quality, a consumer has to know more about other factors. These include the cost of repair, the likely standard of product performance and the potential expense of relying on the guarantee. Some of this information may be available from other sources, such as *Consumer Reports* or *Which?*, but this would inevitably require a greater effort by the consumer to collect this information and then to process it correctly to make a well-informed purchasing decision. These limitations were already noted when the theoretical underpinnings of signalling theory were examined. It was seen that the effectiveness of a signal depends on a bonding component and on bond credibility. Brickey identified further factors which may affect the signalling value of guarantees.

It seems that the MMWA disclosure requirements would be of very little assistance before purchase, because a consumer would not be able to utilise the information that has been disclosed in the manner envisaged by the MMWA, i.e., to ascertain which products are likely to be of a better standard of quality. Instead, it seems that the disclosure requirements will be of more use after the consumer has bought the product and has encountered a quality defect. In that case, clear instructions on how to obtain a remedy are likely to prove useful (Brickey, 1978, p.88).[30]

6.6 Negative regulation: Terms which are not permitted

Finally, the MMWA and the FTC Regulations have specified a number of terms which are not permitted in a guarantee.

Exclusion of jurisdiction of the courts: FTC Regulation 700.8 (§16 C.F.R. 700.8) prohibits terms in a guarantee that would make the guarantor's decision on any complaints under the guarantee final. S.110(d) MMWA expressly grants jurisdiction over guarantee disputes to federal and state courts.

Tie-in for guarantee service: Under s.102(c) MMWA, it is not permitted to require the consumer to use a specific item or service in order to preserve the guarantee. Thus, it is not allowed to state that the guarantee will become void if the product is serviced by somebody other than a service provider authorised by the guarantor. However, such a restriction is acceptable where there is no charge to the consumer for the service in question.[31]

Limited guarantees: No restriction on who can install spare parts: Furthermore, in the case of limited guarantees that do not cover labour costs, s.102(c) MMWA prohibits a condition that requires the consumer to use a service provider authorised by the guarantor to install replacement parts. In such a case, the guarantor has to make the relevant parts available in such a way that the consumer is able to chose who will perform the work that is required to remedy the defect. This prohibition is extended to cover terms that require the use of authorised repair services and authorised replacement parts for service and maintenance that is not provided under the guarantee (§16 C.F.R. 700.10(c)). However, it is permissible for a guarantor to refuse to honour the guarantee if a defect that occurs subsequent to such a service is caused by a non-authorised part or if the defect can be linked to the performance of the non-authorised service.

6.7 Evaluation

This section will examine the impact of the MMWA. It draws on a number of studies that have been carried out over the last 25 years to examine the effect of the Act.

6.7.1 There has been a limited impact on competition

The introduction of the terms "full" and "limited" had the objective of promoting competition in guarantees. The intention was that guarantors would offer full rather than limited guarantees. However, it has been seen that the requirements to be met by full guarantees are quite strict, and it was suggested soon after the passing of the MMWA that there would more limited than full guarantees (Saxe and Blejwas, 1976, p.14). This is confirmed by a 1992 study, in which it was found that there were more than twice as many limited than full guarantees provided by appliance manufacturers in the U.S. (Moore and Shuptrine, 1993, p.30). One suggestion for this is that the criteria for full guarantees may be difficult to interpret by manufacturers, and that therefore more limited guarantees are used. These do not have to meet the minimum federal standards set down in the Act. (*ibid.*, p.33). It may be that the Act simply requires too much for a guarantee to be a "full" guarantee. Thus, a guarantor who may, for example, not want to take responsibility for the labour charges for replacing a defective part, would not be able to offer a "full" guarantee (Eddy, 1977, p.867).

However, although the ratio of full to limited guarantees does not meet the intentions of the Act, Wisdom reported that there had been an increase in the proportion of full guarantees after the MMWA compared to immediately before the Act came into force (Wisdom, 1979, p.1138). He could not find evidence that the shift by some manufacturers within a particular product category caused other manufacturers within the same category to follow suit - there was, therefore, no obvious increase in competition. He concluded that "it does not appear that the Act has caused a dramatic trend towards increased [guarantee] protection." (*ibid.*, p.1140). This also seems to support Eddy's suggestion that competition in guarantees is not a central aspect of a manufacturer's marketing strategy (Eddy, 1979, p.859).

6.7.2 More information is disclosed, but guarantees are not significantly easier to understand

An important objective pursued by the Act was to make guarantee documents easier to understand by consumers in order to enable them to make better informed purchasing decisions. Wisdom's study revealed that guarantee documents had not improved in readability, nor in clarity. Furthermore, research in the early 1990s, almost two decades after the MMWA had come into force, provides evidence that the Act has failed in this objective (Moore and Shuptrine, 1993). This study examined 212 guarantee documents for different categories of consumer products.[32] It suggested that about 13 years of education are required to be able to read and understand the guarantee documents. This is of concern to the authors, because:

> given the fact that the median number of school years completed by persons 25 years or older is 12.7 years, it is evident many people would have difficulty reading and understanding the [guarantees] examined (Moore and Shuptrine, 1993, p.28).

If so, then the Act has not succeeded in making guarantees more accessible to consumers - there would still be a considerable number of consumers who are unable to understand some or all aspects of a guarantee. The conclusions of this study are damning:

> Since 1975 when Congress passed the MMWA, readability levels of [guarantees] have not significantly changed. Clearly, the MMWA has not accomplished its goal of making [guarantees] easy to read and understand (Moore and Shuptrine, 1993, p.33).

However, the disclosure provisions seem to have been a reasonable success. In his 1979 study, Michael Wisdom found that there was some improvement to the description of guarantee coverage, major improvement to the description of the obligation of the guarantor and some improvement in the disclosure of the costs to be borne by the guarantor and the consumer respectively (Wisdom, 1979, p.1131). Those guarantees which were designated as "full" guarantees met the minimum standards (*ibid.*, p.1134). Disclosure of the procedural information required under the Act (name of guarantor and claims procedure) had also improved (*ibid.*, p.1136).

These studies suggest that the Act has been successful in increasing the amount of information that is disclosed to consumers in the guarantee document. However, this has not become any more intelligible, and the success of increased disclosure is all but extinguished by the failure to improve readability. Wisdom takes the view that the success of increased disclosure outweighs the lack of progress as far as readability is concerned (1979, p.1145).

However, it seems that disclosure provisions will only be of limited use if consumers find it difficult to understand fully the information disclosed to them. Therefore, it appears that it may be concluded that the Act has only had a rather limited impact on improving the position of consumers.

It is appropriate to recall Eddy's criticism, discussed above,[33] that greater transparency would not automatically lead to an increase in competition (1977, p.859). As manufacturers do not regard competition on guarantees as central to their marketing strategy, disclosure itself will not lead to greater competition, nor will it induce improvements in product quality (see also Rothschild, 1977, p.365). Furthermore, consumers find it quite difficult to utilise the information which they receive as a result of the disclosure provisions:

> Clarity can improve the information that a consumer receives, but it has no effect at all on the information-handling capacity of the recipient ... a related problem is that to be used intelligently, the information that is provided would have to be coupled with information that is not required (Eddy, 1977, p.860)

The disclosure rules are therefore only useful to the extent that they clarify the entitlements of the beneficiaries under the guarantee. However, in order to be fully effective, the consumer also needs to obtain information about other matters, such as the reputation of the guarantor. This would be consistent with the research findings on signalling theory and guarantees.[34]

Adler (1994) reports that studies that assessed the impact of the FTC rules under the MMWA found that consumers rarely look at or know about guarantees before purchasing products (at p.457). Less than one-third of consumers interviewed for a study carried out in 1979 had read a guarantee before purchase, despite the fact that more than three-quarters of them had been given the opportunity to do so (p.459). In a second study, carried out in 1984, the number of consumers interviewed for this study who read the guarantee before purchase had fallen below 10% (p.460). However, around four in ten consumers in this study read the guarantee at some point after purchase (p.461). This suggests that guarantees remain a minor factor in the pre-purchase context, although guarantees may assume much greater significance in the post-purchase context.

6.8 Conclusions

The MMWA is the primary example of a legal framework that is based on signalling theory. It has been more than a quarter of a century since its adoption, and it is now fairly obvious that it has only been a very limited success. In particular, the requirements for "full" guarantees imposed most of the burden of providing a guarantee on the manufacturer. Had there been a better distribution of obligations between consumer and guarantor (e.g., by sharing between guarantor and consumer the costs for providing a remedy under the guarantee), the MMWA may have stood a better chance of success.

The experience under the MMWA also demonstrates that competition on the basis of guarantees remains limited, despite the very strong encouragement that comes from the Act. Although there are now signs that some manufacturers in particular sectors (such as Japanese car manufacturers) seek to compete more actively on their guarantees, it may be that consumers will focus on aspects other than guarantees when deciding on a purchase.

Notes

1 See chapter 2, section 2.3.1.

2 15 U.S.C. 2301.

3 The Act uses the term "warranty" rather than "guarantee" or "consumer guarantee". In order to maintain coherence, the word "guarantee" has been substituted wherever the Act or any other source referred to uses the word "warranty".

4 See 2.3.1. Exploitation Theory suggests that Guarantees are used to limit or exclude other rights that consumers may have against the guarantor, such as rights under Sale of Goods Legislation, or under Product Liability laws.

5 For a discussion of these problems in a UK context, see 2.3.1.

6 The following is a very brief outline. It is not necessary to consider the Uniform Commercial Code in any detail for present purposes. Braucher (1986) offers a useful discussion of the Code. The Code is currently under review.

7 Louisiana has not adopted the Code.

8 The Magnuson-Moss Act itself is a Federal Act and applies in all the constituent states without further need for adoption. The relationship between the MMWA and the quality warranties implied under state law (i.e., the UCC and specific consumer protection legislation) has given rise to various conceptual difficulties. It is not necessary to consider these here.

9 S.2-318 contains three alternatives: under (a), the right of action extends to family members and house guests; under (b) and (c) to any person who may reasonably be expected to use the goods. (c) is more favourable in relation to the exclusion or limitation of this provision.

10 See 6.5.1, below.

11 It will be seen below that these hopes were overly optimistic. See 6.8 below.

12 These will not be considered in this book, because they are not relevant for present purposes.

13 See chapter 3 at 3.1.1.

14 Indeed, not providing a guarantee may send a signal to the effect that the manufacturer has very little confidence in his products, although the manufacturer does not have to state expressly that no guarantee is provided. This may be contrasted with proposals put forward in the UK by the NCC (1989a; b), which would have introduced such a requirement. See chapter 8.

15 Extended warranties would be classed as "service contracts" under the Act and the FTC rules. S.106 MMWA empowers the FTC to adopt rules for service contracts. These are beyond the scope of the present analysis and will not be considered here.

16 For a discussion of this requirement, see Holdych and Mann (1996), esp. pp.827-828.

17 This contrasts with the position under the Guarantees Directive: see 7.1.

18 A contrary view would suggest that the signal operates to persuade the initial consumer that the product is of a particular level of quality, and that the guarantee is therefore only directed at that consumer and should not be available to subsequent owners. However, although the signal may be directed at the initial consumer, it still relates to the quality of the product, and therefore the guarantee should be available to any owner during the guarantee period. See 5.4.

19 The Guarantees Directive also requires that guarantees must be available before purchase, but does not lay down detailed rules for this purpose. See 7.3.2. It may be that individual Member States will produce more detailed rules, or encourage the development of relevant rules as part of Codes of Practice.

20 A further copy of the guarantee must also be included within the packaging if either or both of the final two options are chosen.

21 See 6.5.1 below.

22 It must also be noted that under s.102(d) MMWA, the FTC is given the power to adopt rules that create substantive guarantee provisions that may be incorporated into actual guarantees by reference. Thus, this provision enables the FTC to create a standardised guarantee. This may be useful for guarantors who may not want to incur the expense of drafting detailed guarantee documents. However, this provision also undermines the disclosure rules in the Act (Saxe and Blejwas, 1976, p.13), because consumers would not be able to establish what exactly the guarantee offered before making a purchase. It is not clear if the pre-sale availability rules would require the guarantor or seller to make available the standard FTC guarantee provisions to allow a consumer to examine these prior to completing the purchase.

23 And see point 7 under heading 6.6 for further discussion of this point.

24 According to s.104(d) MMWA, "without charge" means that the guarantor cannot charge the consumer for any costs that may have been incurred in connection with the provision of a remedy under the guarantee. It does not include incidental expenses (such as the bus fare for taking a product back to the shop where it was purchased), unless such expenses are the result of an unreasonable delay in providing a remedy, or because the guarantor has imposed an unreasonable duty on the consumer as a condition to obtaining a remedy.

If it is required to install the product in question, then the guarantee also has to provide for installation free of charge after the remedy has been provided. This is so even though the consumer may have paid a sum in addition to the product price for the original installation (§16 C.F.R. 700.9).

25 It seems that such a requirement was actually contained in a guarantee document. See Brickey (1978), p.92 and note 97.

26 Although s.104(b)(4) does not permit the limitation of a full guarantee to the first purchaser only, in rule 700.6, the FTC argues that a full guarantee could be limited to the first purchaser if the duration of the guarantee is specified with reference to ownership by the first purchaser ("full guarantee as longs as you own your car"). Brickey (1978, p.91) notes that this interpretation appears to conflict with the Act and the definition of "consumer", in particular. A "consumer" includes a person to whom a product is transferred during the duration of an implied [term] or written [guarantee]" (s.101(e)MMWA), which implies that guarantees must be transferable. The FTC position seems peculiar.

27 The legislative history does not offer any guidance on how to interpret this provision (Brickey, 1978).

28 Saxe and Blejwas (1976) argued that the "implied warranties do not explicitly extend to future performance so that they are breached, if at all, at the time tender of delivery is made. Therefore, it is only logical to conclude that implied warranties have no continued existence, i.e., no duration. By using the phrase 'duration of implied warranty', the writers of the Act must be referring to the statute of limitations" (p.21).

29 This discussion may also offer useful guidance on the scope of Article 5 of the Guarantees Directive, which specifies that a seller is liable for two years after purchase. One view is that this is a limitation period, but the better view seems to be that this is more akin to the idea of "prospective breach", i.e., it imposes liability on a seller for latent defects provided that these become apparent within two years of delivery.

30 This will be examined in more detail in the following chapter.

31 See Eisenach, Higgins and Shughart (1984) for an argument in favour of tie-ins. This suggests that tie-ins could be an efficient means of counteracting the problems of adverse selection and moral hazard.

32 These were: cars, bicycles, tin openers, coffee makers, food processors, hair dryers, lawnmowers, microwave ovens, radios and televisions.

33 See 6.2.2 above.

34 See chapter 3.

Chapter 7

E.C. Law and Consumer Guarantees

7.0 Introduction

In 1993, the European Commission published a Green Paper on Consumer Guarantees (Commission, 1993). This paper set out the options for regulating both "legal" guarantees (now the "conformity with the contract" requirement) and "commercial" guarantees, as well as after-sales services. Three years later, a draft Directive was introduced (COM(95) 520 final) which featured some of the ideas mooted in the Green Paper, but the general consensus at the time was that there had been a considerable watering-down from the original proposal. The draft Directive had a bumpy ride through the legislative process, and the conciliation procedure had to be invoked before Directive 99/44/EC[1] was finally adopted in May 1999 (see Twigg-Flesner, 1999b). This Directive deals with three broad areas: first, it sets down a mandatory requirement that consumer goods must be "in conformity with the contract of sale" (Article 2). Secondly, a set of remedies are made available if goods are not in conformity (Article 3). Finally, there is limited regulation of voluntarily provided guarantees (Article 6). This chapter is only concerned with the final aspect. An overview of the remaining provisions in the Directive is given in chapter 1.

7.1 Defining "guarantee"

Article 1(2)(e) defines a guarantee as:

> any undertaking by a seller or producer to the consumer, given without extra charge, to reimburse the price paid or to replace, repair or handle consumer goods in any way if they do not meet the specifications set out in the guarantee statement or in the relevant advertising.

A number of points can be made about this definition. First, it classifies guarantees as "undertakings", but does not specify more precisely whether such undertakings would be contractual in nature. This ambiguity leaves open the question whether related legislation such as the Unfair Contract Terms Directive (93/13/EEC) could be applied to control the use of unfair terms in guarantees.

Admittedly, the general assumption is that this can be done, but there is at least a lack of clarity in this regard.

It can further be noted that this definition emphasises that a "guarantee" is given free of charge. Thus, extended warranties, which are purchased separately by a consumer, are therefore clearly not within the scope of this definition. In view of the specific problems that have been identified in that context, this seems a sensible decision.[2] However, it is not clear if this definition would encompass "satisfaction guarantees". According to Article 1(2)(e), the guarantee should set out specifications to be met by consumer goods and make available a remedy if this is not the case. In most cases, these specifications will be a statement that the goods are "free from defects in workmanship and material".[3] Satisfaction guarantees do not usually set down any specifications to be met by the corresponding goods, but are rather aimed at consumers' subjective attitudes towards them. This would suggest that satisfaction guarantees fall outside this definition. Yet, the definition covers undertakings "to reimburse the price paid". Most guarantees only offer repair or replacement, rather than refunds. This indicates that there may have been an intention to cover "money-back" guarantees after all. The exact position remains unclear, however.

Moreover, it seems that guarantees need not be limited to a written document, but may also be based on statements made in advertising. The definition itself is phrased somewhat awkwardly, and it is not entirely obvious what "relevant advertising" refers to. The reference to "relevant advertising" was added by the European Parliament (1998) after its first reading (see amendment 14). Read literally, the definition would only cover a guarantee whereby the guarantor undertook to do something if the product did not perform as indicated in *both* the guarantee document itself *and* in any product advertising. In this case, the undertaking given by the guarantor would be linked to the entirety of statements made about the product in both the guarantee document and in advertising. Guarantees which were limited to whatever was said in the guarantee document itself would not, on this reading, be "guarantees" for the purposes of the Directive. This would have the strange consequence of excluding most guarantees from the scope of the Directive. It is clear that such a literal reading of the definition cannot be correct. Instead, it is submitted that, in addition to guarantees purely based on a guarantee document, the definition covers "guarantees" which are only mentioned in advertising, as well as guarantees which are partly based on advertising and partly on a document enclosed with the product.

This reading would be in line with Article 6(1). This states that:

> A guarantee shall be legally binding on the offerer under the conditions laid down in the guarantee statement and the associated advertising.

"Advertising" in this Article can mean two things. First, it undoubtedly covers instances where the guarantee is mentioned in advertising. Should there be a discrepancy between what was said in advertising and what is stated in the guarantee document, it seems that the statements made in advertising will also bind the guarantor. Second, in some cases, there may be a reference to a guarantee in advertising, but then there may not be any information about the guarantee with the actual product. It seems that in this type of situation, Article 6(1) would nevertheless hold the guarantor to the 'guarantee' given in advertising. Therefore, the reference to 'advertising' in the definition of guarantee in Article 1(2)(e) suggests that a guarantee within the meaning of the Directive can be based entirely on advertising.[4] A good example where this may be of significance are the satisfaction guarantees described earlier (although these may not be covered by the Directive at all). In most cases, such guarantees are mentioned in advertising, but usually no further details are provided with the product itself. The only point of reference for a consumer would therefore be the product advertising itself. Under the Directive, such a guarantee would therefore be legally binding, provided that the statement made in the advertisement constitutes an undertaking that the product will perform in a certain manner and that the guarantor will provide a remedy if it does not do so.

The relevance of Directive 84/450/EEC on misleading advertising should be noted. The application of the Directive to guarantees was confirmed in C-373/90 *Criminal Proceedings against X* (the "Bergerac" case). Cars had been advertised for sale as "cheaper" and covered by a one year manufacturer's guarantee. On the facts, no misleading statement about the guarantee had been given, and the ECJ observed at paragraph 17 that a statement about guarantees cannot be regarded as misleading if it is true. By implication, a statement which is not true could therefore be regarded as misleading advertising. The Directive therefore applies to misleading statements about guarantees. If there are misleading statements about guarantees in advertising, it may therefore be possible to ask a court for an order to stop the continued use of the particular statement.

7.2 The legal enforceability of guarantees

Guarantees are given voluntarily and are usually given by manufacturers. They are therefore not usually part of the contract of sale between seller and consumer. It is, of course, possible to suggest that a seller adopts a manufacturer's guarantee and thereby makes it part of the contract of sale with the consumer (see the English decision in *Alexander v Comet Group* (1995)). However, it will often be difficult to establish that a manufacturer's guarantee is, in fact, enforceable. The Commission therefore proposed to introduce a provision that would make guarantees legally enforceable. This was enacted as Article 6(1) of the Directive. During the legislative process, there was some discussion about the need to make guarantees legally enforceable.

7.2.1 Should guarantees be legally enforceable?

Generally speaking, the question of legal enforceability has been more of interest to academics than something that has given rise to large-scale practical difficulties (Lawson, 1992). Thus, a survey conducted by the Office of Fair Trading in

England in 1993 revealed that the uncertainty over the legal enforceability of consumer guarantees, particularly those provided by manufacturers, did not give rise to any practical problems (DGFT, 1996). This is explained by Collins thus:

> The consumer guarantee issue by a manufacturer in the box containing its product may also not be legally binding on the manufacturer unless the consumer can demonstrate that the existence of the guarantee was a reason for purchasing the particular product from a retailer. Nevertheless, manufacturers will invariably comply with their guarantee, albeit strictly construed against the consumer, for failure to do so will result in damage to their business reputation (p.109).

Reputation and adverse publicity are therefore ensuring *de facto* enforceability of manufacturers' guarantees. This may even reflect an assumption among guarantors and consumers that guarantees are always legally binding.[5] It is therefore a little surprising that there has been some resistance to the proposition that guarantees *should* be legally binding. Strong opposition to this view has come from an unlikely quarter: the Consumers' Association (CA). In response to the Commission's proposal to introduce a provision that would make guarantees legally enforceable, CA argued that consumers might not benefit from such a move (Holmes, 1998). The CA expressed concern that consumers would be confused by the existence of two legal schemes and that the balance would shift away from the existing statutory rights. However, the statutory rights do not affect the relationship between the manufacturer and the consumer - the Sale of Goods Act and the Directive put liability on the seller.[6] Guarantees may even offer an alternative mechanism for obtaining a refund when the right of rejection under SoGA is no longer available. The CA instead favoured the introduction of rules which would hold a guarantor responsible for any misrepresentations in guarantees and associated advertising (CA, 1996).

There is some mileage in the confusion argument. In effect, the statutory rights and the consumer guarantee are two alternative mechanisms of obtaining redress for the same problem - faulty goods. The introduction of a detailed legal regime for consumer guarantees could indeed be problematic, because of the likelihood that this may require subsequent interpretation by the courts. The lack of reported consumer cases could be problematic. Yet, this argument does not support the outright rejection of any legal intervention in this area. Rather, the potential confusion to consumers may have a bearing on the extent of legislative intervention and encourage "light touch" regulation.

CA also thought that making guarantees legally binding and introducing further rules on consumer guarantees could lead to the offering of fewer guarantees. Guarantees were offered as part of an overall marketing strategy for a particular product or brand. The willingness to offer guarantees was linked to the relative lack of legislation in this field - and this "finely balanced world" could be upset by provisions such as those on the legally binding nature of guarantees and result in fewer guarantees being offered. This argument does not convince. If guarantees were made legally binding and enforceable, there should be no immediate impact on guarantors. No manufacturer or retailer would be obliged to offer a guarantee.

Those who do offer them tend to honour their guarantees, and it does not follow that making guarantees legally enforceable would cause manufacturers to offer fewer guarantees. If it did, the seriousness of a manufacturer's offer of a guarantee would have to be questioned - why offer a guarantee which might not be legally binding, but not offer a guarantee which would be legally binding? Moreover, it is submitted that ensuring that guarantors are held to their promises is a useful tool for restricting the provision of guarantees in the sense that only those guarantors who intend to stand by their promises will offer one. This could help to filter out those guarantees which would not be honoured at all.

7.2.2 Article 6(1): Guarantees to be legally binding

In a sense, this debate has now been overtaken by events. The Consumer Guarantees Directive will require legislative intervention to make such guarantees binding. Article 6(1) reads as follows:

> A guarantee shall be legally binding on the offerer under the conditions laid down in the guarantee statement and the associated advertising .

There are number points to be made in relation to this provision. First, guarantees will only be legally binding on the "offerer", i.e., the guarantor. A consumer would therefore not be able to enforce a guarantee against a party other than the guarantor, such as a retailer who will be responsible for dealing with guarantee claims.

Secondly, the guarantee can encompass both a document enclosed with a product and additional statements made in advertising. This may be significant if the document itself fails to include a "guarantee promise" made in the relevant product advertising. According to Article 6(1), any additional statement made in advertising will be treated as part of the guarantee and therefore be legally binding on the guarantor. The Directive does not deal with potentially conflicting statements in the guarantee document and in advertising. Malinvaud (2002, para 15) suggests that the principle in Article 2(4)[7] should apply in this context. This would, in effect, mean that the guarantee document would prevail. However, there is nothing in the Directive to support this suggestion, and it is submitted that the better approach to this problem is to resolve any conflict in favour of the consumer and to allow the more favourable provision to prevail.[8] In any event, there would be a significant evidential burden on the consumer to demonstrate that additional or conflicting statements were made in advertising. As the resolution of such a conflict would require the assistance of a court of law, it is unlikely that there will be many instances where this issue will be central.

Thirdly, it must be noted that guarantees will only bind the guarantor "under the conditions laid down in the guarantee statement and the associated advertising". Guarantors, particularly manufacturers, frequently require that the retailer confirms the date of sale from which the guarantee period is to run by putting a stamp in a field on the guarantee document. If this is not done, the guarantee will not bind the guarantor. Retailers often omit to do this, and many consumers may lose the protection offered by a manufacturer's guarantee.

A second condition which is imposed frequently is that the guarantor may require the return of a completed "registration card" within a short period after purchase, and again, if this is not done, the guarantee will not be legally binding. Provided the consumer is made aware of this condition, e.g., by a prominent notice on the cover of the product user's guide, this seems to be unobjectionable. Yet, Howells and Weatherill (1995) argue that a failure to comply with such a condition should not deprive the consumer of the benefit of the guarantee:

> Returning the card can easily be viewed as involving too much trouble for small purchases or can easily be overlooked. The requirement to return the card, as compared to the obligation to provide proof of purchase, seems more closely related to obtaining marketing information than anything which is necessary for the functioning of the guarantee (p.159).

This criticism seems particularly pertinent in the case of those registration cards which ask for a lot of information clearly unrelated to the product; however, it seems less forceful if the registration card only requires the name and address of the consumer and the date of purchase.[9]

Thus, guarantees will become legally binding, but the consumer still needs to be aware of the conditions imposed by the guarantor and make sure that these are complied with. It seems that it is not necessary that a consumer had prior awareness of the guarantee and the provision of consideration for the guarantee by the consumer. Yet, Thomas Holdych (1998) suggests that the wording of Article 6(1) may not have ruled out this altogether. He concedes that the Directive does not mention anywhere that the consumer has to be aware of the existence of the guarantee before purchase for the guarantee to be legally binding. His view is predominantly based on the choice of the word "offerer" in Article 6(1):

> Inclusion of that term implies that the rules of offer and acceptance may apply, subjecting the acceptance of a guarantee to national rules requiring an offeree to know of an offer in order to accept it (Holdych, 1998, p.87).

If this were so, then there would be no point to Article 6(1) at all, because it would do no more than to restate a position found in many Member States. Holdych acknowledges this and concludes that:

> It is questionable, however, whether the EC intended that a buyer might be required to know of a … guarantee for it to be enforceable"(ibid.).

This must be the correct view. A simple explanation may be offered for the use of the word "offerer". It was emphasised earlier that guarantees are legally binding on the conditions stated in the guarantee document. As noted then, this may include "conditions precedent" that need to be complied with before the consumer is entitled to benefit under the guarantee. The word "offerer" may have been used in recognition of the fact that the guarantee is "offered" to the consumer if, in turn, he provides the information requested on the guarantee registration card, for example. It seems highly unlikely that the use of the word "offerer" was to imply that the ordinary rules of contract formation should continue to apply. If this were so, then Article 6(1) would serve not useful purpose. The difficulties of offer and acceptance, and the need to find consideration, are therefore to be rendered irrelevant as far as guarantees are concerned.

A final point to emphasise is that there is no obligation to offer a guarantee (see Malinvaud, 2002, paras 11-13). It is therefore entirely up to manufacturers and retailers whether they wish to offer a guarantee. However, if a decision is made to provide a guarantee, it will bind the guarantor and it will have to comply with the other requirements laid down in Article 6.

7.2.3 The extent of the obligation of distribution network members to honour guarantees

As noted, Article 6(1) requires only the guarantor to honour a guarantee. No other party will be legally bound by a guarantee. This may be unfortunate for consumers who buy goods in another Member State who may need to rely on a guarantee after they have returned to their home state. A well-established principle in the field of EC Competition Law is that guarantees must be available throughout the EC and that members of a distribution system may be required to deal with claims under guarantees on goods bought in another Member State. This section will explore these rules in more depth.

In the context of the Single Market, there is a danger that guarantees may be used to prevent market integration. A consumer who has bought goods in a Member State other than his country of residence may subsequently discover that the terms of the guarantee which he got when he bought the product include a territorial limitation preventing him from invoking the guarantee in his home Member State. As a consequence, consumers may be deterred from going abroad to purchase new goods if they will not be able to rely on a guarantee in their home Member State. This problem was identified by the European Commission in the mid-1970s, and it has adopted a number of decisions under Article 81 to prevent manufacturers from using their guarantees to impede market integration.

The relevant parts of Article 81(1) provide that:

> The following shall be prohibited as incompatible with the common market: all agreements between undertakings, decisions by associations of undertakings and concerted practices which may affect trade between Member States and which have as their object or effect the prevention, restriction or distortion of competition within the common market, and in particular those which: ... (b) limit or control ... markets.

In *Constructa* (1974), involving a distribution system for electrical appliances, the Commission noted that geographical restrictions on a guarantee infringed Article 81(1). This was confirmed in a policy statement which explained that the availability of guarantees were an important consideration for a consumer when deciding to buy a product, and that the territorial restrictions on the availability of a guarantee could be harmful to consumers' interests. Manufacturers' guarantees should therefore be valid throughout the E.C. (Competition Report EC 1977, point 17). Consumers should not be dissuaded from buying products in a Member State other than the one where the product will be used (*Zanussi* (1978)).

The obligation to ensure that E.C. wide availability of a guarantee applies not only to the manufacturer, but can in some situations also extend to the final sellers in a distribution network. A decision by a number of retailers to refuse to honour a guarantee on products imported from another Member State would be a breach of Article 81 (*Ford* (1983)).[10] However, a unilateral refusal by a single retailer not to honour a guarantee on products bought in another Member State is unlikely to be caught by Article 81 because there would be no agreement or concerted practice.[11]

The Commission recognised that the different technical and safety standards in the various member states might require different guarantee policies. A minimum requirement, therefore, is that the guarantee should apply on the terms of the country where the product is used. If a product did not meet the safety standards of the country where the consumer resides, the guarantee would be honoured if the consumer arranged and paid for adaptation (*Moulinex* and *Bauknecht* (1980)). Similarly, if spare parts for a product are not available in the country where the product is used (e.g., because different parts are required to meet safety standards), a consumer may have to return the appliance to the country of purchase at his own cost (*Sony* (1987)) in order to benefit under the guarantee.

The Commission's approach thus aims to strike a balance between market integration and minimising the burden on manufacturers and sellers. Guarantee services may be provided under the conditions prescribed for a particular Member State, provided that all products will be serviced under the guarantee. However, there would be too much of a burden if a guarantee service provider had to be familiar with the safety requirements and product assembly used for all Member States, if technical standards require such differences, and a consumer may have to bear a certain burden if he chooses to exercise his rights in the internal market.

The European Court of Justice (ECJ) has largely confirmed the Commission's approach to guarantees under Article 81. In C-86/82 *Hasselblad v Commission* (1984), a manufacturer of cameras gave a twelve-month guarantee. The sole distributors in the distribution network were to implement the guarantee. The UK distributor introduced a separate 24-month guarantee for cameras sold through the official UK distribution network. This was done with the objective of hindering parallel imports from other EC Member States. The Commission's objections against this practice were rejected as unfounded by the ECJ (at paras 33-35 of the judgment[12]) - the *manufacturers'* guarantee was not affected by this practice. This was put concisely by Advocate General Sir Gordon Slynn thus:

> Although a sole distributor may lawfully combat parallel imports by offering a better or wider range of after-sales services, it may not take steps to *deprive parallel imports of benefits to which they are entitled under a manufacturer's guarantee* (p.930).

In C-31/85 *ETA Fabriques v DK Investment* (1986) ("the *ETA* case"), a manufacturer of watches operated an exclusive distribution system. The system did not attempt to prohibit the parallel import of watches, but the 12-month manufacturer's guarantee was only available if the watches sold in a particular territory had been sold by the distributor based in that territory. It was not available on watches sold by way of parallel imports. The court held that this infringed Article 81(1). ETA had argued that the guarantee was contractual and assigned as part of the distribution agreement. Therefore there was no "unbroken chain of assignments of the contractual guarantee" (para [6]) outside the distribution system. The ECJ rejected this. It therefore seems that Article 81(1) treats the provision of guarantees as more than a purely contractual matter, and that competition law is not concerned about the absence of privity between ETA and consumers who bought the watches from parallel importers (Goyder, 1996).

Restrictions on the availability of manufacturers' guarantees were considered by the ECJ in the context of a selective distribution system in C-376/92 *Metro SB-Großmärkte GmbH & Co.KG v Cartier SA* (1994) ("*Metro-Cartier*"). Although Cartier operated a selective distribution system in the EC, Metro was able to obtain Cartier products lawfully in Switzerland[13] and market them lawfully in the EC, but outside Cartier's selective distribution system. Cartier refused to honour guarantees on watches sold by Metro.

A-G Tesauro argued that as long as sales by parties not part of a selective distribution system were lawful, the guarantee should be available. He based part of his reasoning on consumer protection:

> That view, it seems to me, is also supported by considerations relating to *consumer protection*, which should not be unconnected with the interpretation of Article [81] of the Treaty. To permit a restriction on the guarantee means that consumers who have *lawfully* acquired *original* products from independent dealers are deprived, on that ground alone, of the producer's normal guarantee for manufacturing defects. This constitutes a wholly unjustified form of *discrimination*, at least in so far as the defects are attributable to the producer and not to the independent dealer who sold the product.

The Court did not share this interpretation. It took the view that a restriction on the availability of guarantees to products bought through a selective distribution system is lawful under Article 81:

> [32] ... a contractual obligation to restrict the guarantee to dealers within the network and to refuse to grant it in respect of goods sold by third parties leads to the same result and has the same effect as contractual terms which reserve the right to sell to members of the network ... the restriction of the guarantee is a means whereby the manufacturer can prevent persons outside the network from marketing products covered by the system.

The court thus concluded that:

> [33] Where contractual terms whereby the manufacturer undertakes to sell only through authorised dealers and whereby those dealers themselves undertake to resell only to other authorised dealers or to consumers are lawful, there are no grounds for applying stricter treatment to arrangements for restricting the guarantee by contract to products sold through authorised dealers. Under Article [81] of the Treaty, only the purpose of that restriction and its effect are relevant.

From a competition law perspective, this decision is undoubtedly correct (Goyder, 1996). The important aspect of *Metro-Cartier* is that it involves a selective distribution system, which any retailer who satisfies the qualitative criteria may join - and as selective distribution systems are only acceptable under EC law for a limited category of products (Goyder, 1996),[14] the guarantee should be limited to products obtained in the selective distribution system.[15]

It may be thought that these rules are incompatible with new policy adopted by the European Community to vertical agreements (see Regulation 2790/1999). It is submitted that there is no conflict, because the underlying problem in all these cases was the fact that guarantees were used to separate markets along national lines. Even the much more relaxed attitude of the E.C. towards vertical agreement finds its limits when it comes to market segregation - see Article 4 of the Regulation.

Competition law has primarily focused on ensuring that there are no territorial restrictions in a guarantee. If retailers are responsible for dealing with guarantee claims and refuse to do so, there could be a breach of Article 81(1), but only if retailers act in concert. Moreover, Article 81 imposes obligations on manufacturers and network members, who have to take these into account when drafting their guarantees (Fine, 1989), but it does not create any positive rights for consumers. Article 6(1) of the Directive does not take into account the possibility that a person other than the guarantor may be involved in dealing with guarantee claims. There is clearly a mismatch between competition law jurisprudence on the one hand, and the Directive on the other, and the opportunity to bring the two closer together has been missed.

7.2.4 Transferability

Article 6(1) leaves open the question of whether a guarantee should be freely transferable to subsequent owners of the corresponding goods. It does not expressly state that guarantees are transferable, nor is this ruled out. It is therefore up to the Member States to decide whether guarantees should be transferable. In contrast, in the *ETA* case, the ECJ appeared to assume that all such guarantees should be transferable. At paragraph 8 of its judgment, the Court endorsed the Commission's view that:

> the guarantee must ... be granted to every user holding a guarantee certificate, irrespective of which retailer supplied the product.

This clearly envisages that a consumer may transfer a guarantee with the corresponding goods and thereby pass on the benefit of such a guarantee to subsequent owners. There seems to be a further lack of co-ordination between the Directive and existing ECJ jurisprudence here. However, Member States can decide to make guarantees transferable. Article 6(1) only requires that guarantees should be legally binding. The means by which this is achieved in the domestic legal orders may permit transferability. It would have been preferable for this to have been made clear in the Directive itself.

7.3 Procedural requirements

The Guarantees Directive contains two procedural requirements: guarantees have to be provided in plain intelligible language and guarantees must be made available in durable form on request by the consumer.

7.3.1 Guarantees to be provided in plain intelligible language

Article 6(2) requires that the contents of a guarantee should be set out in plain intelligible language. This may be compared with Article 5 of the Unfair Contract Terms Directive (UCTD). This requires that all contract terms must be written in plain and intelligible language. In addition, the UCTD includes a provision according to which ambiguous contract terms are to be given an interpretation which is most favourable to a consumer. Article 6(2) of the Guarantees Directive does not contain this additional provision, but there is no reason why the rule of interpretation in Article 5 of the UCTD should not be followed in the specific context of guarantees (see also Malinvaud, 2002, para 29).[16]

Member States are given the option in Article 6(4) to require that guarantees are drafted in one or more of the official languages of the European Community. This might be particularly relevant for Member States whose language is not widely used, unlike French, German or English, for example. It will also be important in those Member States where use of the national language is to be given preference, such as France. Moreover, Malinvaud (2002, para 22) notes that many consumers only know their native language and that it would therefore be desirable to ensure that a guarantee is provided in the language of the country where the guarantee is given.

7.3.2 Guarantee to be available in durable form

Article 6(3) states that:

> On request by the consumer, the guarantee shall be made available in writing or feature in another durable medium available and accessible to him.

A consumer may request to see the guarantee in some kind of durable medium. Unfortunately, the Directive does not define "durable medium". Such a medium may be a paper-based guarantee document, or some other medium which satisfies the requirement of "durability", such as a CD-ROM or a floppy disk. It is not clear if it is sufficient to place the text of the guarantee on a website (but see Malinvaud, 2002, para 18). It may be stretching the meaning of "durable" too far if it were to include websites. It may be possible to look to other Directives which use the same concept for guidance. Thus, Article 2(f) of Directive 2002/65/EC concerning the distance marketing of consumer financial services[17] defines "durable medium" as follows:

> "Durable medium" means any instrument which enables the consumer to store information addressed personally to him in a way accessible for future reference for a period of time adequate for the purposes of the information and which allows the unchanged reproduction of the information stored.

The definition given above requires that the information is "personally addressed" to the consumer. This seems to be more relevant for the area covered by Directive 2002/65/EC, i.e., financial services, in which the personal circumstances of the consumer are relevant. This would not be essential in the context of guarantees. The remainder of the definition may be of greater assistance. This suggests that the medium need not allow for indefinite retention of the information, but at least for a period during which the consumer needs to access the information in an unchanged form. This would, in principle, allow the publication of this information on a website, provided that the website remains unchanged for the period during which the consumer requires the information. However, the definition of "durable medium" in Article 2 (l) of the Directive on Insurance Mediation[18] suggests otherwise. This definition is the same as the one set out above, but contains the following second sentence:

> In particular, durable medium covers floppy disks, CD-ROMs, DVDs and hard drives of personal computers on which electronic mail is stored, but it excludes Internet sites, unless such sites meet the criteria specific in the first paragraph.

There is a somewhat circular argument in relation to websites in this - such sites are not durable media as defined in the previous paragraph unless they meet the definition in the first paragraph. This fails to clarify the position of websites. It may be that websites are only then included if the particular page can only be accessed by the particular consumer.

However, this second sentence clarifies that it would be sufficient to e-mail information to the consumer, provided that the consumer uses e-mail software which stores messages on the hard drive. Overall, it can be said that the exact meaning of "durable medium" remains unclear. This may be intentional to allow for inclusion of new media which are currently not widely available.

What, then, is the scope of application for Article 6(3)? Although it is not limited to the pre-sale context, it seems that it will have the greatest relevance there. A consumer may wish to consult the guarantees given on a number of competing products as part of his purchasing decision. In the context of distance selling transactions, Article 5(1) of the Distance Selling Directive[19] requires that a consumer is given written information about any guarantees which exist after conclusion of the contract and by the time the goods are delivered. Article 6(3) of the Guarantees Directive adds to this by giving the consumer the right to ask for information about guarantees before a contract is made.

These provisions may be useful for those consumers who take guarantees into account as part of their purchasing decision. However, as suggested elsewhere in this book,[20] the number of such consumers is likely to be small. If the primary function of guarantees is to provide an informal means of obtaining redress, then a consumer will only be interested in the terms of the guarantee if and when a problem has arisen.

7.4 Regulation of guarantee substance

In chapter 5, it was seen that there are two basic forms of substantive regulation: positive and negative. In E.C. law, there is only very limited positive regulation, and this is generally restricted to disclosure provisions.

7.4.1 Disclosure by category

The Guarantees Directive contains two provisions on the substance of a guarantee. First, Article 6(1) states that guarantees are to be legally binding under the *conditions laid down in the guarantee statement and the associated advertising*. It has already been observed that "conditions" can refer both to the conditions that need to be fulfilled by the consumer before he can rely on the guarantee and the conditions on which the guarantor will honour the guarantee. Article 6(1) therefore confirms that the terms and conditions on which a guarantee is provided can be determined freely by the guarantor.[21]

Second, Article 6(2) requires that the guarantee:

> set[s] out in plain intelligible language the contents of the guarantee and the essential particulars necessary for making claims under the guarantee, notably the duration and territorial scope of the guarantee as well as the name and address of the guarantor.

There are a number of points to note: first, there is no elaboration of what constitutes the "contents" of the guarantee, other than the specific items mentioned in this Article. It may be assumed that this covers the guarantee promise itself,[22] the remedies for non-fulfilment,[23] and other important terms and conditions.[24] In addition, there is an express obligation to state the duration of the guarantee and its territorial scope. The final provision may be a nod in the direction of EC Competition Law, which requires the EC-wide availability of guarantees.

Furthermore, it is necessary to provide contact details for the guarantor, as well as details on how to make a claim. The phrase "essential particulars" is surprisingly imprecise and it is not clear what would constitute "essential particulars". It seems that details on who to contact in order to claim under the guarantee, as well as details on postage and allocation of costs, should all be regarded as "essential particulars". However, this is far from clear.

Despite these reservations, the disclosure rules generally support the use of guarantees as an informal redress mechanism. First, they require a clear statement of what the guarantee provides. Second, there has to be a clear explanation of the procedure which has to be followed to make a claim. Armed with this information. consumers will be able to judge whether it would be worth their while to use the guarantee to solve their problem, or whether it would be better to rely on their statutory rights. If the procedure for making a claim is easily accessible and appears fair, consumers may be encouraged to seek redress under the guarantee first.[25]

7.4.2 Minimum duration of guarantees to obtain ECO-Label

One of the items that must be disclosed according to Article 6(2) is the duration of the guarantee. There appears to be no requirement anywhere that a guarantee has to be of a particular duration.[26] Despite this apparent lack of prescription on the duration of guarantees, a measure from a different area of E.C. Law may have an impact on the duration of guarantees. Regulation 1980/2000[27] ("The Eco-Label Regulation") provides for the establishment of a voluntary Community Eco-Label which is intended to promote products which have a reduced environmental impact during their life-time. The label is to provide a signal to consumers that a particular product meets the scientific criteria laid down by the Community and therefore has a reduced environmental impact compared to other products in the same group which do not meet these criteria. The Regulation enables the Commission to specify the scientific criteria that have to be met by a particular product group in order to qualify for the award of the label. The Commission has adopted a number of such decisions, including criteria for personal computers (Decision 2001/686/EC),[28] portable computers (Decision 2001/687/EC)[29] and dishwashers (Decision 2001/689/EC)[30]. Most of the criteria laid down in these Decisions relate to environmental issues. However, Section 2 of the Annex to Decision 2001/686/EC also requires that a manufacturer of a personal computer:

> shall offer a commercial guarantee to ensure that the personal computer system unit will function *for at least three years*. This guarantee shall be valid from the date of delivery to the customer.[31]

An identical provision can be found in Decision 2001/697/EC. In the case of dishwashers (2001/689/EC), the minimum guarantee period is two years.[32]

A manufacturer who wishes to obtain the Eco-label will therefore be required to offer a guarantee that has a duration of at least the period required by the relevant Eco-labelling decision. This restricts the manufacturer's freedom of determining the scope and extent of his guarantee. He is faced with the choice either to forego the use of the Eco-label, or to offer a guarantee that is of the minimum duration required by the relevant decision. If he decides not to use the Eco-label, he may risk a drop in sales, because consumers increasingly favour products that meet strict environmental standards (see Thogersen, 2000). If he decides to comply with the criteria, he may have to provide a guarantee of longer duration than he would otherwise have done.

The motivation behind the Eco-label decision is to ensure that the life-time of a product is of reasonable duration in order to reduce the number of products that need to be disposed of. From this perspective, the provision of a medium-term guarantee to cover repairs seems sensible. However, setting a minimum duration would not support the use of guarantees as a redress mechanism, because it may distort the degree of responsiveness which a consumer could perceive on the basis of the guarantee. This provision may therefore have an adverse impact on the use of guarantees in the context of dispute resolution, and it is desirable that this requirement in the Eco-labelling decisions were removed.

7.4.3 Negative regulation: Directive 93/13/EEC on unfair terms in consumer contracts

Directive 93/13/EEC[33] (the Unfair Contract Terms Directive) was adopted to deal with the problem of unfair terms in standard-form consumer contracts. It has already been noted that Article 5 of the Directive imposes a general requirement that all contract terms are provided in clear and intelligible language.

Moreover, all contract terms which have not been individually negotiated and which are unfair (Article 3(1)) will not be binding on a consumer (Article 6(1)). A term is unfair:

> If, contrary to the requirement of good faith, it causes a significant imbalance in the parties' rights and obligations arising under the contract, to the detriment of the consumer.

The Annex to the Directive provides an indicative and non-exhaustive list of the terms which may be regarded as unfair. Article 4 specifies that the unfairness of a particular contract term should be assessed by taking into account the nature of the goods or services for which the contract was concluded and all the relevant circumstances at the time of contracting. However, this assessment should not relate to the definition of the main subject matter, nor the consideration provided (Article 4(2)), provided that these terms are written in plain intelligible language.

It is, of course, not entirely clear whether guarantees are "contracts" for the purposes of the Unfair Contract Terms Directive. As noted previously, the definition of guarantee describes these as "undertakings", and Article 6(1) requires these to be legally binding, but does not specify their legal form. However, there is a general assumption that the Unfair Contract Terms Directive should apply. If it did not, then there would be no control over unfair terms in consumer guarantees, which cannot have been the intention of the European legislator. It is therefore submitted that the provisions of the Unfair Contract Terms Directive can be applied to control the terms of consumer guarantees. Consequently, it may be possible to render ineffective those terms in a guarantee which would fail the test of fairness. It was demonstrated in chapter 5 that "negative regulation" is an important aspect of the fairness principle which should be adopted as part of a legal framework for consumer guarantees. Applying the "significant imbalance" test, it will be possible to control those terms in a guarantee which would impose too heavy a burden on a consumer who wishes to take the benefit of a guarantee.[34]

7.5 Relationship between guarantee and legal rights

A further point to be examined is the relationship between guarantees and consumers' legal rights (i.e., the "conformity" requirement). In the Green Paper (1993), and also in the first draft of the Directive (COM(95) 520 final), it was suggested that guarantees should have to provide something 'additional'. Thus, the Commission recommended that:

> [The] guarantee should confer additional benefits on the consumer over and above the rights already arising from the [statutory rights] (p.96).

There is, of course, some vagueness in this - it is far from clear how a guarantee could provide an additional benefit to the statutory rights. At its most basic, it must be the fact that a guarantee may be offered by a manufacturer rather than a seller. A consumer would gain the additional benefit of being able to pursue a second party if something was wrong with the goods.

Although such a requirement was still included in the first draft, the Directive itself no longer contains such a rule. Guarantees are therefore not required to provide additional benefits for consumers. This is to be welcomed. A requirement that a guarantee must put the consumer into a better position than under the statutory rights would amount to a covert method of positive regulation. Thus, if a range of remedies is required by law, a guarantee would have to include all these remedies *plus* some additional benefit. It may be hard to imagine what this could be, if the range of remedies available in law already include repair, refund, price reduction and replacement. The impact of such a provision may have a greater impact on retailers providing a guarantee than on manufacturers, who are not (currently) directly liable to consumers.

There is, of course, a danger that consumers might be lead by a guarantee which is more restrictive than their statutory rights to believe that the guarantee constitutes the full extent of their rights in cases of non-conformity. Article 6(2) of the Directive specifies that each guarantee must contain a statement that the consumer has legal rights under applicable national legislation governing the sale of consumer goods and make clear that those rights are not affected by the guarantee. This is important because it will make consumers aware of the fact that a guarantee is not their only means of obtaining redress if goods are defective.

Although Article 6(2) is expressed only as a rule requiring disclosure of the fact that the consumer has statutory rights and that these remain unaffected, it seems that this provision should be read as encompassing a prohibition on any attempt to restrict these rights. Moreover, under the Unfair Contract Terms Directive, a term in a guarantee which seeks to restrict or exclude the consumer's statutory rights would probably always fail the test of fairness and therefore not be binding on the consumer. There is therefore some control over attempts to restrict the consumer's legal rights.

Furthermore, Article 7 states that any contract term or agreement between consumer and seller to limit or exclude the statutory rights are not binding on the consumer. Some commentators (e.g., Malinvaud, 2002, para 36) take the view that this effectively requires all guarantees to meet the minimum level of protection set by the statutory rights, whether given by a seller or manufacturer. If such guarantees offered less than the statutory level of protection, the guarantee would operate as a limitation clause. Although this reasoning may seem attractive, it has no support either in Article 6 or Article 7. Article 7 merely requires that there are no express attempts to exclude the statutory rights, and Article 6(2) reduces the risk of confusion by mandating a clear statement that consumers enjoy protection in addition to the guarantee. It is submitted that the Article 7 does not constitute a requirement that guarantees meet at least a level of protection equivalent to the statutory rights. Although such a requirement may be justifiable on the basis that it would ensure that guarantees are not used to deflect consumers from their rights under the relevant legal position, this can adequately be achieved by the requirement to provide a clear reference to the legal rights in the guarantee document.[35] This would preserve the ability of consumers to gauge how responsive a guarantor is likely to be by considering the remedies offered under the guarantee. If a seller offers a guarantee which is more restrictive than the statutory rights, the consumer can interpret this as reflecting the seller's limited willingness to deal with complaints. In that case, it may be preferable for the consumer to base his complaint on the statutory quality standard.

7.6 Enforcement

Article 6(5) states that a failure to comply with the requirements in Article 6 does not affect the validity of a guarantee and consumers can still rely on it. However, there are no sanctions for a failure to comply with Article 6. This has been lamented by commentators (see e.g. Micklitz, 1999, p.488). The only sanction envisaged in the Directive is mentioned in Article 10, which amends the Injunctions Directive to include the Consumer Guarantees Directive within its scope.

7.6.1 The injunctions directive

Although there are no specific sanctions in the Directive for a failure to comply with the requirements laid down in Article 6, Article 10 of the Directive has amended Directive 98/27/EC[36] (the Injunctions Directive) to bring the Guarantees Directive within the scope of the Injunctions Directive. This short Directive requires that the Member States enable qualified entities, such as public bodies or private associations involved in consumer protection, to apply for an injunction to prevent the infringement by a trader of any of the rules included in the consumer protection directives. One requirement is that the injunction must seek to protect the collective interests of consumers (Article 1(1)). An infringement is an action that harms these collective interests (Article 1(2)). An application may therefore only be made where the infringement affects the interests of a sizeable number of consumers. It will not be available in isolated cases. However, if a guarantee fails to comply with the rules of Article 6, it seems likely that a significant number of consumers will be affected, i.e., everybody who has bought a product with a guarantee that does not meet the minimum requirements of the Guarantees Directive. In such circumstances, it may be possible to apply for an injunction to stop the guarantor from continuing to give such guarantees. Unfortunately, there were no examples of the application of the Directive in the context of guarantees available at the time of writing.

7.6.2 The E.C. green paper on European Union consumer protection

As a final observation, it is necessary to mention the developments that may happen at the European level in the years to come. In October 2001, the European Commission presented a green paper on European Union consumer protection (COM(2001) 531 final). This paper launched a debate about the future direction of E.C. Consumer Protection. One of the options mentioned in the paper is that a general "framework" Directive could be adopted which would introduce a general requirement that businesses should not engage in unfair commercial practices when dealing with consumers. This seems to extend beyond infringements of existing consumer protection rules and could cover unfair, yet lawful, behaviour. Furthermore, the Commission seems to favour a strengthened public enforcement base to ensure that businesses treat consumers fairly.

In June 2002, the Commission presented a follow-up communication to the Green Paper (COM (2002) 289 final). This states that there is support for reform and that there will be detailed research into the operation of the Single Market for consumers. It also announces that the Commission will work on a proposal for a framework Directive based on the idea of "fair commercial practices" (at p.8). There would be a general clause which could consist of an unfairness element and a consumer detriment test. However, at this point, the Commission is still considering the options and more detailed proposals are expected at a later stage. This development is welcome. The framework for guarantees developed in this book would very probably fit into the new consumer protection landscape which may eventually emerge.

7.7 Conclusions

The E.C. rules on guarantees are largely uncontroversial, and generally support the function of guarantees as an informal route to obtaining redress if goods are faulty. However, there are problems in the detail of these rules. It is desirable that the Commission should clarify the relationship between the ECO-Label Regulation and Article 6 of the Guarantees Directive. The Guarantees Directive is the main piece of E.C. legislation on consumer guarantees, and it seems very unusual to introduce substantive requirements on duration through a separate measure which is not even referred to in the Directive. Similarly, the Regulation and the various decisions adopted under it do not refer to the Guarantees Directive. This creates a rather confusing picture for those wishing to provide guarantees. More importantly, it may distort the "signal" emitted by a guarantee, in that a guarantor who wishes to obtain the ECO-Label for his goods has to provide guarantees of a minimum duration, even where that guarantor may have preferred a shorter duration.

The substantive rules in Article 6 are welcome, because these will create greater transparency in the provision of guarantees. The one grip is the rather superficial requirement that there must be a reference to the legal (or statutory) rights of consumers in the guarantee, but there is no indication how this should be phrased. A clear model summary statement of these rights would have been a useful addition to the Directive.

Interesting developments may yet occur within the next five years or so. The Commission will undoubtedly pursue its *Green Paper on EU Consumer Protection* initiative. This may lead to the adoption of a general fairness principle, which would be a significant step forward for consumer protection and one that would be in line with the framework proposed in this book. Moreover, by 2006, the Commission has to consider the question of direct producer liability. This may have an impact on the provision of guarantees. These future developments are awaited with great interest.

Notes

1. (1999) O.J. L 177/12.
2. See 2.1.2, above. The first draft of this definition covered extended warranties: see COM(95)520 final, p.10.
3. In contrast, Malinvaud (2002) appears to assume that guarantees are effectively given against a lack of conformity within the meaning of Article 2. This is difficult to reconcile with the definition of "guarantee", and also with every-day practice.

4 This might also explain the provision in Article 6(5) of the Directive, which states that the failure of a guarantee to comply with the rules laid down in Article 6 should not deprive it of its legally binding nature. It seems unlikely that guarantees that are solely based on advertising would provide all the detail that is required, and it is therefore important to make clear that the consumer can nevertheless enforce that promise.

5 Although it was seen in the previous section that this assumption may be slightly misguided.

6 See chapter 1, section 1.5.5.

7 Article 2(2)(d) states that public statements can be taken into account in considering whether goods are in conformity with the contract. Article 2(4) provides a defence for the seller if he can show that such statements were not correct and had been corrected at the time of sale. See chapter 1 at 1.4.

8 See the second sentence of Article 5 of the Unfair Contract Terms Directive (93/13/EEC).

9 One solution might be the introduction of a proportionality requirement, although this may be unworkable in practice.

10 In this case, a number of Ford dealers had published an advertisement in newspapers stating that they would no longer provide guarantee service on cars purchased in another Member State. Interestingly, the advertisement also stated that legally, guarantee work could only be required from the original seller.

11 By definition, an agreement or concerted practice requires the involvement of at least two persons.

12 Notably in para 35: "[Reserving a special advantage for its own customers] cannot be regarded as restricting the supply of parallel imports of cameras where such cameras are fully covered by the manufacturer's normal guarantee which the distributor is under an obligation to provide."

13 Swiss law did not permit restrictions on the reselling of products, as envisaged under the selective distribution system.

14 These are primarily luxury products or technically complex products. See Whish (2001), p.558.

15 Following this case, the Commission had to admit in reply to a question by the European Parliament that a purchaser of a product from a non-network retailer when that product comes with a manufacturer's guarantee would have no protection under E.C. Law (Tenreiro, 1995).

16 Moreover, if guarantees are legally binding as contracts, Article 5 UCTD would apply in any event.

17 (2002) O.J. L 271/16.

18 Adopted on 30 September 2002. At the time of writing, the Directive had not yet been published in the Official Journal. An unofficial version published on the DG Internal Market website was used as the basis for this section.

19 Directive 97/7/EC on the Protection of Consumers in Respect of Distance Contracts (1997) O.J. L 144/19.

20 See chapter 3, in particular.

21 This is, of course, subject to the qualification that certain terms would not be acceptable under Directive 93/13/EEC. See below.

22 See 2.1.1.

23 See 2.1.2.

24 See 2.1.3.

25 See 2.2.

26 There has been some confusion with regard to the rules in the Consumer Guarantees Directive. The two-year manifestation period has sometimes been interpreted as requiring a two-year manufacturers' guarantee. This is clearly not the case, and there are no rules on the duration of a guarantee in the Directive.

27 (2000) O.J. L. 237/1.

28 (2001) O.J. L 242/4.

29 (2001) O.J. L 242/11.

30 (2001) O.J. L 242/23.

31 Emphasis added.

32 The dishwasher decision also requires a "spare parts guarantee", i.e., a guarantee that replacement parts are to be available for a specific time after production of the product ceases. The decision requires such availability for a period of twelve years after production has ceased.

33 (1993) O.J. L 95/29.

34 The detailed application of the legislation implementing the Directive into English law is considered in the next chapter.

35 This could be phrased along the lines of: "The law provides you with a right to repair or replacement, and in certain circumstances a right to price reduction or refund. This guarantee does not affect these rights."

36 (1998) O.J. L 166/51.

Chapter 8

Consumer Guarantees in English Law

8.0 Introduction

This chapter will examine the legal framework for guarantees in English law. There are very few specific provisions on guarantees, and most of these are based on the Consumer Guarantees Directive, discussed in the previous chapter. The Directive was finally implemented in December 2002 by the Sale and Supply of Goods to Consumers Regulations 2002 (see generally, Howells and Twigg-Flesner, 2003). In addition to these rules, there are various provisions which are relevant in the context of consumer guarantees, and this chapter will demonstrate that there is a fairly complex legal framework of relevance guarantees currently in place. The first part of this chapter will review a reform proposal made in 1989 which would have introduced a detailed code on guarantees. Although this failed and there have been no attempts to resurrect it, it is nevertheless interesting to examine these proposals. This will be followed by a detailed discussion of the legal rules that have an impact on consumer guarantees.

8.1 A failed reform proposal: *Competing in quality*

The National Consumer Council (NCC) in the U.K. put forward proposals in 1989 which resemble the framework under the Magnuson-Moss Warranty Act 1975 (MMWA).[1] The NCC had similarly been influenced by signalling theory. Para 1.5 of the Report duly stated that:

> In this country there is little law requiring the disclosure of information about the quality of products. One way consumers try to gauge the reliability of a product is by the guarantee offered with it. Yet there are no laws that help to distinguish a good guarantee from a worthless one. This distorts competition and misleads consumers (NCC, 1989b, p.1).

This is continued into para 1.7 where the NCC stated that manufacturers should be required to state whether or not they are offering a guarantee.

> In this way, consumers will be able to see which manufacturers are prepared to stand by their products. This in turn we believe will force manufacturers to address the issues of product quality and customer service diligently.

The parallels in the objectives pursued by the MMWA and the NCC's proposals are readily apparent. The gist of the NCC's approach was that the quality of consumer goods can be improved by promoting competition on guarantees, because consumers use guarantees to gauge product quality. The pitfalls of this argument were dealt with in chapter 3.

The NCC set out in some detail its view that improved information and the resultant increase in competition would benefit consumers, because this would encourage manufacturers to improve the quality of their products. It also found that the majority of consumers regard accurate information about reliability and durability at the point of sale as vital (p.20). It concluded that many consumers were confused both with regard to their statutory rights and to any additional protection they might enjoy under a guarantee (p.19).

Interestingly, the NCC recognised that the Sale of Goods Act 1979 (SoGA) - then before the 1994 reforms that introduced the "satisfactory quality" standard - had many shortcomings, including its focus on a bi-partite relationship (buyer and seller) and the limited range of remedies, both of which made the SoGA unsuitable for consumer transactions (NCC, 1989, p.9-11). It rejects reforms to the SoGA because:

> [T]hese laws are based on common standards for all products and as such they cannot reflect the different types of defects in different types of products. Secondly, they cannot play a role in stimulating competition. Thirdly, we consider that raising product quality should be the first objective of consumer law. Prevention is better than cure ... (p.21, para 5.1.2).

This view appears to reflect a somewhat rigid adherence to the notion that improvements to product quality can only be achieved through competition. This would require consumers to use guarantees as a quality signal and manufacturers to compete on the terms of their guarantee, as well as improve quality in order to be able to offer a competitive guarantee. Yet, the NCC not only failed to provide sufficient evidence to demonstrate what happens in practice, it also seemed unaware of the research published by then, which only gave cautious support to signalling theory.

The NCC made detailed recommendations for a legislative framework for guarantees. It proposed that there should be specific terminology for guarantees, and that guarantors should have to follow this terminology. Thus, a guarantee that met all the requirements specified by the NCC should be a "consumer guarantee" (para 6.1.1). There could be four different designations: "consumer guarantee: x months", "consumer guarantee plus: x months", "retailer's consumer guarantee: x months" and "no consumer guarantee" (para 6.1.5). Clear information about which type of guarantee is offered would have to be displayed with the product (para 6.1.12). Such guarantees should be available free of charge, because a guarantee is a "statement by the producer about how far he stands by his product" (para 6.1.2). A guarantee would run with the product and therefore not be restricted to the purchaser (para 6.1.3). The criteria for the "consumer guarantee" would be minimum criteria, and a guarantor who offered more than the minimum level of protection would be entitled to use the label "consumer guarantee plus".

Although the NCC accepted that the existing public law controls[2] were sufficient to control the provision of guarantees, one new criminal offence was recommended. Some retailers had adopted a practice of removing details of the manufacturer's guarantee in order to persuade consumers to take out an extended warranty. In order to control this, NCC proposed that removing a manufacturer's guarantee should be a criminal offence (para 6.1.10).[3]

A consumer guarantee should have been available for all products, but special rules were to apply to motor vehicles, white and brown goods. The NCC proposed the terms of the consumer guarantee. First, a consumer guarantee should be binding as a statutory contract (para 6.2.2). Furthermore, a consumer guarantee should last for at least 12 months, and the duration should be clearly indicated (para 6.2.3). The definition of "defect" would have been identical to the definition of satisfactory quality in the SoGA (para 6.2.4).[4] However, there should be no liability under a consumer guarantee where the defect is due to misuse by the consumer or improper maintenance (para 6.2.5). A defective product should be repaired by the guarantor at no cost to the consumer and the guarantee should be extended by the period that the product was under repair (paras 6.2.7-8). If three attempts at repair had been unsuccessful, or the product had been out of use for more than thirty days within a twelve month period, the consumer should be offered a replacement or a refund (para 6.2.10). If a replacement or refund were given more than twelve months after purchase, a deduction for use could have been made (para 6.2.12). Finally, guarantees should not be subject to unreasonable conditions, having regard to all the relevant circumstances (para 6.2.14).

Although the influence of the MMWA in the NCC proposals is clearly evident, the NCC sought to avoid some of the problems encountered under the MMWA. Thus, rather than to introduce a two-tier system of "full" and "limited" guarantees, the NCC instead set a basic level of protection that anybody seeking to offer a consumer guarantee would have had to meet. No specific designation was proposed for guarantees that did not meet the minimum standard.

However, the NCC proposals are as flawed in their approach as the MMWA. The argument that promoting clarity over guarantee terms would result in increased competition and product quality is not sufficiently supported by research evidence. Both the MMWA and the NCC proposals are based on an approach which is too heavily biased towards signalling theory. Not only do both presuppose that guarantees are accurate signals of product quality, but furthermore that guarantors will compete on the terms of their guarantees and that there will therefore be improvements in product quality. Had the MMWA and NCC been based on a more balanced approach which had taken into account other uses of guarantees,[5] rather than being based almost entirely on signalling theory, they may have had a stronger impact.

8.2 The legal status of manufacturers' guarantees

It is now appropriate to turn to the current rules on consumer product guarantees in English law. There will first be a consideration of the legal status of such guarantees, followed by a detailed analysis of the relevant legal provisions.

8.2.1 The legal definition of "guarantee"

Originally, the only definition of guarantee could be found in the Unfair Contract Terms Act 1977 ("UCTA"), section 5. This section renders ineffective any clause in a guarantee which purports to exclude or restrict liability for loss or damage caused by goods as a result of negligence by the manufacturer or distributor. For the purposes of UCTA, 'guarantees' are defined in section 5(2)(b) thus:

> Anything in writing is a guarantee if it contains or purports to contain some promise or assurance (however worded or presented) that defects will be made good by complete or partial replacement, or by repair, monetary compensation or otherwise.

The final part of section 5(1)[6] refers to a "contract term ... contained in ... a guarantee". The references to a "contract term" is contained in a guarantee, must mean that the guarantee itself must also be a contract. Therefore, UCTA classifies guarantees as contracts. At one stage during the implementation process, the Department of Trade and Industry (DTI) proposed to replace the UCTA definition with a definition based on the Guarantees Directive, but this proposal was abandoned. In any event, it should be noted that the Law Commission has suggested that section 5 should be repealed (Law Commission, 2002).

The term "consumer guarantee" is defined in Regulation 2 of the Sale and Supply of Goods to Consumers Regulations 2002 ("SSGCR") thus:

> 'Consumer guarantee' means any undertaking by a person acting in the course of his business to a consumer, given without extra charge, to reimburse the price paid or to replace, repair or handle consumer goods in any way if they do not meet the specifications set out in the guarantee statement or in the relevant advertising.

This definition follows closely the definition of "guarantee" found in Article 1(2)(e) of the Guarantees Directive. Consequently, there is the same uncertainty with regard to its scope as identified previously in relation to Article 1(2)(e), and in particular whether "satisfaction guarantees" are covered.[7]

It is also not clear why it was decided to call this a "consumer guarantee", rather than simply a "guarantee" - perhaps the DTI felt that there was a risk of confusion if there were two different definitions for the same term. In the remainder of this chapter, the term "guarantee" will be used and includes "consumer guarantees" within the meaning of Regulation 2 SSGCR.

Moreover, in contrast to UCTA, the SSGCR definition does not specify the legal nature of consumer guarantees. For this, it is necessary to look to Regulation

15(1) SSGCR. However, it is useful first to review to position before the implementation of the Guarantees Directive. The subsequent discussion may continue to be relevant for those "guarantees" which are not covered by Regulation 2 SSGCR.

8.2.2 Were guarantees legally enforceable in English law prior to the implementation of the consumer guarantees directive?

Manufacturers' guarantees often come as part of the overall package of goods. However, the consumer will have concluded his contract with a retailer and not with the manufacturer, and will therefore not be in a direct legal relationship with that manufacturer. The legal enforceability of a guarantee in English Law, before the implementation of the Consumer Guarantees Directive, depended on whether this could be construed as a contract between guarantor and consumer under the common law rules of contract formation (cf. Willett, 1992).[8] If a guarantee is to be a contract, it must comply with the rules on contract formation. A number of elements must be present before a legally binding contract is concluded: There has to be an offer by the guarantor to provide the consumer with a guarantee for a particular product. This offer must then be accepted by the consumer. In return for the guarantee, the consumer will have to provide some form of consideration, i.e. something of value. The conclusion of the contract of sale may in itself be sufficient consideration, and the completion of a registration document which contains some statistical information might also fulfil this requirement.[9] Indeed, there may be a variety of acts by a consumer which may be sufficient consideration, such as the obligation to pay for the return of the goods to the manufacturer (Lowe and Woodroffe, 1999, p.59). Finally, the guarantor must intend to create a legal relationship.

However, it is a general principle that a person can only accept an offer if he was aware of this before providing his consideration (*Williams v Carwardine* (1833)). If a consumer only discovered the guarantee after purchase, and if the only consideration he might have provided is entering into the contract for the sale of the product itself, it is unlikely that this would be sufficient for the guarantee to be legally enforceable. If the consumer has to return a registration card it is arguable that he provides sufficient consideration for the guarantee to become enforceable by returning it. This technical requirement caused an unnecessary lack of certainty. Consumers may often not enquire whether a product is covered by a guarantee, nor may they be given information about the availability of a guarantee before purchase. Indeed, a consumer may expect that a particular product is covered by some sort of manufacturer's guarantee. Although it is unlikely that he will be aware of its individual terms, he will nevertheless anticipate that a guarantee will be given. It seems odd, to say the least, and perhaps even unfair to require prior knowledge of the guarantee when it is common for products to be accompanied by some sort of guarantee. The editors of *Benjamin's Sale of Goods* argued that it:

> may be sufficient if the goods are of such a general type (for example, a television set or a video recorder) as would normally be accompanied by a manufacturers' guarantee (at para 14-020).

There could therefore be a presumption that products within particular categories are sold with a manufacturers' guarantee. However, it may then be necessary to consider whether consumers should be told before purchase if a product is not guaranteed.[10] However, this difficulty should not be overstated. In many cases, a consumer will have been aware of the guarantee before he decided on a purchase. The retailer may have mentioned the manufacturer's guarantees before the consumer completed his purchase. Also, the guarantee is often mentioned in advertisements and promotional material (Lowe and Woodroffe, 1999, p.58). It is arguable that this may be sufficient in order to constitute an offer that a guarantee will be given by the manufacturer if the consumer subsequently buys the product. However, the guarantor may dispute the extent to which a particular statement by the guarantor, e.g., in an advertisement, was intended to constitute a term of the 'guarantee contract', although this seems highly unlikely in practice.

It is therefore at least arguable that a guarantee would, in some circumstances, be enforceable as a contract between guarantor and consumer and that this is collateral to the main contract of sale. In this way, a guarantee would be enforced if it constituted a contractual warranty, which would be collateral to the main contract of sale. Although there are no cases specifically on manufacturers' guarantees, there is a reasonable body of case-law on collateral warranties generally.[11] It will be useful to review this to appreciate the difficulties of establishing collateral contracts in this context.

The legal standard for establishing collateral contracts is high. In *Heilbut, Symons & Co. v Buckleton* (1913), Lord Moulton stated that:

> Collateral contracts ... must be proved strictly. Not only the terms of such contracts but the existence of an *animus contrahendi* on the part of all the parties to them must be clearly shown (p.47).

The difficulty, therefore, is whether a particular statement was intended to give rise to a legally binding obligation. Thus, in *Brown v Sheens and Richmond Car Sales* (1950), motor car dealers assured the claimant that a car was in perfect condition and "good for thousands of trouble free miles". The car was then acquired through hire-purchase.[12] It was not in perfect condition and required substantial repairs. It was held by Jones, J that the dealers had given an express contractual warranty as to the condition of the car. This had induced the purchaser to enter into the hire-purchase agreement. The car dealers were found liable for the breach of their warranty. Similarly, in *Andrews v Hopkinson* (1957) the sales manager of a second-hand car dealer told the claimant that a car was "a good little bus" and that he would "stake [his] life on it". This was held to be a collateral warranty to the hire-purchase agreement. McNair J found that the plaintiff would not have bought the car or entered into the hire-purchase agreement without this warranty. The consideration in this case was the entering into of the hire-purchase agreement. In *Shanklin Pier v Detel Products LD* (1951), a director of Detel Products made representations to the owners of Shanklin Pier about the quality of their paint. The claimants then specified that contractors repairing the pier had to use Detel's paint. McNair J. held that Detel had given a collateral warranty to Shanklin Pier. The judge summed up the legal principle underpinning this and the previous cases thus:

> If ... the consideration for the warranty in the usual case is the entering into of the main contract in relation to which the warranty is given, I see no reason why there may not be an enforceable warranty between A and B supported by the consideration that B should cause C to enter into a contract with A.

In *Wells (Merstham) Ltd. v Buckland Sand and Silica Ltd.* (1965) a representation was made by the defendant sellers about the suitability of a particular type of sand for the claimant's business. The claimants placed an order with another company which was supplied by the defendants. Edmund Davies J held that the defendants' statement was an express warranty. There was evidence of contractual intention, as it was in the contemplation of both parties that a contract based upon the promise would be entered into.

A direct offer of a guarantee made by a manufacturer to a specific purchaser in the situation described above could give rise to a contractual guarantee, the consideration being the conclusion of the contract for the sale of the product with the retailer. However, manufacturers will rarely, if ever, make such direct offers. Manufacturers generally try to make consumers aware of their products and any guarantees through advertising. A sufficiently precise and clear reference to a guarantee in such materials might amount to an "offer" of a guarantee. However, the manufacturer will not realistically expect each consumer who has been targeted to buy his product. It is therefore less likely that a general statement in advertising would give rise to an enforceable obligation. A manufacturer does not know who will buy his products and who will rely on the promise he has made in his advertisement. It will be seen in the analysis of the case-law which follows that the courts have found it difficult to construe a contract on the basis of general publicity material.

The usual position at common law is that statements made in advertisements cannot give rise to enforceable obligations because there is normally no intention to be legally bound (*Partridge v Crittenden* (1968)). Yet, an exception to this general rule was established in that most famous contract case of all, *Carlill v The Carbolic Smoke Ball Company* (1893). An advertisement promised everybody who used the smoke ball according to instructions a reward of £100 if they contracted influenza. Mrs Carlill successfully claimed her award in the Court of Appeal because the advertisement constituted a unilateral offer which had been accepted by performing the required act. There had been an intention to create legal relations on the part of the Smoke Ball Company, which manifested itself in the statement that a sum of money had been deposited with a specific bank. Bowen LJ suggested that the question the courts should consider was this:

> [The advertisement] was intended to be issued to the public and to be read by the public. How would an ordinary person reading this document construe it?

This test suggests an approach which is favourable to consumers - if an ordinary person could construe the advertisement or the reference in a brochure as something by which the manufacturer should stand, then the courts should seek to apply the law accordingly, rather than insist on strict requirements of contractual formation.[13] Similarly, in *Wood v Letrik* (1932), the defendants stated in an advertisement that their electric comb would cure grey hair after 10 days' use and guaranteed that they would pay £500 if it failed to do so. The judge placed considerable emphasis on the use of the word "guarantee" in the advertisement, construing it according to the plain meaning which ordinary sensible people would attach to it. A consumer reading the word "guarantee" would understand that the person using it was offering to bind himself to be responsible for a certain state of facts. The judge rejected claims that reliance had been unreasonable and that the plaintiff did not use the comb properly. The "guarantee" in this case was therefore enforceable.

However, even in more recent times, claims in advertisements could give rise to collateral contracts. Thus, in *Esso Petroleum Co. Ltd. v Customs and Excise Commissioners* (1976), a promotion promised each customer a coin bearing the head of one of the members of the English football squad for each 4 gallons of petrol purchased. A majority of the House of Lords thought that this could give rise to a collateral contract. Lord Simon observed *obiter*:

> It seems to me in general undesirable to allow a commercial promoter to claim that what he has done is a mere puff, not intended to create legal relations. The coins may have been themselves of little intrinsic value; but all the evidence suggests that Esso contemplated that they would be attractive to motorists and that there would be a large commercial advantage to themselves from the scheme (p.5).

There was a collateral contract, with consideration being provided by entering into the main contract to purchase the petrol. Lord Simon's observations are significant because they are indicative of an attitude that seeks to give effect to the legitimate expectations of consumers. It suggests a less doctrinal approach in respect of manufacturers' statements-why should a manufacturer (or a retailer) be allowed to hide behind the traditional rule of contractual intention and thus reject a customer's claim under a guarantee? It seems that there is a clear case for holding manufacturers liable for their statements in principle, subject perhaps to a test of clarity - only where a statement is so vague that it could not possibly have been intended to be a serious statement should it be possible to classify it as mere puff.[14]

Yet, this has not been universally accepted. In *Lambert v Lewis* (1982), manufacturers of towing hitches had claimed in advertising leaflets that their towing hitches were fool-proof and required no maintenance. The claimants, relying on *Shanklin Pier* and *Carlill*, argued that these statements had been made seriously and that there was an intention that they would be relied on. The Court of

Appeal agreed with the defendants that there was insufficient evidence of an intention to create a contract. Stephenson LJ confirmed that the difficulty is whether statements made in promotional literature are intended to be legally binding. *Shanklin Pier* was distinguished, because in that case, the statement was given to a particular person to enter into a particular contract. Stephenson LJ emphasised that in *Lewis*, the manufacturers were unaware of the subsequent contracts. In the earlier line of cases there had been an express (oral) statement to the subsequent purchaser, and both parties were clearly contemplating the conclusion of a specific contract. This is rarely the case where a manufacturer sends out general advertising leaflets, because no specific contract will be in his contemplation. The court was clearly concerned about the wider implications of holding that the statement in the brochure was legally enforceable. This could have been interpreted as creating strict liability for all types of losses suffered by a buyer following a breach of a promise in advertisements (Hervey, 1981). Although this may be so, it is arguable that a sufficiently precise statement such as the one in *Lewis* (that the hitches "required no maintenance"), should have become binding on the manufacturer.[15]

More recently, the Court of Appeal in *Bowerman v Association of British Travel Agents (ABTA)* (1995) held that publicity material could give rise to a legally enforceable obligation. ABTA travel agents displayed a notice in their offices describing ABTA's scheme of protection against financial failure of ABTA members. Ms Bowerman claimed that this notice constituted a contractual offer by ABTA to those who booked their holidays through an ABTA agent to protect them financially should the agent go out of business. ABTA denied this and relied on *Carlill*. The Court of Appeal by a majority accepted Ms Bowerman's arguments. Hirst LJ, who dissented, and Hobhouse LJ accepted that *Carlill* applied to the present case. Hirst LJ thought that the wording of the notice, unlike the advertisement in *Carlill*,[16] was too vague to constitute an offer.[17] The majority found that the wording of the notice was precise enough and provided sufficient evidence of an intention to create legal relations. Consideration was provided by the consumer by entering into a contract with an ABTA member, as this would be a gain to the commercial purposes for which the association was created. Hobhouse LJ observed that rather than engaging in a fine analysis of the language used, the document as a whole and its impact on the general public should be considered. As such, it would reasonably be read by a member of the public as containing an offer of a promise. The notice satisfied the requirements for a collateral contract.

This decision is very significant. Its immediate effect is that trade associations may be bound in a direct contractual relationship with a consumer, where these associations appear to promise something to customers dealing with members of such associations (Oughton and Lowry, 2000, p.102). But the decision may be "of considerable value beyond the holiday industry and in relation to shop displays generally" (Whincup, 1996). It seems to confirm that "the collateral contract device can confer direct rights upon consumers as against manufacturers ... who offer inducements to the public to purchase their goods ... from their retailers ..." (McMeel, 1997). If it can reasonably be expected that a consumer will rely on a manufacturer's statement regarding the availability of a guarantee, the guarantee promise should be binding on the manufacturer.[18]

It seems, therefore that the common law of contract could recognise the enforceability of guarantees. However, as discussed above, if a consumer was not aware of a guarantee before buying the corresponding product and there is nothing the consumer needs to do to activate the guarantee, it may still not be enforceable. The collateral contract argument only works if the consumer can at the very least be deemed to have been aware of the guarantee before he bought the relevant product. Following *Bowerman v ABTA*, it appears that it is sufficient if a consumer could have become aware of it through general advertising.[19] Some uncertainty therefore remains. The position has now been clarified in respect of guarantees which meet the definition of "consumer guarantee" by virtue of Regulation 15(1) SSGCR, discussed in the following section. However, in relation to other "guarantees", such as satisfaction guarantees, the discussion above will continue to be relevant.

8.2.3 Guarantees are legally enforceable

Regulation 15(1) of the SSGCR will ensure that guarantees are legally enforceable:

> Where goods are sold or otherwise supplied to a consumer which are offered with a consumer guarantee, the consumer guarantee takes effect at the time the goods are delivered as a contractual obligation owed by the guarantor under the conditions set out in the guarantee statement and the associated advertising.

Regulation 15(1) only refers to an obligation owed by the guarantor to the consumer, rather than simply a contract between guarantor and consumer. It is not clear if this was a deliberate decision.[20] Perhaps there was an intention to avoid the creation of obligations on the consumer that might be enforceable by the guarantor.[21] Thus, if a consumer did not follow the conditions in the guarantee, it would be strange if a guarantor would then seek to enforce these against the consumer. Rather, the guarantor's obligation would be subject to the consumer's compliance with these conditions, and the wording of the Regulation 15(1) seems to confirm this.

This wording might also have been chosen in recognition of the fact that guarantees are unlike other forms of contract in that a consumer makes no positive step (except, perhaps, the return of a registration card, where required) to enter into it. Although most consumer contracts are based on standard-form contracts, a consumer still needs to take the active step of agreeing to a particular transaction. However, a guarantee becomes available automatically when purchasing a particular product. A consumer may have taken a guarantee into account in deciding to buy a particular product,[22] but it seems unlikely that a consumer would choose not to buy a product which met his needs in all other aspects simply because the guarantee did not appeal to him. If the consumer were not happy with the guarantee, he would probably simply ignore it. In this sense, a guarantee is very unlike other types of contract. Yet, treating guarantees as something akin to a contract ensures that these are binding in a way that is instantly recognisable to an

English lawyer, and, more importantly, enables the application of other contract law measures, notably the legislation on unfair contract terms.[23]

It is now appropriate to examine the elements of the legal framework on guarantees in English law.

8.3 General principles: Fairness

In chapter 5, it was argued that a general fairness principle which covers fairness in procedure, substance and performance is desirable. It will be see below that there are well-established provisions dealing with procedural and substantive fairness. As far as fairness in performance is concerned, English law is less well-developed. This aspect of fairness is relevant to the extent that it is desirable that the discretion given to a guarantor is exercised in a non-arbitrary manner. In effect, this requires that a guarantor should be required to perform his obligations under a guarantee in good faith. However, English law does not (yet) recognise an over-riding principle of good faith, or fairness, in the performance of contractual obligations. There are, however, signs that the courts are moving towards the development of such a principle. In *Abu Dhabi National Tanker Co. v Product Star Shipping, The Product Star* (1993), the question of control over contractual discretion arose in the context of a charter party. Leggatt LJ made the following observations:

> Where A and B contract with each other to confer a discretion on A, that does not render B subject to A's uninhibited whim. In my judgment, the authorities show that not only must the discretion be exercised honestly and in good faith, but, having regard to the provisions of the contract by which it is conferred, it must not be exercised arbitrarily, capriciously or unreasonably (p.404).

This is a significant dictum. It accepts that discretion may be given to a contracting party, but that party cannot exercise this discretion in an arbitrary fashion. More recently, in *Gan Insurance v Tai Ping Insurance Co* (2001), in the context of a reinsurance arrangement, the Court of Appeal was prepared to imply a term into a contract which required an insurer not to withhold approval to a particular transaction arbitrarily. Significantly, Mance LJ said:

> The right to withhold approval ... is a right to be exercised in good faith after consideration of and on the basis of the facts giving rise to the particular claim, and not with reference to considerations wholly extraneous to the subject-matter of the particular reinsurance or arbitrarily (para 76).

A similar approach was adopted in the context of a consumer transaction in *Nash v Paragon Finance plc* (2001). The case involved the power of a lender to set interest rates for loans. It was claimed that the lender's power to vary interest rates was subject to an implied term that this would be exercised reasonably. Dyson LJ was prepared to imply such a term. He emphasised that this was not a term that the lender would not impose unreasonable rates. Rather, the term implied was that a lender would not exercise his discretion in a way that no reasonable lender would do (para 41). The difficulty with *Nash* is that Dyson LJ suggested that the test for reasonableness in this context should be the same as that developed in *Associated Provincial Picture Houses v Wednesbury Corporation* (1948) ("Wednesbury unreasonableness"). However, the *Wednesbury* test was developed in the area of judicial review of administrative action and may not be appropriate in a consumer context. *Gan Insurance* did not suggest that *Wednesbury* would be relevant. Clarification of this point in a subsequent case is therefore desirable.

These decisions are, without doubt, very significant (cf. Sims and Goddard, 2002, p.271). Although in a narrow sense, they do no more than imply a term into the type of contract at issue in the respective cases, it is submitted that these decisions are a clear indication that English law is (slowly) moving towards the adoption of a good faith standard in the exercise of contractual discretion. Consequently, these cases may be of much wider application and could be relevant to all types of contract (including guarantees). In the context of consumer product guarantees, the cases could provide a basis for controlling the exercise of a guarantor's discretion under the guarantee. This would require that guarantors act in accordance with the terms of the guarantee and that they do not refuse to honour a consumer's claim without a good reason.

8.4 General principles: Transparency and clarity

It was noted in chapter 5 that a crucial requirement for a legal framework for manufacturers' guarantees is that there is clarity and transparency with regard to the terms and conditions of such guarantees. There are a number of specific provisions which seek to ensure that guarantees are transparent and that consumers are not misled by guarantees.

8.4.1 Transparency and clarity in the guarantee

First, there is no requirement to draw any conditions that have to be satisfied to the consumer's attention at the time of purchase. The most common requirements are that a consumer may have to return a guarantee registration card or that the guarantee document has to be date-stamped by the seller. Although most guarantors would not insist on compliance with such a requirement (cf. Howells and Weatherill, 1995, p. 159), it seems that such pre-conditions are acceptable provided that these are clearly drawn to the consumer's attention at the time of purchase. There is a gap in English law because it does not ensure that such conditions are adequately drawn to the consumer's attention. However, Regulation 15(3) SSGCR provides that a consumer can ask to see the guarantee and that it must be made available to him either in writing or in another durable medium available and accessible to him.[24] Thus, a consumer who wishes to examine a guarantee before he commits himself to a purchase has to be given the opportunity to do so. This provision has a distinct signalling theory flavour. Although not limited to the pre-purchase context, Regulation 15 (3) enables consumers to consider the guarantees offered with a number of products he may be interested in and to take the guarantee into account in his overall purchasing decision.[25]

Furthermore, where a consumer concludes a contract through distance communication means, Regulation 8 of the Consumer Protection (Distance Selling) Regulations 2000 ("the Distance Selling Regulations") requires that a consumer is given details of guarantees, in writing or in another durable medium available and accessible to him, either before the contract has been concluded or, at the latest, by the time the goods covered by the guarantee are delivered to him. There is an overlap between the SSGCR and the Distance Selling Regulations. A consumer can request details of the guarantee under Regulation 15(3) before he decides on a purchase. A response to such a request would, presumably, be sufficient to comply with Regulation 8. However, even where no such request is made, the consumer still needs to receive information about the guarantee by the time his goods are delivered to him.[26] Unfortunately, it is not clear whether, for example, the guarantee card that is enclosed with the product would be sufficient. This may depend on the amount of information given on the card. However, the obligation to provide the relevant information is on the *supplier* of the goods, and the guarantee card will, in most cases, have been prepared by the *manufacturer*. If the manufacturer is also the supplier, the card may suffice, but in most cases, this will not be so. The supplier may therefore have to provide information about the guarantee to the consumer himself.

8.4.2 Transparency and clarity in advertising

Guarantees may be referred to in advertising. Indeed, under the Consumer Guarantees Directive and the SSGCR, it is envisaged that some guarantees may be based exclusively on advertising. It is therefore necessary to ensure that references to guarantees in advertising do not mislead consumers. The Control of Misleading Advertisements Regulations 1988[27] ("Misleading Advertising Regulations") provide a suitable control mechanism. Regulation 2(2) defines advertising as misleading if in any way, it deceives or is likely to deceive the person to whom it is addressed or whom it reaches and if because of this, it is likely to affect their economic behaviour. Thus, in the context of guarantees, a consumer who bought a particular product in reliance on statements about the guarantee made in advertising, could claim the advertisement was misleading if the guarantor fails to honour the statements made in advertising. Misleading advertising is controlled through an administrative framework. The Director-General of Fair Trading ultimately has the power to ask for an injunction to prevent the continued use of such advertising. In the Enterprise Act 2002, this power is given to other bodies with an interest in consumer protection.

8.5 Procedural regulation: Who can benefit under the guarantee?

It was concluded in chapter 5 that, in order to ensure fairness in the substance of guarantees, a guarantee should be available to anybody who owns the relevant product during the guarantee period. It should therefore be transferable.

The Guarantees Directive left open the possibility that the benefit of a guarantee may be transferred to a subsequent owner of the corresponding goods, such as a second-hand purchaser or a person receiving the goods as a gift. It is at least arguable that Regulation 15(1) SSGCR makes it possible that a subsequent owner can enforce the guarantee.[28] According to Regulation 15(1), where goods are sold or supplied[29] to a consumer, the guarantee takes effect as a contractual obligation owed by the guarantor. "Consumer" is defined in Regulation 2 as:

> Any natural person who, in contracts covered by these Regulations, is acting for purposes which are outside his trade, business or profession.

The phrase "contracts covered by these Regulations", presumably, includes the contractual guarantee created by Regulation 15(1). Crucially, there is no requirement in Regulation 15(1) that the goods are sold or supplied by a person acting in the course of a business. So if a consumer (A) sells or supplies goods to another consumer (B) (a second-hand purchaser or a donee), then B would also be a consumer for the purposes of Regulation 15(1) and could therefore enforce the guarantee in the same way that A could. However, all this is subject to the conditions set out in the guarantee document and the associated advertising. A term in the guarantee which limits the guarantee to the first consumer purchaser would, presumably, mean that the guarantee could then not be enforced by a second-hand purchaser or donee. So although Regulation 15(1) opens up the possibility that a guarantee may be transferred to a subsequent owner of the goods, it does not create an absolute rule to that effect. It is therefore appropriate to consider alternative means of transferring the benefit of a guarantee to subsequent owners.

It is clear that subsequent owners are unlikely to have an automatic right of enforcement against the guarantor, because they will not be a party to the "guarantee contract". However, there may be two potential solutions to this: first, it may be possible for the original consumer to assign his rights under the guarantee to a subsequent owner. Second, it may be possible to utilise the Contracts (Rights of Third Parties) Act 1999 to secure the benefit of the guarantee for a subsequent owner. These are now considered in turn.

8.5.1 Assigning the benefit of the guarantee to a subsequent owner

It may be possible for the original consumer to assign his rights under the guarantee under s.136(1) of the Law of Property Act 1925 ("LPA"). Such an assignment would have to be absolute, i.e., the original consumer would have to give up all entitlements under the guarantee. It also has to be made "by writing under the hand of the assignor [the person making the assignment, i.e. the original consumer]", although no particular wording has to be used. It may be that a reference to the guarantee in a written contract for the sale of the product covered by the guarantee may be enough to satisfy this requirement.[30] Furthermore, the assignment has to be communicated to the assignee, i.e., the third-party consumer. The guarantor has to be given written notice of the assignment (s.136(1) LPA). This may be given either by the original consumer or the third-party consumer. It has to be given before a claim under the guarantee can be made.

Assignments generally relate only to the benefit of a contract. In the context of a guarantee, the assignment would therefore only cover the entitlement to the specified remedy (free repair or replacement) if the product is faulty. However, the guarantee will include terms and conditions on which it is provided, and these may impose a burden on the consumer who seeks to rely on the guarantee.[31] It seems that such terms could be regarded as a "condition of the enjoyment of the benefit" (Treitel, 1999, p.648), and as a consequence, the third-party consumer would have to comply with these in order to benefit from the guarantee.

However, it will not be possible to assign the benefit of a guarantee where the guarantee itself includes a term which provides that the guarantee cannot be assigned. It will be seen below that the Office of Fair Trading, in applying the Unfair Terms in Consumer Contracts Regulations, has taken the view that such a term may be unfair and therefore not binding on a consumer.[32]

The procedure for effecting an assignments is unlikely to be of use in the context of most situations where a consumer transfers ownership of a product under guarantee to another consumer. Consumers are unlikely to follow the correct procedure because it would be unnecessarily burdensome. Moreover, most consumers will not be aware of the legal requirements to effect a valid assignment. Similarly, guarantors are unlikely to be particularly keen on the widespread use of assignments, because this could result in a significant number of notifications that would have to be processed by the guarantor. The alternative offered by the Contracts (Rights of Third Parties) Act 1999 may offer a better solution.

8.5.2 Enabling a subsequent owner to enforce the guarantee

A second possibility may be provided by the Contracts (Rights of Third Parties) Act 1999. This Act enables a person who is not a party to a contract, but mentioned as a potential beneficiary under that contract (the "third party"), to enforce the relevant terms and obtain that benefit. S.1(3) of the Act requires that the third party is identified in the contract "by name, as a member of a class or as answering a particular description but need not be in existence at the time the contract is entered into". Under s.1(1) of the Act, a third party may enforce a term in a contract (a) if the contract provides for this expressly, or (b) if the term in question purports to confer a benefit on the third party. However, alternative (b) is not available where on a proper construction of the contract it appears that the parties to the contract did not intend the term to be enforceable by the third party. Thus, it seems that the transferability of the guarantee would depend on the intentions of the guarantor. Although a guarantee is a contract between guarantor and consumer, the consumer will have had no input in drafting its terms - the guarantor has drafted the guarantee, and it is provided on his terms. There will therefore not be any agreement between consumer and guarantor with regard to the enforceability of the guarantee by a third party. The guarantor has the opportunity to provide for this expressly. If there is no express term, then the guarantor can rebut the presumption in s.1(1)(b).

If a guarantee is to be enforceable by another person, that person would have to be identified in some form in the guarantee. S.1(3) does not require a particularly precise identification. A term which referred to "subsequent owners" would therefore satisfy the definition of a third party, because this is clearly either a class or a particular description. The fact that it will not be possible to say in advance who a "subsequent owner" might be is not a problem because it is not required that the third party is in existence at the time the contract is made.

It must be noted that the Act provides merely a "default setting" (MacMillan, 2000, p.723), i.e., it only applies to the extent that the parties to the contract have not included a term that modifies or disapplies altogether the operation of the Act. Thus, a term in a guarantee that limits the benefit of the guarantee to the original purchaser would be evidence that the Act was not intended to apply to this particular guarantee.[33] On the other hand, if the guarantee included a term that expressly allowed both the original consumer and "subsequent owners" to benefit from the guarantee, then it may be possible for any such subsequent owner of the product covered by the guarantee to use the provisions in the Act to enforce the guarantee against the guarantor.

However, what about the situation where the guarantee does not expressly state who can benefit under the guarantee? It may be possible to argue that the guarantee purports to confer a benefit on any subsequent owner. This possibility requires closer examination. It is important first of all to note that s.1(1) only applies to a particular *term*, rather than to a *contract as a whole*. However, as far as a manufacturer's guarantee is concerned, it is the guarantee as a whole which a consumer would wish to enforce rather than a particular term. If there is an express term by which the benefit of the guarantee is to be made available to all subsequent owners, it may be possible to interpret this provision as a statement that each term of the guarantee should be treated as enforceable by the third party. Where there is no such term, it seems difficult to consider the guarantee as a whole in determining whether it purports to confer a benefit on a third party; rather, it would be necessary to examine each term in turn to establish that it purports to confer a benefit on a third party (cf. MacMillan, 2000, p.725). A distinction would then have to be drawn between terms in a contract the purpose of which is to *confer* a benefit and terms which may merely *be of* benefit to a third party (Adams et.al., 1997, p.241 and p.251). Clearly, most terms in a guarantee will *be of* benefit to a subsequent owner, but it is far from clear that these are intended to *confer* a benefit on a third party. The application of the Act may therefore fail at this stage. Should it be possible to mount this initial hurdle, it is then still necessary to consider if a subsequent owner could enforce the guarantee against the guarantor. The problem is that the guarantee will be silent on the rights of third parties (cf. Roe, 2000, p.891). If so, the test of identification in s.1(3) cannot be satisfied. If a third party is not identified in the way envisaged in s.1(3), it cannot enforce the contract. Thus, a guarantee which is altogether silent on any third parties cannot include terms which purport to confer a benefit on a third party even where they are clearly of benefit to a third party.

This analysis therefore reveals that the 1999 Act will only then be of assistance where there is an express term in the guarantee which states that subsequent owners of the product covered by the guarantee can also benefit from the guarantee. If there is no mention at all of subsequent owners then the Act cannot apply. So unless there is an express term conferring a right of enforcement on a subsequent owner, it will be difficult to show that both guarantor and consumer intended the guarantee to be of benefit to a subsequent owner.

8.5.3 How can the benefit of a guarantee be secured for subsequent owners?

The preceding analysis considered three routes by which a guarantee could benefit persons other than the consumer who bought the relevant product from the seller. Regulation 15(1) SSGCR provides one, albeit limited, route. Neither of the other two routes is particularly useful for consumers. The procedure that has to be followed to effect a valid statutory assignment is cumbersome, and it would be impractical to require a consumer to go through this process when he decides to sell or otherwise transfer a product to another person. The assignment procedure may be of use for long-term guarantees on products such as double-glazing or fitted kitchens, which are the types of products a consumer is likely to leave in a property he is selling. For most consumer products, however, assignment seems to be of little, if any, use.

The 1999 Act is more useful, but its application is also limited. It can only operate where there is a term in the guarantee that could be construed as purporting to confer a benefit on a third party. This party must have been identified. However, the Act is important because it illustrates a vital shift in policy. It is a trite observation that the doctrine of privity and its limitations have been much criticised, particularly in the context of consumer transactions. Indeed, it has been remarked that "seen against the background of a consumer transaction ... the significance of privity of contract is very much reduced" (Jolowicz, 1969, p.3).[34] The 1999 Act indicates that in certain circumstances, this can be overcome and a third-party consumer may benefit from a guarantee. There is no reason why this should not apply to all guarantees. It would therefore be desirable to clarify Regulation 15(1) to ensure that manufacturers' guarantees are freely transferable. Limitations to the original consumer should be rendered unenforceable, although it may be acceptable to allow the guarantor to require notification of the transfer.

8.6 Procedural regulation: Only the Guarantor is required to honour the guarantee

Having considered who can legally benefit from a guarantee, it is now necessary to examine upon whom the law imposes the responsibility to honour the guarantee. In chapter 5, it was suggested that anybody mentioned expressly in the guarantee document should be so responsible.

English law is rather restrictive in this regard. Under Regulation 15(1) of the SSGCR, a guarantee is legally binding only on the guarantor. A consumer cannot enforce a guarantee against any other party.

The decision by Trowbridge County Court in *Alexander v Comet Group plc.* (1995) suggests that a seller could be bound by a manufacturer's guarantee because the guarantee formed an express term of the contract of sale. In *Alexander*, the manufacturer's guarantee included a term which provided that the *retailer* would exchange a faulty product returned within one year of purchase. The judge held that the terms of this guarantee formed express terms of the contract of sale with the retailer, and that the consumer was entitled to rely in law on the retailer, as supplier of the defective product, to act as the manufacturer's agent in providing a replacement. Had the retailer not wanted to be bound by the conditions attached to a guarantee, he should have stated clearly that the guarantee was not part of the terms of the contract of sale. This judgment has not been fully reported and as a County Court judgment is of limited value. It seems that the decision rests on two facts: first, the guarantee document specified that the consumer should contact the retailer if the product in question developed a fault and had to be replaced, rather than the manufacturer. Second, the consumer had emphasised that his purchasing decision had been influenced by the existence of the guarantee and the retailer's pricing policy. Unfortunately, the case is not fully reported, and its correctness may be doubted (see Howells and Weatherill, 1995, p.159).

In chapter 5, it was suggested that there may be network distribution agreements in place which may contain an obligation on network members to honour guarantees on products bought from any member of the network. It has been argued elsewhere (see Twigg-Flesner, 1999c) that in a domestic context, the Contracts (Rights of Third Parties) Act 1999 may operate to provide consumers with a direct right of enforcement against any member of such distribution networks.[35] In such a situation, the consumer would be seeking to enforce the relevant term in the distribution agreement between the manufacturer and an individual member of the distribution network by which that member is required to honour the manufacturer's guarantee, regardless of where the consumer bought the product. On closer analysis, it seems unlikely that the 1999 Act would apply in this context. The term in question may be of benefit to a consumer, but it would be difficult to argue that a term which imposes an obligation on a network member could be regarded as purporting to confer a benefit on a consumer. Although there may be a practical benefit in having an increased number of defendants, but it is unlikely that the term was intended to confer a benefit on the consumer. It is unlikely that the test of enforceability in s.1 of the Act would be satisfied in this case. Furthermore, the relevant term in the distribution agreement may not even refer to the consumers in any way, and as a consequence, the identification requirement in s.1(3) would also not be satisfied.

It can be seen that the analysis of guarantees as contracts has some limitations. In particular, because of the doctrine of privity of contract, the consumer only has a direct claim against the guarantor. This may cause problems in cases where the guarantor has arranged for the retailers in his distribution network or for independent repair service providers to deal with consumer claims under a guarantee. If a retailer or repairer refuses to honour the guarantee, then the consumer would have to bring an action against the guarantor to enforce the guarantee. It is, of course, highly unlikely that a consumer would take either the guarantor or the retailer to court. However, if legal liability for the guarantee is only imposed on the guarantor, the fact that a remedy is often provided by a retailer would be ignored. It would therefore be preferable if the law was modified to make a guarantee binding on any person mentioned in the guarantee document. The 1999 Act demonstrates that there is a willingness to remove the rigidities of the doctrine of privity in particular circumstances and it is submitted that manufacturers' guarantees are also an area where privity should be modified.

8.7 Dealing with claims under a guarantee

In chapter 5, the conclusion was reached that there should be no specific rules for the allocation of costs for claiming under a guarantee, nor for the impact of a claim on the guarantee period. Instead, this should be left to the discretion of the guarantor. There are no specific provisions in English Law for claims made under a guarantee. Specific rules on the extension of the guarantee period whilst a product is examined by a guarantor or on guarantees for goods that are provided as replacements under a guarantee are therefore left to be decided by the guarantor, or through negotiation between consumer and guarantor. However, it may be regarded as unacceptable that the consumer should have to bear the cost of returning goods to the guarantor, and such terms may be unfair under the Unfair Terms in Consumer Contracts Regulations 1999. This does not constitute a universal principle, but rather depends on the circumstances of the particular situation. Yet, any such intervention may make it more difficult for a consumer to gauge the response he is likely to expect from the guarantor. The allocation of costs is an important factor to be taken into account by the consumer in perceiving the willingness of the guarantor to respond to the consumer's problem. Regulating this would take away this factor and make it more difficult for consumers to establish the likely response of the guarantor to his claim. The absence of specific rules for these aspects is therefore not a problem.

8.8 Substantive regulation

It was argued in chapter 5 that in order to enable consumers to assess the usefulness of a particular guarantee mechanism in complaining informally, substantive regulation should be limited to disclosure rules only. Moreover, it was accepted that terms which could be detrimental to consumers should be subject to negative regulation and be removed or declared ineffective.

8.8.1 Positive regulation

There were no specific rules affecting the substance of guarantees in place before the implementation of the Consumer Guarantees Directive. It was seen above that attempts to introduce detailed rules modelled on the MMWA in the Consumer Guarantees Bill 1990 were unsuccessful. The SSGCR are a modest addition to English law. They are limited to promoting the disclosure of the essential details of the guarantee, rather than to set down specific rules as to what a guarantee should provide.

8.8.2 Clear reference to the statutory rights

Prior to the implementation of the Consumer Guarantees Directive, there were few rules in English law which affected the substance of guarantees. Section 5 of the Unfair Contract Terms Act 1977 prohibits the use of certain types of exclusion clauses. The only measure that required a positive addition to a guarantee document is the Consumer Transactions (Restrictions on Statements) Order 1976 ("the 1976 Order"). It was adopted under Part II of the Fair Trading Act 1973, which allows the adoption of secondary legislation to deal with practices which could threaten consumers' economic interests.[36] In essence,[37] the Order requires that where a consumer is supplied with goods and there is a guarantee,[38] there has to be a statement which is clear and conspicuous and to the effect that the guarantee does not affect the statutory rights of a consumer. The impact of this measure has been very limited. Generally, all that has been added to guarantees is a statement along the lines of "This does not affect your statutory rights". This is not a particularly informative statement, and unlikely to be of much use to consumers.[39]

8.8.3 Additions made by the SSGCR 2002

The SSGCR add very little. Regulation 15(2) requires that the guarantee sets out in plain and intelligible language:

> The contents of the guarantee and the essential particulars necessary for making claims under the guarantee, notably the duration and territorial scope of the guarantee as well as the name and address of the guarantor.

This reproduces the provision in Article 6(2) of the Consumer Guarantees Directive. The same points made in relation to Article 6(2) in the previous chapter also apply here and need not be restated. There is therefore very little by way of substantive regulation in English law.

8.8.4 Summary: Positive regulation of the substance of guarantees

There is only a limited degree of positive regulation of the substance of guarantees. It is required that a guarantor provides clear details of the essential aspects of the guarantee, including the procedure for bringing a claim. It is important not to forget the relevance of the EC's ECO-Label.[40] Although there is no general requirement with regard to the duration of a guarantee, manufacturers who wish to obtain the ECO label need to introduce a minimum period for their guarantees. Finally, guarantees must include a statement that a consumer has rights under statute. This is also an important requirement, although a more comprehensive statement of these rights may be of greater use. The rules on what a guarantee must include are therefore not particularly extensive; however, the next section will demonstrate that there are many terms which may *not* be included in a guarantee because they might be unfair.

8.9 Negative regulation

One of the key principles of the legal framework developed in this book is that it should be fair. A fundamental aspect of fairness is that there should not be any unduly burdensome terms in manufacturers' guarantees. It was seen in chapter 2 that there may be terms which seek to restrict the statutory rights of consumers, as well as terms which make it very difficult to obtain the benefit of the guarantee.[41] It was concluded in chapter 5 that these are most suitably dealt with through what has been termed "negative regulation". It is now necessary to consider the existing framework for the negative regulation of manufacturers' guarantees. There are two measures of relevance in this context, the Unfair Contract Terms Act 1977, and the Unfair Terms in Consumer Contracts Regulations 1999. The focus will be on the Regulations. The Law Commission (2002) is working on proposals to combine both measures into one set of rules on unfair terms.

8.9.1 Combating unfair terms: The Unfair Terms in Consumer Contracts Regulations 1999

These Regulations implement Directive 93/13/EEC on Unfair Terms in Consumer Contracts. The Regulations apply to contractual terms which have not been "individually negotiated" (Regulation 5(1)). This is defined in the Regulations as terms which have been drafted in advance and the substance of which the consumer has not been able influence (Regulation 5 (2)). Clearly, this covers a manufacturer's guarantee - the terms and conditions of such a guarantee are drafted by the guarantor and the consumer has not opportunity to negotiate the terms on which the guarantee is provided.

A pre-drafted term will be regarded as unfair "if, contrary to the requirement of good faith, it causes a significant imbalance in the parties' rights and obligations under the contract, to the detriment of the consumer" (Regulation 5). Much has been written about the meaning and potential scope of the term "good faith", but it is not necessary to consider this for present purposes.[42] It is sufficient to note that in *Director-General of Fair Trading v First National Bank plc* (2001), the House of Lords explained that "good faith" covers both procedural and the substantive elements of a contract (per Lord Bingham, paragraph 17).[43] With regard to the procedural elements, it requires that a consumer is made aware of all the relevant terms, and that particular attention is drawn to important or onerous terms. In the context of a guarantee, this could, for example, apply to conditions which require a consumer to maintain a product in a specific manner, particularly if this goes beyond what a consumer would ordinarily expect to do. If this is hidden away in the terms and conditions, the term may be regarded as unfair, but if it is clearly highlighted and easily identifiable by the consumer, it may not be unfair.

As for the substantive element, the House of Lords noted that there are some terms which always create a significant imbalance to the detriment of a consumer (per Lord Steyn, paragraph 37). An example is given by Beale (1995, p.245), who refers to terms which seek to exclude liability for personal injury. Such terms are inherently contrary to the requirement of good faith and therefore unfair. Similarly, in the context of guarantees, a term that seeks to restrict or exclude consumers' rights under the Sale of Goods Act 1979 would be contrary to the good faith requirement in its substantive sense and therefore be unfair.

In assessing whether a particular term is unfair, it is necessary to take into account the nature of the good or services covered by the contract, to consider all the circumstances attending the conclusion of the contract and to the other terms of the contract (Regulation 6(1)). If a term is regarded as unfair, then it will not be binding on the consumer (Regulation 8(1)).

It must be observed that there will not be an assessment of the fairness of a term which defines the main subject matter of the contract, nor of the adequacy of the consideration provided by the consumer (Regulation 6(2)). However, it is nevertheless possible to refer to these aspects when assessing the fairness of other terms in the contract (see Bradgate, 2000, p.92). At one point, the OFT appeared to take the view that the conditions on which a guarantee is provided are not subject to the test of unfairness and could therefore not be reviewed under the Regulations:

> Regulation 3(2) [of the 1994 Regulations] provides that terms which define the subject matter of the contract cannot be assessed for fairness, provided that they are in plain and intelligible language. The conditions of a [guarantee] are likely to come within this exemption (OFT, 1996(d), p.30).

On this view, most of the terms of a guarantee would not be reviewable under the Regulations. In fact, if this particular interpretation of "subject matter of the contract" were correct, then it would logically follow that exclusion clauses in guarantees would similarly not be assessed as to their fairness, because such exclusions would, on this interpretation, also have to be regarded as one of the conditions on which the guarantee is provided. It is submitted that the guarantee promise itself and the remedies for failing to comply with this promise are the "subject matter" of the contract. The terms and conditions on which the guarantee is to be implemented, however, cannot be regarded as falling within the exclusion in Regulation 3(2). This narrow interpretation of the core terms exception is also supported by the House of Lords in *Director-General of Fair Trading v First National Bank plc.* (2001).

However, conditions that may have to be complied with before the guarantee becomes available are unlikely to be subject to the Regulations. This may be either because there is no contract until the conditions have been complied with,[44] or because these could be regarded as core terms.[45]

The Regulations contain a set of rules for their enforcement by public authorities and other organisations with a legitimate interest in protecting consumers (see Twigg-Flesner, 2000b). It is possible for such organisations to challenge terms perceived to be unfair outside the context of a specific case. This enforcement mechanism is co-ordinated by the Office of Fair Trading (OFT),[46] which also publishes a regular *Unfair Contract Terms Bulletin* that provides details of terms which have been challenged successfully. In the following paragraphs, the OFT's approach to guarantees will be examined in more detail to identify the likely scope of the Unfair Terms in Consumer Contracts Regulations 1999 in the context of manufacturers' guarantees.

8.9.2 Limitations and exclusions of statutory rights

An observation that can be made at the outset is that exploitation theory in the context of guarantees continues to be of relevance.[47] This was emphasised by the OFT in its third Bulletin on Unfair Contract Terms:

> Guarantees can be used as a way to cut down on the consumer's legal rights to redress. This can occur where they are in such a way as to exclude all other warranties or implied terms. This can leave consumers without important legal protection, and in a way which is entirely unclear to the consumer without legal advice. (OFT 1997a, p.9, para 2.6).

Indeed, such exclusion clauses have been challenged repeatedly by the OFT. In *Goodalls Caravans Ltd.* (1996), the exclusion clause was very broad:

> The Seller undertakes to assist the purchaser in obtaining from the manufacturer the benefit of any warranty or guarantee given by such manufacturer in respect of the goods; this undertaking of assistance is given an accepted instead of, and expressly exclude, any other guarantee condition or warranty whether express or implied by statute, common law or otherwise.

The OFT objected to the exclusion of the implied terms. A similar term was at issue in *Dampco (UK) Ltd.* and was changed to a statement that clearly referred to the statutory rights of consumers and the fact that these remained unaffected by the guarantee. Similarly, in *Hidden Hearing* (1999), a term in a guarantee which sought to exclude the statutory rights was amended to make it clear that the guarantee did not supersede the rights under the Sale of Goods Act 1979 (SoGA).

In *Laport Garages* (1999), an exclusion of the SoGA implied terms was challenged and the term changed to emphasise that any manufacturer's guarantee was issued in addition to the consumer's statutory rights.[48]

The OFT has also been concerned about the use of the phrase "This does not affect your statutory rights".[49] This is used in most guarantees to indicate that the guarantor does not seek to restrict the rights of consumers under SoGA. However, the phrase on its own is often meaningless and can be confusing, particularly in a context where the guarantee differs significantly in its scope from the system of protection under SoGA. The OFT has therefore begun to encourage traders to revise this statement and be more precise about the nature of the statutory rights. Thus, in *The Babies Paradise Nursery* (1999), the OFT persuaded the trader that the statement was not in plain and intelligible language, and it was amended to give a basic indication of what the statutory rights are.[50]

In *ISL Renosystems* (1999), the standard phrase also contained a clause limiting the amount and type of any damages claim. This was contradictory and confusing and the term was amended simply to make it clear that the guarantee was additional to the consumer's statutory rights. A similar problem arose with the proposed standard contract prepared by the *Glass and Glazing Federation* (1999), a trade association. Again, the guarantee operated as an exclusion clause, but included a reference to the statutory rights. This term was revised to make it clear that the guarantee did not supersede the consumer's statutory rights.

Where there is no such statement, but a likelihood of confusion, the OFT will encourage the inclusion of a clear statement that the statutory rights remain unaffected by the guarantee. This happened in *Dyno-Rod* (2000) and *Town and Country Driveways plc.* (2001).

A slightly different, yet equally confusing statement, was included in *Multiyork Furniture Ltd.* (2000). Here, the guarantee referred to a "statutory one-year guarantee". There is, of course, no such guarantee and the term was amended to clarify that the guarantee was not statutory and that the consumer's statutory rights remained unaffected by the guarantee.

8.9.3 Exclusion clauses in guarantees: The Unfair Contract Terms Act 1977

It should also be noted that the Unfair Contract Terms Act 1977 (UCTA) includes a specific provision on exclusion clauses in manufacturers' guarantees in section 5, for which a separate definition of "guarantee" applies.[51] Section 5(1) prohibits the use of a clause by which a manufacturer seeks to exclude or limit his liability for damage or loss caused by negligence during the manufacturing or distribution process. As noted previously, the Law Commission considers this provision to be redundant.

The 1999 Regulations do not only cover exclusion and limitation clauses, but may also apply to terms which are unfair because they are detrimental to consumers by imposing an unduly high burden upon them. However, in contrast to UCTA, the 1999 Regulations do not render any terms automatically ineffective.

8.9.4 Mandatory arbitration of guarantee disputes

In *Ford Motor Company* (1996), the OFT objected to a clause in a motor vehicle guarantee that required a consumer to accept a term that a dispute under the guarantee would be referred to an arbitrator. It was felt that this was unfair, based on paragraph 1(q) of Schedule 3 to the Regulations.[52] Under the Arbitration Act 1996, consumers cannot be required to agree to arbitration if the amount at issue is below £5,000.[53] A similar term was also challenged in *Dampco (UK) Ltd.* (1999) and in *Vauxhall Motors Ltd* (2000).

8.9.5 Repair and maintenance restrictions

In *Dyno-Rod* (2000), a term in a guarantee was vague and potentially misleading in that it gave the impression that the guarantee would become void unless all repairs and maintenance were carried out by the guarantor. This term was changed to make it clear that routine maintenance did not have to be provided by the guarantor.

8.9.6 Charge to obtain benefit of guarantee

In *Kenwood Damp Proofing* (2000), a term in the guarantee required the consumer to pay a fee to request an inspection of the work that has been carried out. This was revised to provide that this fee would be refunded if the inspection revealed that further work was necessary to complete the contract satisfactorily.

8.9.7 Restrictions on transferability

In *East Yorkshire Aluminium* (1997), a guarantee was offered on double glazing. This guarantee was not assignable. This was felt to be unfair because the guarantee added substantial value to the product and it would be detrimental to consumers if they could not pass on the benefit of the guarantee if they sold their house. The guarantee was amended to provide for assignment subject to conditions.[54] Similarly, in *Rimacroft Ltd.* (2000) a guarantee for a car engine was not transferable. This was changed to provide for the transfer of the guarantee on payment of a fee to cover administrative costs. In this instance, the OFT reserved its position on the amount of the transfer fee, although it accepted that a fee may be charged to process the transfer.[55]

8.9.8 Allocation of costs for providing service under a guarantee

In *Garland Electronics* (1998), a term required that all repair items under guarantee had to be returned to the shop and collected by the customer once repaired. The OFT challenged this term and it was deleted. It was argued that the term had the effect of removing a customer's right to claim back the expenses of returning goods that were faulty at the time of purchase. Here, the guarantee therefore provided less protection to the consumer than the statutory rights. There are a number of points to note about this example. It appears that the guarantee in question was issued by the retailer, rather than by the manufacturer. The retailer is, of course, directly bound by the statutory rules in the SoGA and the guarantee therefore operated as a limitation clause in that the consumer's right to consequential damages was limited. However, if this is seen in the light of the conclusions reached with regard to rules on the allocation of costs for claiming under a guarantee, this decision causes some problems. It was concluded in chapter 5 that the allocation of such costs should be determined by the guarantor. This would enable a consumer to see how willing the guarantor is to deal with complaints. If a term in a guarantee which seeks to allocate at least some of the relevant costs to the consumer is regarded as unfair and therefore unenforceable, it becomes more difficult for consumers to ascertain the responsiveness of that seller to informal complaints. It may have been preferable to require the inclusion of a statement that the retailer would be responsible for all the costs associated with repairs carried out under the SoGA.

8.9.9 Confusing references to guarantee

In *Olympic Warranties* (1996), a term in a vehicle guarantee required that the car had to be serviced every 3,000 miles, or the guarantee would become void. This particular term only appeared on a sticker on the back of the policy document. The term was deemed unfair because the term was not properly drawn to the attention of the consumer.

Microsoft UK (1998) highlights a problem of a different kind. The guarantee in this decision was a software guarantee, but the problem identified here is of wider application. Many consumer products are imported from the United States, and carry guarantees that are designed to comply with the U.S. rules.[56] The guarantee in question in *Microsoft* read as follows:

> Limited Warranty: Microsoft warrants that the support provided hereunder shall be substantially as described. This warranty is exclusive and is in lieu of all other warranties and Microsoft disclaims all other warranties, express or implied, including but not limited to, warranties of merchantability and fitness for a particular purpose.

There are a number of problems with this guarantee: It seeks to exclude liability for the implied terms. This is clearly unfair under the Unfair Contract Terms Regulations. Furthermore, it is also an offence under the Consumer Transactions (Restrictions on Statements) Regulations 1976. In addition, the guarantee refers to "merchantability". This was replaced with "satisfactory quality" in 1994. Reference to the old standard was likely to mislead consumers.

However, it is interesting to note that the OFT did not require a change to the title of the guarantee, and this continues to be known as a "limited warranty". This is despite the fact that this designation is all but meaningless in the United Kingdom. The guarantee in question had clearly been drafted for the U.S. market and complied with the rules of that jurisdiction. This is a problem which appears with some regularity - often, products marketed in the U.S. and the UK will have the same guarantee, despite the fact that U.S.-style guarantees would fall foul of UK legislation. Consequently, consumers may be confused by the terminology used and the existence of exclusion and limitation clauses, which are illegal in the UK but may be acceptable under U.S. rules. It is desirable that this problem is addressed by the OFT in the near future.

8.9.10 Other terms which may be unfair

The survey of unfair terms in this section has focused on those terms which have been the subject of OFT enforcement under the 1999 Regulations. However, there are other terms which may be regarded as unfair under the regulations. Thus, it seems likely that a requirement to return a product under guarantee in the original packaging may be regarded as unfair - it would undoubtedly be sufficient if the consumer were required to take adequate care in packaging the product before returning it to the guarantor.[57]

8.9.11 Usefulness of the 1999 regulations for dealing with unfair terms

Following this discussion, a number of conclusions can be drawn on the application of the Regulations to manufacturers' guarantees. First, it must be emphasised that the view the OFT has taken of a clause in a particular guarantee is not necessarily of general application. For example, in a number of cases, the OFT regarded a restriction on the transfer of a guarantee as unfair. The products in those cases were double glazing and a car engine, and the guarantees had a duration of several years. Both products are usually expensive, but are also likely to be "sold" on, e.g., when the consumer moves house or sells his car. In such circumstances, the guarantee is of great value. The position may be less clear-cut in the context of every-day consumer products, which are often used more intensively and have a greater likelihood of breaking down. However, it was noted before that it would in any event be desirable that guarantees are freely transferable. The important point is that a term which may be unfair in one guarantee may not be so in another.

Moreover, the scope of the Regulations is such that some terms may be regarded as unfair and therefore as unenforceable where the retention of such a term would, in fact, indicate to the consumer that the guarantor may not be particularly receptive to complaints and therefore use the particular term as a barrier to reduce the number of claims under the guarantee. Thus, terms which require the consumer to assume some or all of the costs related to the implementation of a guarantee are likely to be regarded as unfair. However, as explained in chapter 5, a consumer may draw conclusions as to the responsiveness of the guarantor to a complaint from such terms, and it would be preferable if these were retained. It may seem strange to advocate the retention of terms which may be significantly unfavourable to consumers. It must be borne in mind that this only relates to a few specific terms in a guarantee, i.e., those which set out the rules on bringing a claim under the guarantee. If these are restrictive, then it seems likely that the guarantor would be less responsive to a complaint than if these were generous to the consumer. If all such restrictive terms were unfair and therefore ineffective, the signalling function of such terms would become ineffective, and consumers may find it more difficult to obtain redress.

Generally, the existence of a regime to control unfair terms in a guarantee is vital in promoting the use of guarantees to seek redress informally. As noted before[58], the problem with guarantees as an informal redress mechanism is that it has been drafted by the person who will also have some responsibility for the product defect covered by the guarantee. Although the terms on which guarantees are provided enable consumers to ascertain how responsive the guarantor is likely to be to informal complaints, there also has to be a reflection of fundamental expectations of fairness within these terms. The 1999 Regulations provide a useful means of preserving fairness in the substance of guarantees, although there are some terms which might be regarded as unfair under the Regulations and yet be valuable in establishing guarantor responsiveness.

8.10 The relationship between guarantees and statutory rights

In chapter 5, it was argued that there should be no direct link between guarantees and the statutory rights and that both should operate concurrently. Thus, a consumer who has decided to rely on a guarantee should not be deprived of invoking his statutory rights if his complaint is not resolved to his satisfaction under the guarantee.

8.10.1 The position at common law: Guarantees and statutory rights are distinct

It has already been seen that in English law, guarantees and statutory rights are treated as distinct matters. Thus, where a guarantee is given, it is not permissible to try to limit the statutory rights of consumers, and it is necessary to include a statement in the guarantee that these statutory rights are not affected by the guarantee. However, there is no requirement that the guarantee must offer a benefit at a level which is equal to, or even exceeds, the statutory rights. It is therefore possible to offer a guarantee that only promises repair for a period of six months, which is a considerably shorter period than under the statutory rights.[59] The seminal judicial exploration of the relationship between guarantees and the statutory rights is provided by Mustill LJ in *Rogers v Parish* (1987). In this case, the claimants had bought a Range Rover which cost £14,000. This was defective but the claimants agreed to a replacement vehicle. However, there were numerous problems with the replacement car, and the claimants eventually sought to reject the car and obtain a refund. One of the questions to be considered by the Court of Appeal was whether the existence of a manufacturer's guarantee had an impact on the application of the quality standard in s.14(2).[60] Mustill LJ observed:

> I am far from satisfied that [the argument that the existence of a manufacturer's guarantee suggests that the consumer would have to accept some types of defects] is open to the defendants at all, having regard to the express disclaimer in the contract of sale, and also in the [guarantee], of any intention to vary the buyer's rights at common law... Nor am I convinced that this objection can satisfactorily be answered by saying that the argument founded on the [guarantee] operates not to deprive the buyer of his common law rights but rather as a relevant circumstance for the purposes of s.14(6) operating simply to diminish the reasonable expectations of the buyer. ... Can it really be right to say that the reasonable buyer would expect less of his new Ranger Rover with a [guarantee] than without one? Surely the [guarantee] is an addition to the buyer's rights, not a subtraction from them, and, it may be noted, only a circumscribed addition since it lasts for a limited period and does not compensate the buyer for consequential loss and inconvenience. If the defendants are right a buyer would be well advised to leave his guarantee behind in the showroom. This cannot be what the manufacturers and dealers intend or what their customers reasonably understand.

This passage makes two important points: first, it cannot be accepted that a guarantee should be taken into account when determining whether a particular product is of satisfactory quality.[61] Otherwise it would follow that goods which are defective but could be repaired under the guarantee would still be of satisfactory quality. Second, Mustill LJ notes that a guarantee operates in addition to the statutory rights, but does not have to provide greater benefits - he accepts that guarantees can be more restrictive in the rights they offer to consumers. *Rogers v Parish* therefore confirms that guarantees and statutory rights are to be treated separately. This is subject to the requirement already discussed, that a guarantee must not seek to exclude the statutory rights of consumers. This position was also adopted in *Alexander v Comet Group plc* (1995). Here, a judge at Trowbridge County Court held that a consumer was free to choose whether to bring a claim under the SoGA against the retailer or under a manufacturer's guarantee. Although not of value as a precedent, it nevertheless illustrates the general attitude in English law that statutory rights and guarantees operate concurrently, yet independently.

It should also be noted that the fact that a consumer requires a seller to repair goods which do not meet the standard of satisfactory quality will not be regarded as an acceptance of these goods, and a consumer would not lose his right of rejection if he agreed to a repair (or replacement) by the seller (s.35(6)(a) SoGA). Unfortunately, this section is limited to repairs made by or under an arrangement with the seller. If repairs are carried out under a manufacturers' guarantee, this section will not apply, because the repair would be made by or under an arrangement with the manufacturer.[62] It would be beneficial if this section were amended to include repairs agreed to under a manufacturer's guarantee.

A problem which has not been addressed in the Sale and Supply of Goods to Consumers Regulations 2002 is the relationship between the remedial regime introduced into the Sale of Goods Act 1979 as Part 5A, and remedies provided under a guarantee. A difficulty may arise where a seller to deal with claims under a manufacturer's guarantee by providing repair or replacement of the defective goods. Under the new Part 5A, the seller is already required to repair/replace non-conforming goods. It may therefore be difficult, if not impossible, to identify whether a particular repair is carried out under the guarantee or by virtue of the seller's obligations under the Sale of Goods Act 1979. This may, however, be significant, e.g., if the seller takes longer than expected to provide a remedy. Under Part 5A, the consumer may then claim a price reduction, or even rescission of the contract of sale, but he would not be entitled to do so if the repair was delayed under the guarantee. This may not be of great practical significance, but it is nevertheless a point which may, on occasion, cause confusion. Clarification of this aspect would have been welcome.

8.11 Enforcement

In chapter 5, it was seen that there are a number of enforcement mechanisms and sanctions. A distinction was made between general and specific mechanisms, and a further distinction between private (e.g., contractual) and public (criminal or administrative) ones. It was argued that a general principle of good faith, or fair dealing, together with an administrative enforcement mechanism would suffice in the context of manufacturers' guarantees. There appears to be no need to introduce specific sanctions, or to introduce criminal penalties.

In this section, all the relevant enforcement mechanisms and the available sanctions either for a failure by a guarantor to comply with the legal framework for guarantees or for a refusal to honour his guarantee will be considered. It must be noted that most of the measures considered below are of a general nature and are not limited to manufacturers' guarantees.

8.11.1 Private enforcement

Private enforcement in the context of guarantees would be an action for breach of contract. This would require a consumer to launch a claim against the guarantor on the basis that the guarantor has failed to comply with the terms and conditions of the guarantee. It has already been remarked that this is unlikely to be utilised by consumers.

Moreover, the SSGCR provide that a failure to meet the requirements set down in Regulation 15 does not deprive the guarantee of its legally binding nature, and the consumer can still enforce this against the guarantor. It will be seen further below that there is a possibility to take action under other measures. Furthermore, Regulation 15 contains a specific procedure for the enforcement of the provisions on guarantees.

8.11.2 Regulatory enforcement: Criminal

It was concluded in chapter 5 that no criminal sanctions would be required. Yet, a number of measures which fall within the category of criminal enforcement apply to manufacturers' guarantees. One of these has already been discussed. Failure to comply with the Consumer Transactions (Restrictions of Statements) Order 1976 is a criminal offence under s.23 of the Fair Trading Act 1973. A further measure is the Trade Descriptions Act 1968.

8.11.3 The Trade Descriptions Act 1968

The Trade Descriptions Act 1968 (TDA) is a general measure which may apply to the provision of manufacturers' guarantees. Section 14 of the Act makes it an offence for any person in the course of any trade or business to make a statement which he knows to be false or recklessly to make a statement which is false, with regard to the matters specified in that section.[63] These include the provision of any services and the nature of any services. It may be that guarantees could fall within the scope of that section, provided that guarantees are regarded as a service for the purposes of s.14. Unfortunately, the case-law under s.14 is far from clear. In *Breed v Cluett* (1970), a vendor of a house had falsely stated that the house was covered by the National House-Builders' Registration Council ten-year guarantee. In a very brief judgment, Lord Parker CJ suggested that this statement fell within s. 14(1) of the Trade Descriptions Act 1968. If so, the provision of a guarantee would, indeed, be a "service", and false statements about a guarantee could be dealt with under this section. This question was revisited in *Ashley v London Borough of Sutton* (1994). In this case, a book containing a betting strategy was advertised in a mailshot. The mailshot contained a satisfaction guarantee:

> Our guarantee is straightforward and unmatched by any other publication known today. [We] invite you to try out the complete Formula 2 strategy for a whole 90 days. Then if you *for any reason* feel it is not the most powerful and profitable strategy you have ever seen, just return it. We'll be happy to buy it back from you right away, for the full price you paid.

When consumers who bought the book tried to invoke the guarantee, this was refused by the defendant. He was convicted by magistrates of a breach of s.14(2)(b). The Divisional Court was asked whether it was correct to decide that the guarantee constituted a service within the meaning of s.14 TDA. Unfortunately, Scott Baker J. did not consider whether the guarantee itself constituted the service, but rather focused on whether a consumer who bought the book had bought "goods" or a service, i.e., the betting strategy contained in the book. Surprisingly, he concluded that the book was a service and that s.14 applied. This decision has been much criticised. Oughton and Lowry (2000, p.524) take the view that it was incorrect to find that the book was a service, and instead, there was merely the supply of goods, that is, the book itself. This view is shared by Cartwright (1996, p.60). This appears to be the correct view. The Divisional Court clearly misunderstood the question it had been asked. However, the case is still of some value for the present discussion. *Ashley* concerned a money-back (or "satisfaction") guarantee,[64] and it is difficult to describe the service provided in this context. Indeed, in *Dixons Ltd. v Roberts* (1984), the Court of Appeal held that an offer by Dixons to pay the difference in price should a customer be able to find a product purchased at Dixons at a lower price elsewhere did not constitute a provision of a service. In *Newell and Taylor v Hicks* (1984), it was noted that a service should be regarded as "doing something for somebody" (Goff LJ at p.313). The promise to provide a refund did not constitute a service within that definition. Cartwright comments that had this been cited to the court in *Ashley*, it would have come to the conclusion that the money-back guarantee would not be a service within the meaning of s.14 after all (Cartwright, 1996, p.61).

In contrast, manufacturers' guarantees do not normally promise a refund, but instead offer repair or replacement of products which are not working in the way promised by the guarantor. Surely, there can be no doubt that this *would* constitute the provision of a service, or a facility, within the meaning of s.14, and therefore any failure to honour a guarantee could be a breach of this section.

Harvey and Parry (2000, p.404, n.6) query whether the failure by Ashley to honour the money-back guarantee, rather than being a criminal offence under the TDA, should be treated simply as a breach of contract. There can be little doubt that such a refusal to honour a guarantee will be a breach of contract, and that it may be possible to rely on regulatory enforcement instead.[65] Indeed, the use of regulatory enforcement was preferred over criminal ones in chapter 5.

However, the possibility of a criminal conviction for a failure to honour a guarantee is a powerful sanction which could be a final resort if a particular guarantor persistently refuses to honour his guarantees. Still, the existence of administrative mechanisms may render the need for a criminal enforcement mechanism unnecessary.

8.11.4 Regulatory enforcement

In chapter 5, it was argued that a general "good faith" or "fairness" principle is required to control the application of a guarantee in a particular case. Such a principle could be used to ensure that a guarantor would not exercise the discretion under his guarantee in an unfair and arbitrary manner. It was also argued that such a principle would best be enforced by a public body. It has already been seen that procedural and substantive fairness is reflected in various disclosure rules and in the Unfair Terms in Consumer Contracts Regulations 1999. This section will consider the extent to which a general principle of fairness in performance is enforced in English law.

8.11.5 Fairness in performance: Dealing with unfair conduct

Before the enactment of the Enterprise Act 2002 (which is due to come into force in 2003), there were two measures which provided for regulatory powers in the field of consumer protection to promote fairness: Part III of the Fair Trading Act 1973 ("FTA") and the Stop-Now Orders Regulations 2001 (SNORs), which implement Directive 98/27/EC. In 1999, the UK government presented its White Paper *Modern Markets: Confident Consumers*, in which it announced that it would reform these powers. The Enterprise Act received Royal Assent on 7 November 2002. Part 8 of the Act will make available the relevant regulatory powers to protect consumers. Rather than to discuss the nuts-and-bolts of the current and new provisions in detail, this section will instead focus on the key aspects of these measures.

Section 34 FTA empowered the Director-General of Fair Trading (DGFT) to take action where a trader has persisted in a course of conduct which is (a) detrimental to the interests of consumers and (b) to be regarded as unfair to consumers. Ss.34 (2) and (3) FTA explain that "unfair conduct" covers a course of conduct which contravenes a measure imposing duties, prohibitions or restrictions on the trader which are enforceable by criminal sanctions, as well as a course of conduct by the trader that involves a breach of contract or a breach of a duty, both at common law and under statute, which can be enforced by civil proceedings. S.211 of the Enterprise Act 2002 (EA) no longer refers to this as "unfair conduct", but instead calls this "domestic infringements". The section empowers the Secretary of State for Trade and Industry to make Regulations specifying what constitutes a domestic infringement, and provides broad examples. In short, "domestic infringements" under the EA would still be some kind of infringement of relevant legal provisions. This significantly restricts the usefulness of the Act as it does not cover unfair conduct which is technically lawful. Furthermore, the infringement must cause harm to the collective interests of consumers (s.211(1)(c) EA). The Act (like the FTA) will therefore have no application to isolated consumer disputes.

The SNORs only applied to so-called "community infringements", which are infringements by a trader of the measures that implement specific E.C. directives. S.212 EA re-enacts these simply as "community infringements". Such infringements are a breach of the rules implementing an EC directive, and any rules going beyond the directive but adopted or retained as part of the implementation. This must also harm the collective interests of consumers. The test is taken from the Injunctions Directive (98/27/EC), but it is not further defined. It seems that, as a minimum, it must require that more than one consumer is affected by the conduct in question.

In the context of guarantees, therefore, the Enterprise Act will only be relevant if there is a failure to comply with the rules set out in Regulation 15 SSGCR, and only if this harmed the collective interests of consumers. Under the Act, any qualified entity[66] is entitled to bring proceedings, although the Office of Fair Trading is to assume a co-ordinating role. The enforcement authority is required to make the trader concerned aware of its intention to apply for a court order to prevent the continuation of the unfair conduct, and undertakings by the trader to cease the conduct may be accepted instead.

The difficulty with the Enterprise Act (as with the FTA/SNORs) is that each requires that a rule of law is infringed in some way. This limits their usefulness in the context of guarantees. Frequently, a dispute between guarantor and consumer will be in respect of the exercise of the guarantor's discretion regarding the remedy to be provided. A guarantor may have exercised his discretion in a manner that may be regarded as unfair, but this may not be unlawful. In such circumstances, there would be no grounds for action. The problems that consumers have to deal with are neatly summarised by the National Consumer Council thus:

> None of [Part III] helps the consumers who have complained of unfair treatment. They are unlikely to have got any satisfaction from making their complaint. They are confused by the apparent inaction while the Director General waits for enough complaints to mount up to prove 'persistence'. They may even find out that what seemed to them to be unfair is acceptable under the law (NCC, 1997, p.2).

It is therefore not surprising that there have been repeated calls for the reform of Part III FTA, of which the NCC's report cited above is a recent one. The NCC itself made a number of recommendations. In particular, it argued that the regime should be extended not only to cover behaviour which is oppressive or deceptive, yet not against the law, but also place a duty on traders not to engage in unfair practices. Furthermore, the NCC envisaged the use of codes of practice for "problem sectors". Such codes would set down minimum acceptable benchmarks for fair trading in that sector.

The Enterprise Act continues with the requirement that there must be a breach of relevant civil or criminal provisions, and the Secretary of State for Trade and Industry is given the power to make Regulations detailing the provisions which may be relevant. Furthermore, the conduct must harm the collective interests of consumers. Thus, court orders would only be available for practices that are against the law, and only where such practices harm the collective interests of consumers. A recurring failure to comply with the legal framework for guarantees could satisfy this requirement. If the recent development towards treating the unfair exercise of contractual discretion as a breach of an implied term continues to develop (see 8.3, above) then it would be possible to regard the arbitrary exercise of discretion in a guarantee as a breach of contract. This would be a welcome development. However, there would still have to be some sort of impact on the collective interests of consumers. It may therefore be concluded that the regulatory enforcement mechanism will only be of limited assistance.

8.11.6 Designated enforcement basis in the SSGCR

Regulations 15(6) and 15(7) of the SSGCR provide a further basis for regulatory enforcement of the implementing provisions. Regulation 15(6) specifies that an enforcement authority (defined as the DGFT and every weights and measures authority) may apply for an injunction. Under Regulation 15(7), a court may grant an injunction on terms it thinks fit. This provision would allow regulatory enforcement authorities to apply for an injunction without having to satisfy the requirement that the collective interests of consumers are harmed or that the guarantor has persisted in conduct which amounts to a failure to comply with Regulation 15. At this stage, it is not possible to say how this provision will operate in practice. This enforcement mechanism seems to be more readily available than under the Enterprise Act. It is not clear if in practice, the enforcement authorities will only intervene if there are several complaints about a particular guarantor, and even then it seems probable that attempts will be made to persuade the guarantor to amend his guarantee or to give undertakings to the enforcement authority to do so.[67]

8.12 Conclusions

This chapter has undertaken a detailed analysis not only of the impact of the Consumer Guarantees Directive on the English rules on guarantees, but of the vast array of different legal rules which have an impact on consumer product guarantees. It is evident from this that the framework for guarantees in English law is such that it largely supports the use of guarantees as one way of obtaining redress informally if there is a quality problem with consumer goods.

There are, however, several uncertainties in respect of particular aspects of this legal framework. Thus, despite the apparent wide scope of Regulation 15(1) SSGCR, it is still not clear that a guarantee could be transferred to a subsequent owner of the corresponding goods. It is desirable that this is clarified by a clear provision which makes guarantees transferable to subsequent owners.

Moreover, although there are strong signs that the English courts are finally accepting the need to adopt a good faith criterion, at least in the context of contractual discretion, this development is not yet complete. It is hoped that subsequent cases will firmly establish a principle that any form of contractual discretion must be exercised in good faith, and that a failure to do so is to be treated as a breach of an implied term to that effect.

Finally, it is desirable that the relationship between Part 5A SoGA and guarantees is clarified. Currently, it may not be clear whether a seller repairs goods in pursuance of his statutory obligations, or under a manufacturer's, or his own, guarantee. As the consequences of inadequate repair may differ, there is a real danger of confusion.

All in all, however, the legal framework on guarantees in English law is not particularly restrictive, and gives sufficient freedom to guarantors to use their guarantees to indicate their willingness to deal with consumer complaints informally.

Notes

1 See chapter 6.

2 The Trade Descriptions Act 1968 or the Fair Trading Act 1973 (the latter replaced by the Enterprise Act 2002); see 8.11, below.

3 However, it was seen in chapter 2 that it seems to be a common practice for some large retailers to "buy-out" a manufacturers' guarantee and to offer products at lower prices (at 2.2). Presumably this should be acceptable as long as consumers are aware that no manufacturer's guarantee is provided with a particular product.

4 There seems to be an inherent contradiction in the NCC's report. On the one hand, the NCC rejected reforms to the SoGA because it contains a flexible quality standard common to all products (at para 5.1.2), but then it sought to require guarantees to adopt the same standard for the defects that would trigger the manufacturer's guarantee.

5 Such as their function as a redress mechanism - see chapter 4.

6 "(1) In the case of goods of a type ordinarily supplied for private use or consumption, where loss or damage -
(a) arises from the goods proving defective while in consumer use; and
(b) results from the negligence of a person concerned in the manufacture or distribution of the goods,
liability for the loss or damage cannot be restricted by reference *to any contract term or notice contained in or operating by reference to a guarantee of the goods.*" (my emphasis - see main body of text).

7 See chapter 7 at 7.1.

8 In the case of a guarantee offered by a retailer, there is normally no question that any such guarantees are legally binding. Retailers' guarantees are guarantees offered at the same time that the contract for the sale of the actual product is concluded. Either the guarantee becomes a term of the contract of sale itself, or it will be a collateral contract, based on a direct representation by the retailer to the consumer, who then enters into the contract for the sale of the product.

9 In *Chappel & Co. Ltd. v Nestle Co. Ltd.* (1960), three chocolate wrappers were held to be sufficient consideration for a record. See *Benjamin's Sale of Goods*, para. 14-020.

10 The National Consumer Council's proposal for such a rule (NCC, 1989b) was ultimately rejected by the government at the time.

11 For a more detailed consideration of this case law, see Bradgate (1991).

12 Under a hire-purchase arrangement, the seller sells the car to a finance house which in turn enters into a contract with the consumer. The consumer is therefore not in a contractual relationship with the seller, but with the finance house.

13 In the terminology of Adams and Brownsword (2000) this would be a consumer-welfarist realist approach. Realists feel able to adapt the rules of contract law to ensure a fair outcome. Those realists who could be described as consumer-welfarists seek to ensure that consumers are treated fairly.

14 If the statement were ambiguous, it would, presumably, have to be construed in favour of the consumer.

15 It must be noted that statements in advertising are to be taken into account in assessing whether a product has met the statutory quality standard under the Consumer Guarantees Directive. See chapter 1 at 1.4. Also, statements about guarantees made in advertising will now be enforceable.

16 "*£100* will *be paid* ..." (emphasis added)

17 e.g., "*seeks to arrange*", "*ensures*", "*arranges*" etc.

18 The decision is also significant in that it highlights a conflict in the law of contract when its general principles are to be applied in a consumer context. The distinction between the wording of the notice in *Bowerman* and the advertisement in *Carlill* drawn by Hirst LJ may be appropriate in a commercial context, where attention to fine detail may be crucial in determining the contractual status of certain statements, but it seems nonsensical to require the same degree of precision in a consumer context.

19 However, it should be noted that in none of the cases where a collateral contract was found did the trader hand over a document which contained his promise (which would be akin to a guarantee document) and then deny liability.

20 The consultation document offers no explanation (see DTI, 2002).

21 Although this would be very unlikely ever to happen.

22 But see chapter 3 for evidence that most consumers are unlikely to do so.

23 See 8.9.1 and following.

24 See the discussion in chapter 7 at 7.3.2.

25 Regulation 15 (3) of SSGCR 2002 states that "on request by the consumer to [the guarantor and any other person who offers to consumers the goods which are the subject of the guarantee for sale or supply - Regulation 15(4)], the guarantee shall within a reasonable time be made available in writing or in another durable medium available and accessible to him".

26 These broad rules may be contrasted with the much more detailed rules adopted under the Magnuson-Moss Act 1975 - see chapter 6.

27 These implement Directive 84/450/EEC on misleading advertising.

28 This point was made by Robert Bradgate in his response to the DTI's second consultation. I am grateful to Professor Bradgate for providing me with a copy of his response.

29 "Supply" is defined in Regulation 2 as including supply by way of sale, lease, hire or hire-purchase. However, this is not an exhausting definition, and there is nothing to suggest that a supply by way of gift would fall outside the meaning of "supply" in the SSGCR.

30 However, it is unlikely that there will be many such written contracts in practice.

31 This may include the need to provide the relevant marketing information on a guarantee registration card, or to provide proof of purchase.

32 See below.

33 See 2.1.3 for examples of such terms.

34 This is true both for vertical and horizontal privity. Thus, the adherence to a system of front-line retailer liability under the SoGA and the Guarantees Directive lacks a convincing justification other than the existence of privity between retailer and consumer. In the same vein, restrictions of the statutory rights to the original consumer appear outdated. See chapter one (at 1.5.5) and Bradgate and Twigg-Flesner (2002).

35 See also Flechtner (1998), p.427 for a U.S. case where a third-party consumer was able to enforce a seller's promise to the manufacturer to perform guarantee service. Flechtner noted that, if correct, the inevitable consequence of such an approach would be the introduction of exclusion clauses to cover this eventuality. Indeed, the operation of the 1999 Act in English law could, presumably, be displaced by a suitably worded exclusion clause.

36 The complex procedure in the Act has resulted in its being called a "failure" - see Howells and Weatherill (1995), p.503. Part II will be repealed when the relevant provisions of the Enterprise Act 2002 come into force, probably in the summer of 2003. The 1976 order will be preserved, as will the enforcement mechanism under ss.23-33 FTA. The Act provides that ss.23-33 may be repealed by Statutory Instrument should the 1976 order be repealed.

37 Regulation 4 applies to sellers, Regulation 5 to manufacturers and distributors. This summary combines the two Regulations into one.

38 Of course, the Order does not only apply to guarantees. It covers all instances where sellers or manufacturers give a specific promise about what they will do if goods are defective in some way.

39 The Office of Fair Trading has taken the view that it is not sufficiently clear and precise under the Unfair Terms in Consumer Contracts Regulations 1999, unless there is at least an additional statement either summarising the statutory rights or directing the consumer to a Trading Standards Department for further advice.

40 See chapter 6.

41 See 2.3.1.

42 See e.g., the collections edited by Beatson and Friedman (1995), Brownsword, Hird and Howells (1999) and Forte (1999).

43 This was also the view taken by the Court of Appeal and the judge at first instance. As far as the procedural element is concerned, the lower courts followed the analysis by Hugh Beale (1995) and observed that the intention was to prevent "unfair surprise". In this respect, the "good faith" concept would regard a term as unfair if it introduced an obligation or restriction on the consumer which he would not normally expect in the particular contract, unless special steps were taken to draw this term to the consumer's attention.

44 If these are regarded as "contingent" conditions; i.e., that there cannot be a binding contract until that condition is fulfilled.

45 It would be a core term because compliance with the condition would be the consideration provided by the consumer. However, there may be a difficulty in reconciling this with Regulation 15(1) SSGCR. This deems all guarantees to be legally enforceable as a contractual obligation, and thereby overrides the need to identify offer, acceptance, intention to create legal relations and consideration. In that sense, a consumer may not provide any "consideration" at all. If so, then these conditions could not be treated as core terms, but would have to be regarded as conditions precedent. There would therefore be no contract until the consumer has complied with them, and the Regulations could not apply to deal with any such requirements.

46 Strictly speaking, it is the Director-General of Fair Trading and his office which has this responsibility. The Enterprise Act 2002 will convert the Office of the Director-General into the Office of Fair Trading.

47 See 2.3.1.

48 Similar problems were dealt with in *Kenwood Damp Proofing* (2000), *Aspen Windows Group* (2000), *Emanuel Spence Ltd* (2000), *Haygate Engineering Company Ltd* (2000), *R C Woodhouse* (2000) and *Nationwide Security Blinds* (2002).

49 See above.

50 This policy has been pursued further, and changes to clarify the relationship between a guarantee and the statutory rights were also effected in *Adorn Supplies* (1999), *Hidden Hearing* (2001), *Yakamoto Futon Centre* (2001) and *Timberland Flooring Company* (2002). In *Comet Group plc* (2001) an extended warranty was challenged in a similar way. The revised term is "The contents of this policy do not affect your statutory rights. If you have any doubts about your statutory rights, please contact your local Trading Standards Department or Citizens' Advice Bureau".

51 The definition of "guarantee" in this section has already been discussed. See above.

52 It also failed to comply with the requirements of the Consumer Arbitration Act 1988 (now replaced by the Arbitration Act 1996).

53 Under s.91 of the Arbitration Act 1996, the Regulations apply to arbitration agreements. The Unfair Arbitration Agreements (Specified Amount) Order 1999 (SI 1999/2167) creates a conclusive presumption that arbitration agreements are unfair and therefore unenforceable against a consumer if the amount in dispute is below £5,000.

54 The relevant term in that contract provides that the company will not accept liability under the guarantee unless a claim is made by the original purchaser, or by a person who can produce a chain of documentary evidence that shows that the benefit of the guarantee was transferred to subsequent owners. This still seems to be a fairly onerous term.

[55] See also the earlier discussion on assignment. The contract term in question only sought to prevent the assignment of the guarantee. The inherent restriction of guarantees to the original purchaser, which flows directly from the classification of guarantees as contracts, is not affected. If it were, then the doctrine of privity would in itself be contrary to the requirement of good faith. Although this may be an interesting line of thought to pursue, it falls outside the scope of this book.

[56] Discussed in detail in chapter 6.

[57] The European Commission is compiling unfair contract terms in its CLAB database. This contains further examples of unfair terms in manufacturers' guarantees. These are not considered in this book because the most common unfair terms have been dealt with in the text, and little to advance the argument would be added to the discussion in this chapter by an examination of additional unfair terms.

[58] See chapter 4.

[59] Under the Consumer Guarantees Directive, such a right exists for at least two years. See 1.4.

[60] See chapter one (at 1.5). This case arose before the 1994 amendments, when the test to be applied under s.14(2) was that of "merchantable quality".

[61] Contrast this with Bridge (1999).

[62] However, if the seller is responsible for repairs under guarantee as well, s.35(6)(a) SoGA may apply.

[63] In its White Paper *Modern Markets: Confident Consumers*, the UK government proposed to amend the Trade Descriptions Act to remove the requirement in s.14 that the trader must have acted knowingly or recklessly. No changes to the Act have been made.

[64] For a discussion, see 2.4.

[65] Indeed, Clayson (1995) notes that Ashley also gave an undertaking under the Control of Misleading Advertisements Regulations 1988.

[66] "Qualified Entities" are organisations designated by the Secretary of State as representing the interests of consumers.

[67] Although the DGFT can obtain an injunction to prevent the continued use of unfair terms without having to demonstrate harm to the collective interest to consumers or persistence, only one case has been heard so far. It seems unlikely that there would be an influx of cases involving guarantees.

Chapter 9

Consumer Product Guarantees - Conclusions

Overview

The purpose of this book has been to examine consumer product guarantees, to consider their function and to develop a suitable legal framework for guarantees. It has been seen that signalling theory, which postulates a link between product quality and guarantees, is only useful to a limited extent. In most cases, guarantees do not accurately reflect the likely level of quality to be expected from a product. Instead, guarantees are most likely to be of relevance when a consumer is seeking to obtain redress when a product has developed a fault which can be attributed to the manufacturing process. Empirical evidence reveals that almost all consumers will seek to obtain redress themselves without taking legal advice and the assistance of a dispute resolution mechanism which involves a third-party (such as mediation or the small-claims court procedure). This is not due to a lack of awareness, but primarily because the cost of utilising such mechanisms often exceeds the benefit of resolving the dispute. Furthermore, the literature on consumer complaining behaviour has identified a number of factors which have a bearing on how consumers respond to particular problems. These include the extent to which an addressee of a complaint will respond and how he will treat the consumer. Manufacturers' guarantees can provide a vital indication to consumers as to the likely responsiveness of the manufacturer to consumer complaints through their terms and conditions, and the procedure for bringing a claim, in particular.

On the basis that the crucial function of guarantees is to help a consumer obtain redress for a faulty product, it was then considered what the legal framework for guarantees should be. The relevant elements fall into four broad categories: procedural rules, substantive rules, rules on the relationship between guarantees and statutory rights, and rules on the enforcement of the legal framework. The key principles on which this framework is based are transparency and fairness. Fairness is relevant in three ways: first, consumers need to be aware of all the terms and conditions on which the guarantee is provided, particularly any conditions that need to be satisfied to obtain the benefit of the guarantee. In this sense, fairness and transparency overlap. Second, the terms of the guarantee itself should be fair and not contain unnecessary exclusions or overly burdensome conditions. Finally, there needs to be fairness in the exercise of the guarantor's discretion. A guarantor should not reject a claim under a guarantee if the consumer has complied with all the relevant conditions, nor should he exercise any discretion he may have as to the appropriate remedy in an unfair manner. Existing English law already contains many of these elements, although as seen in chapter 8, several improvements could be made.

Manufacturer liability and signalling theory: Grasping the wrong nettle?

An important aspect of this analysis was a consideration of the relationship between consumers' statutory rights and manufacturers' guarantees. Consumers are entitled to claim a remedy from the seller if a product they have bought is not of the required quality. Although the seller is similarly liable for defects which existed at the time of purchase, the statutory quality standard extends beyond defects in workmanship and materials and also covers, amongst others, the appearance and expected performance of the product. At present, a manufacturer is not directly liable to a consumer if a product fails to meet the statutory quality standard. It was argued that statutory rights and manufacturers' guarantees should be kept separate, and that the existence of one should have no bearing on the scope of the other. However, because the statutory rights cover more aspects of quality than most manufacturers' guarantees, and because these rights reflect the desirable level of protection for consumers against faulty goods, guarantees need to make it clear that the statutory rights are not affected by the guarantee. Furthermore, it needs to be ensured that sellers do not seek to avoid their liability with reference to the limitations in a manufacturers' guarantee. Finally, because a consumer receives a guarantee automatically with the corresponding product and has no choice as to whether to "accept" the guarantee, an alternative route for obtaining redress needs to be preserved.

Both the Magnuson-Moss Warranty Act (MMWA, see chapter 6) and the National Consumer Council's proposals (NCC, 1989b; see chapter 8) concern the substantive regulation of manufacturers' guarantees. The overt reason for the introduction of detailed substantive rules was the desire both to improve the information about product quality that is available to consumers and to raise the standard of product quality by encouraging competition on guarantees. However, it seems that there is also a covert reason which may have had a much stronger influence on these proposals than has been acknowledged. It is generally the case that a consumer has no direct claim against a manufacturer under the statutory rights. The real desire behind the MMWA and the NCC proposals may have been an intention to introduce direct producer liability.

The NCC proposals were part of the Consumer Guarantees Bill 1990 which completed most of its stages in Parliament before being lost when the Government of the day decided not to support the Bill. Willett argued that the main reason for its failure was that the Government did not accept the need to support consumers who are in a weak bargaining position in their relations with commercial interests

(1990, p.552). Willett emphasises that the Bill, by imposing some liability on manufacturers, would have introduced significant improvements to consumer protection:

> Making the manufacturer directly responsible to the consumer for poor quality products is a significant conceptual development in itself and has been advocated for several decades. It duly recognises the reasonable expectations of consumers as to who should bear responsibility for defects of quality (p.553).

This is undoubtedly correct. Most quality defects will be the result of the manufacturing process and therefore be the responsibility of the manufacturer, rather than the seller (cf. Bradgate and Twigg-Flesner, 2002). However, it was not considered if the statutory rights should be extended to cover the manufacturer, as well. By linking the definition of "defect" in the Bill to that of "satisfactory quality" in the Sale of Goods Act 1979 (SoGA), the Bill came very close to suggesting that the producer should be liable under sale of goods legislation. However, the NCC adhered to the notion that guarantees are provided voluntarily only, and only those manufacturers who chose to offer a guarantee would have been required to comply with these rules. Perhaps the reason the NCC did not propose the introduction of direct producer liability was because it hoped that the element of voluntariness would increase the chances of enacting the Bill. However, if the real objective was to hold the manufacturer responsible for quality defects, then it might have made more sense to introduce this with the framework of the SoGA.

Of course, the Bill would have gone further by seeking to improve the informational inequality between consumer and manufacturer by drawing to the consumer's attention the remedies under the guarantee against the manufacturer should there be a quality defect (Willett, 1990, p.556). Furthermore, it would have mitigated resource inequality by improving information about quality and post-purchase rights (p.557). Nevertheless, the objectives pursued by the Bill were not acceptable to the Government, and the Bill failed. Clearly, making the producer responsible for faulty goods was a very laudable objective. However, the means by which the Bill sought to achieve this do not seem adequate. It would have been much better to address this issue head-on by considering a change to the SoGA.

Furthermore, in some respects, the minimum standard set down for a full guarantee (MMWA), or a consumer guarantee (NCC), contains rules one would more likely expect to see as part of the general law on the sale of consumer good. Thus, rules that require defects to be remedied quickly and without charge to the consumer by repairing or replacing the product in question, provisions on alternatives if repair or replacement are unsuccessful and the possibility for subsequent owners or users to enforce the guarantee would improve the current rules on the sale of goods.

Perhaps the relative failure of the MMWA (and the total failure of the NCC proposals) can be explained on the basis that the legislators were grasping the wrong nettle, and what was really needed was a fundamental reform of the laws relating to the sale of goods to provide for the direct liability of the manufacturer to the final consumer for quality defects. When the European Commission reports on the operation of the Consumer Guarantees Directive in 2006, it is required to reconsider the case for direct producer liability. Interesting times lie ahead.

Conclusion

Consumer product guarantees are a useful means by which consumers can obtain a remedy for faulty goods. Relying on a guarantee may be better if a consumer wishes to seek redress informally, because a guarantee can indicate whether the guarantor is willing to respond to consumer complaints. If a guarantee is not available, or if the guarantee is not particularly favourable to consumers, then it may be better for a consumer to complain to the seller on the basis of a breach of his statutory rights. This may make it more cumbersome to obtain a remedy because there is greater scope for disagreement between consumer and seller as to whether there is, in fact, a legal entitlement for the consumer to a remedy. As most consumers seek to resolve quality problems informally, it may be more difficult to obtain a remedy under statutory rules than under a guarantee. This function of guarantees should be promoted.

Bibliography

Adams, J.N. and Brownsword, R. (1988). "Law Reform, Law Jobs, and Law Commission No.160", 51, Modern Law Review, 481-492.

Adams, J.N. and Brownsword, R. (1990). "Privity and the Concept of a Network Contract", 10, *Legal Studies*, 12.

Adams, J.N. and Brownsword, R. (1995). *Key Issues in Contract* (London: Butterworths).

Adams, J.N. and Brownsword, R. (1999). *Understanding Law*, 2nd edition (London: Sweet & Maxwell).

Adams, J.N. and Brownsword, R. (2000). *Understanding Contract Law*, 3rd edition (London: Sweet & Maxwell).

Adams, J.N., Beyleveld, D. and Brownsword, R. (1997). "Privity of Contract - the Benefits and the Burdens of Law Reform", 60, *Modern Law Review*, 238.

Adler, R.S. (1994). "The Last Best Argument For Eliminating Reliance From Express Warranties: 'Real-World' Consumers Don't Read Warranties", *South Carolina Law Review*, 429.

Agrawal, J., Richardson, P.S. and Grimm, P.E. (1996). "The Relationship Between Warranty And Product Reliability", 30, *Journal of Consumer Affairs*, 421-443.

Akerlof, G. (1970). "The market for "Lemons": Quality Uncertainty and the Market Mechanism", 84, *Journal of Law and Economics*, 488-500.

Ash, S.B., Kennedy, J.R. and Thirkell, P. (1979). "Consumer Satisfaction With Product Warranties: A Study of Canadian Automobile and Appliance Owners", in Hunt, H.K. and Day, R.L. (eds) *Refining Concepts and Measures Of Consumer Satisfaction and Complaining Behaviour* (Bloomington: Indiana University).

Astola, T. (1984). "Manufacturers' Guarantees and EEC Competition Law", 7, *Journal of Consumer Policy*, 65-80.

Atiyah, P.S. (2000). *The Sale of Goods*, 10th edition (eds J.N. Adams and H. MacQueen) (London: Pitman Publishing).

Balachander, S. (2001). "Warranty Signalling and Reputation", 47, *Management Science*, 1282-1289.

Baldwin, J. (1997). *Monitoring the Rise of the Small Claims Limit: Litigants' Experiences of different forms of adjudication*, LCD Research Paper No. 1/97 (London: Lord Chancellor's Department).

Beale, H. (1995). "Legislative Control of Fairness: The Directive on Unfair Terms in consumer Contracts" in Jack Beatson and Daniel Friedman (eds), *Good Faith and Fault in Contract Law* (Oxford: Clarendon Press).

Beale, H. (1996). "Customers, Chains and Networks", in Willett, C. (ed.), *Aspects of Fairness in Contract* (London: Blackstone Press).

Beale, H. and Howells, G. (1996). *Memorandum for the House of Lords European Communities Select Committee*, Minutes of the Report.

Beale, H. and Howells, G. (1997). "EC Harmonisation of Consumer Sales Law - A missed opportunity?", 12, *Journal of Contract Law*, 21.

Bearden, W.O. and Mason, J.B. (1984). "An Investigation of Influences on Consumer Complaints Reports", 11, *Advances in Consumer Research*, 490-495.

Bearden, W.O. and Shimp, T.A. (1982). "The use of extrinsic cues to facilitate product adoption", 19, *Journal of Marketing Research*, 229-239.

Beatson, J. and Friedman, D. (1995). *Good Faith and Fault in Contract Law* (Oxford: Clarendon Press).

Benjamin's Sale of Goods (1992). 4th edition (London: Sweet & Maxwell).

Bernstein, L. (1992). "Opting Out of the Legal System: Extralegal Contractual Relations in the Diamond Industry", 21, *Journal of Legal Studies*, 115-157.

Best, A. and Andreasen, A.R. (1977). "Consumer Response to Unsatisfactory Purchases: A Survey of Perceiving Defects, Voicing Complaints and Obtaining Redress", 11, *Law and Society Review* 701-742.

Beyleveld, D. and Brownsword, R. (1991). "Privity, Transitivity and Rationality", 54, *Modern Law Review*, 48.

Birds, J. and Hird, N.J. (2001). *Modern Insurance Law*, 5th edition (London: Sweet & Maxwell).

Bixby, M.B. (1984). "Judicial Interpretation of the Magnuson-Moss Warranty Act", 22, *American Business Law Journal*, 125-163.

Blodgett, J.G. and Anderson, R.D. (2001). "A Bayesian Network Model of the Consumer Complaint Process", 2, *Journal of Service Research*, 321-338.

Blodgett, J.G., Wakefield, K.L. and Barnes, J.H. (1995). "The Effects of Customer Service on Consumer Complaining Behaviour", 9(4), *Journal of Services Marketing*, 31-42.

Borrie, G. (1984), "A Duty To Trade Fairly?", 7, *Journal Of Consumer Policy*, 197.

Boulding, W. and Kirmani, A. (1993). "A consumer-side experimentation of signalling theory: do consumers perceive warranties as signals of quality?", 20, *Journal of Consumer Research*, 111-123.

Bourgoignie, T. (1979). "New Patterns Of Consumer Protection Under Warranty Law: Lessons From The U.S. Magnuson-Moss Warranty Act", 3, *Journal of Consumer Policy*, 266.

Bourgoignie, T. (1984). "The Need to Reformulate Consumer Protection Policy", 7, *Journal of Consumer Policy* , 307-321.

Bradgate, R. (1991). "Misrepresentation And Product Liability In English Law" *in* Howells, G. and Phillips, J. (eds) *Product Liability - Anglo-American Law Review Special Edition* (Chichester: Rose).

Bradgate, R. (1995). "Harmonisation of Legal Guarantees: A Common Law Perspective", *Consumer Law Journal*, 94.

Bradgate, R. (1997) "Consumer Guarantees: The EC's draft Directive", *Web Journal of Current Legal Issues*, <http://webjcli.ncl.ac.uk/1997/issue1/bradgate1.html> [last accessed 27 January 1998].

Bradgate, R. (2000). *Commercial Law*, 3rd edition (London: Butterworths)

Bradgate, R. and Twigg-Flesner, C. (2002). "Expanding the Boundaries of Liability for Quality Defects", 25, *Journal of Consumer Policy*, 345-377.

Bradgate, R. and White, F. (1995). "Rejection and Termination in Contracts for the Sale of Goods", in Birds, J., Bradgate, R. and Villiers, C. (eds) *Termination of Contracts* (Chichester: Wiley Chancery).

Braucher, J. (1985). "An informal resolution model of consumer product warranty law", *Wisconsin Law Review*, 1405-1480.

Braun, J. (1984). "Principles of Conduct for the Direct Selling Business in Europe", 7, *Journal of Consumer Policy*, 300-305.

Brickey, K.F. (1978). "The Magnuson-Moss Act - An Analysis of the Efficacy of Federal Warranty Regulation as a Consumer Protection Tool", 18, *Santa Clara Law Review*, 73-118.

Bridge, M. (1990). "The Evolution of Modern Sales Law", *Lloyds Maritime and Commercial Law Quarterly*, 52-69.

Bridge, M. (1997) *The Sale of Goods* (Oxford: Oxford University Press).

Broadbridge, A. and Marshall, J. (1995). "Consumer Complaint Behaviour: The case of electrical goods", 23(9), *International Journal of Retail & Distribution Management*, 8-18.

Brownsword, R. (1993). "Towards a Rational Law of Contract?", in Wilhelmsson, T (ed.) *Perspectives of Critical Contract Law* (Aldershot: Dartmouth).

Brownsword, R. (1996). "'Good Faith in Contracts' Revisited", 49, *Current Legal Problems*, 111-157.

Brownsword, R. (2000). *Contract Law: Themes for the Twenty-First Century* (London: Butterworths).

Brownsword, R., Hird, N.J. and Howells, G. (1999). *Good Faith in Contract: Concept and Context* (Aldershot: Ashgate).

Brownsword, R., Howells, G. and Wilhelmsson, T. (eds) (1994). *Welfarism in Contract Law* (Aldershot: Dartmouth).

Bryant, W.K. and Gerner, J.L. (1982). "The Demand for Service Contracts", 55(3), *Journal of Business*, 346-366.

Bureau Européen des Unions de Consommateurs (1994) *BEUC Opinion on the Commission's Green Paper on Guarantees for Consumer Goods and After-Sales Service*, BEUC/21/94 final (Brussels: BEUC).

Bureau Européen des Unions de Consommateurs (1997a) *BEUC Comments on the proposal for a European Parliament and Council Directive on the Sale of Consumer Goods and Associated Guarantees*, BEUC/014/97 final (Brussels: BEUC).

Bureau Européen des Unions de Consommateurs (1997b) *Proposed Directive on the Sale of Consumer Goods and Associated Guarantees - Briefing Note to the BEUC General Assembly*, BEUC/401/97 (Brussels: BEUC).

Cartwright, P. (1996), "A Service Fault in the Divisional Court", *Journal of Business Law*, 58-63.

Cartwright, P. (2001) *Consumer Protection and the Criminal Law* (Cambridge: Cambridge University Press).

Cave, M. (1985), "Market Models and Consumer Protections", 8, *Journal of Consumer Policy*, 335-351.

Chapman, K. and Meurer, M.J. (1989). "Efficient Remedies for Breach of Warranty", 52, *Law and Contemporary Problems*, 107-131.

Chen, Z. and Ross, T.W. (1994). "Why are Extended Warranties so Expensive?", 45, *Economics Letters*, 253-257.

Christie, N. (1977). "Conflicts as Property", 17(1), *The British Journal of Criminology*, 1-15.

Clark, A. (1992). "Product Liability and Pure Economic Loss: A Radical Proposal", *Journal of Business Law*, 383.

Clark, B. and Davis, M.J. (1975). "Beefing up Product Warranties: A New Dimension in Consumer Protection", 23, *Kansas Law Review*, 567.

Clayson, C. (1995). "Consumer Protection: Money-back guarantees and the Trade Descriptions Act 1968", 5, *Trading Law*, 387-391.

Cohen, M.A. and Lee, H.L. (1990). "Out of Touch with Customer Needs? Spare Parts and After-Sales Service", *Sloan Management Review*, 55-66.

Collins, H. (1999). *Regulating Contracts* (Oxford: Oxford University Press).

Commission of the European Communities (1993). *Green Paper on Guarantees for Consumer Goods and After-Sales Services*, COM (93) 509 final.

Commission of the European Communities (2001). *Green Paper on European Union Consumer Protection*, COM(2001) 531 final.

Consumers' Association (1994). *Extended Warranties: A consumer appraisal* (London: CA).

Consumers' Association (1996). *Memorandum for the House of Lords European Communities Select Committee*, Minutes of the Report.

Consumers in Europe Group (CEG, 1996). *Consumer Guarantees* (CEG 96/18).

Cranston, R. (1995). "The Green Paper on Guarantees", *Consumer Law Journal*, 110.

Davis, S., Gerstner, E. and Hagerty, M. (1995). "Money Back Guarantees in Retailing: Matching Products to Consumer Tastes", 71 *Journal of Retailing*, 7-22.

Day, E. and Fox, R.J. (1985). "Extended Warranties, Service Contracts and Maintenance Agreements - A Marketing Opportunity?", 2, *Journal of Consumer Marketing*, 77-86.

Deards, E. (1998). "The Proposed Guarantees Directive: Is it Fit for the Purpose?", 21 *Journal of Consumer Policy*, 99-119.

Denicola, R.C. (1975). "The Magnuson-Moss Warranty Act: Making Consumer Product Warranty A Federal Case", 44, *Fordham Law Review*, 273-300.

Department of Trade and Industry (DTI, 1992). *Consumer Guarantees Consultation Paper.*

Department of Trade and Industry (DTI, 2001a). *Consumer Knowledge Survey.*

Department of Trade and Industry (DTI, 2001b). *Consumer Knowledge Performance Monitor.*

Department of Trade and Industry (DTI, 2002). *Sale of Consumer Goods Directive - The Second Consultation on EC Directive 1999/44/EC on Certain Aspects of The Sale of Consumer Goods and Associated Guarantees*, URN 02/538.

Devience, A. (1990). "Magnuson-Moss Act: Substitution for UCC Warranty Protection?", 95, *Commercial Law Journal*, 323-337.

Dick, A.S., Hausknecht D.R. and Wilkie W.L. (1995) "Consumer Durable Goods: A review of post-purchase issues", 8, *Journal of Consumer Satisfaction, Dissatisfaction and Complaining Behaviour* 111-123.

Dickie, J. (1997). "A Step Closer to European Sale of Goods Law? - Commission Draft Directive on the Sale of Consumer Goods", *Journal of Business Law*, 167.

Director-General of Fair Trading (DGFT, 1996a). *Memorandum for the House of Lords European Communities Select Committee*, Minutes of the Report.

Director-General of Fair Trading (DGFT, 1996b) *Supplementary Memorandum for the House of Lords European Communities Select Committee*, Minutes of the Report.

Dobson, P. (1990a). "Consumer Guarantees", *Journal of Business Law*, 139-141.

Dobson, P. (1990b). "Consumer Guarantees and Reform of Sales Law", *Journal of Business Law*, 181.

Douglas, E.J., Glennon, D.C. and Lane, J.I. (1993). "Warranty, Quality and Price in the US Automobile Market", 25, *Applied Economics*, 135-141.

Eddy, J.A. (1977). "Effects of the Magnuson-Moss Act upon Consumer Product Warranties", 55, *North Carolina Law Review*, 835-877.

Eisenach, J.A., Higgins, R.S. and Shughart II, W.F. (1984). "Warranties, Tie-Ins and Efficient Insurance Contracts: A Theory and Three Case Studies", 6, *Research in Law and Economics*, 167-185.

Emons, W. (1989). "On the Limitation of Warranty Duration", 37, *Journal of Industrial Economics* 287-301.

Ervine, W.C.H. (1985). "Protecting New Car Purchasers: Recent United States And English Developments Compared", 34, *International and Comparative Law Quarterly*, 342-358.

Estelami, H. (2000). "Competitive and Procedural Determinants of Delight and Disappointment in Consumer Complaint Outcomes", 2, *Journal of Service Research*, 285-300.

European Consumer Law Group (ECLG, 1983). "Non-Legislative Means Of Consumer Protection", 6, *Journal of Consumer Policy*, 209-224.

European Consumer Law Group (ECLG, 1989). "Servicing of Cars and Electrical Goods", 12, *Journal Of Consumer Policy*, 485-517.

European Consumer Law Group (ECLG, 1994). "The EU Green Paper on Guarantees for Consumer Goods and After-Sales Services - a response", 17, *Journal of Consumer Policy*, 363-368.

European Consumer Law Group (ECLG, 1998). "Opinion on the Proposal for a Directive on the Sale of Consumer Goods and Associated Guarantees", 21, *Journal of Consumer Policy* 91-97.

European Parliament (1998). *First Report on the Proposal for a Directive on the Sale of Consumer Goods and Associated Guarantees*, A4-0029/98 of 10 March 1998.

Farnsworth, E.A. (1995). "Good Faith in Contract Performance", in Jack Beatson and Daniel Friedman (eds), *Good Faith and Fault in Contract Law* (Oxford: Clarendon Press).

Feldman, L.P. (1976). "New Legislation and the Prospects for Real Warranty Reform", 40, *Journal of Marketing*, 41-47.

Fine, F. (1989). "EEC Consumer Warranties: A new anti-trust hurdle facing exporters", *European Competition Law Review*, 233.

Flechtner, H.M. (1998). "Enforcing Manufacturers' Warranties, "Pass Through" Warranties, and the Like: Can the Buyer Get a Refund?", 50, *Rutgers Law Review*, 397-471.

Folkes, V.S. (1984). "Consumer Reactions to Product Failure: An Attributional Approach", 10, *Journal of Consumer Research*, 398-409.

Forte, A.D.M. (ed.) (1999). *Good Faith in Contract and Property Law* (Hart Publishing: Oxford).

Fox, R.J. and Day, E.D. (1988). "Enhancing The Appeal Of Service Contracts: An Empirical Investigation of Alternative Offerings", 64(3), *Journal of Retailing*, 335-352.

Gerner, J.L. and Bryant, W.K. (1981). "Appliance Warranties as Market Signals", 15, *Journal of Consumer Affairs*, 75-86.

Gibson, L. (1992). "Access to Justice and Consumer Redress Within a Single Market", 15, *Journal of Consumer Policy*, 407-415.

Goyder, J. (1996). "Consumer Guarantees and Competition Issues", in Lonbay (ed.) *Enhancing the legal position of the European Consumer* (London: BIICL).

Grether, D.M., Schwartz, A. and Wilde, L. (1986). "The Irrelevance Of Information Overload: An Analysis of Search and Disclosure", 59, *Southern California Law Review*, 277-303.

Grønmo, S. and Ölander, F. (1991). "Consumer Power: Enabling and Limiting Factors", 14, *Journal of Consumer Policy*, 141-169.

Grossman, S. (1981). "The Informational Role of Warranties and Private Disclosure about Product Quality", 24, *Journal of Law and Economics*, 461-483.

Grundman, S. and Bianca, C.M. (eds.) (2002), *EU Sales Directive - Commentary* (Oxford: Intersentia).

Guerin, K.R. (2001). "Clash of the Federal Titans: The Federal Arbitration Act v The Magnuson-Moss Warranty Act: Will the Consumer Win or Lose?", 13, *Loyola Consumer Law Review* 4.

Gunter, M.E. (2000). "Can Warrantors Make an End Run? The Magnuson-Moss Act and Mandatory Arbitration in Written Warranties", *Georgia Law Review*, 1483.

Hadfield, G.K., Howse, R. and Trebilcock, M.J. (1998). "Information-Based Principles for Rethinking Consumer Protection Policy", 21, *Journal of Consumer Policy*, 131-169.

Halstead, D., Dröge, C. and Bixby Cooper, M. (1993). "Product Warranties and Post-Purchase Service: A Model of Consumer Satisfaction With Complain Resolution", 7, *Journal of Services Marketing*, 33-40.

Harland, D. (1995). "Consumer Guarantees-The Relevance for Europe of the Australian Experience", *Consumer Law Journal*, 153.

Heal, G. (1977). "Guarantees and Risk-sharing", 44, *Review of Economic Studies*, 549-560.

Hedley, S. (2001). "Quality of Goods, Information, and the Death of Contract", *Journal of Business Law*, 114-125.

Hervey, T. (1981). "Winner takes all", 44, *Modern Law Review*, 575-580.

Hewitt, S.W. (1987). *Manufacturers' Liability for Defective Products* (London: BSP Professional).

Hogarth, J., English, M. and Sharma, M. (2001). "Consumer Complaints and Third Parties: Derterminants of Consumer Satisfaction With Complaint Resolution Efforts", 14, *Journal of Consumer Satisfaction, Dissatisfaction and Complaining Behaviour*, 74-87.

Holdych, T.J. (1998). "Warranties and Conditions in the Sale of Goods: A Market Based Assessment of English and European Community Warranty Law", 29, *Cambrian Law Review*, 73-92.

Holdych, T.J. and Mann, B.D. (1996). "The Basis of the Bargain Requirement: A Market and Economic Based Analysis of Express Warranties - Getting What you Pay for and Paying for What you Get", 45, *DePaul Law Review*, 781-857.

Holmes, A. (1998). "Consumer Guarantees", 8, *Consumer Policy Review,* 45.

Hondius, E. (1997). "Kaufen ohne Risiko: Der europäische Richtlinienentwurf zum Verbraucherkauf und zur Verbrauchergarantie", *Zeitschrift für Europäisches Privatrecht,* 130.

House of Lords (1997). *Consumer Guarantees - Tenth Report of the Select Committee on European Communities*, 4 March 1997 (London: HMSO).

Howells, G. (1994). "Guarantee Law", in F. Maniet and B. Dunaj (eds.), *The Scope and Objectives of Consumer Law* (Louvain-la-Neuve: CDC Publications).

Howells, G. (1998a). *Consumer Product Safety* (Aldershot: Ashgate).

Howells, G. (1998b). "'Soft Law' in EC consumer law", in Craig, P. and Harlow, C. (eds.) *Lawmaking in the European Union* (Dordrecht: Kluwer).

Howells, G. (1999). "The Move From Soft to Hard Law", in Stauder, B. and Stauder, H. (eds) *La Protection Des Consommateurs acheteurs à distance* (Zürich: Schulthess Polygraphischer Verlag).

Howells, G. and Bryant, C. (1993). "Consumer Guarantees: Competition or Regulation?", *Consumer Law Journal*, 3.

Howells, G., James, R. and Spiller, P. (2001). "Making The Alternative Appropriate: ADR For Consumers", 7, *New Zealand Business Law Quarterly*, 204.

Howells, G. and Twigg-Flesner, C. (2003). "Much Ado about Nothing? The implementation of Directive 1999/44/EC into English Law", in Schermaier, M.J. (ed.), *Verbraucherkauf in Europa - Altes Gewährleistungsrecht und die Umsetzung der Richtlinie 1999/44/EG* (Munich: Sellier ELP).

Howells, G. and Weatherill, S. (1995). *Consumer Protection Law* (Aldershot: Dartmouth).

Howells, G. and Wilhelmsson, T. (1997a). *EC Consumer Law* (Aldershot: Ashgate).

Howells, G. and Wilhelmsson, T. (1997b). "EC and US Approaches to Consumer Protection - Should the Gap be Bridged?" , *Yearbook of European Law*, 207.

Huyse, L. and Parmentier, S. (1990). "Decoding Codes: The Dialogue Between Consumers and Suppliers Through Codes of Conduct in the European Community", 13, *Journal of Consumer Policy*, 253-272.

Ilmonen, K. (1987). "From Consumer Problems to Consumer Anomie", 10, *Journal of Consumer Policy*, 25-38.

Jarmin, A. (1994). "Consumer Product Testing", in R. John (ed.), *The Consumer Revolution - Redressing the balance* (London: Hodder & Stoughton).

Jolowicz, J.A. (1969). "The Protection of the Consumer and Purchaser of Goods under English Law", 32, *Modern Law Review*, 1-18.

Kelley, C.A. (1988). "An investigation of Consumer Product Warranties as Market Signals of Product Reliability", 16, *Journal of the Academy of Marketing Science*, 72-78.

Kelley, C.A., Conant, J.S. and Brown, J.J. (1988). "Extended Warranties: Retail Management and Public Policy Implications", in G.Frazier et. al., *American Marketing Association Educator's Proceedings* (American Marketing Association:Chicago, 1988).

Kelley, C.A. and Conant, J.S. (1991). "Extended Warranties: Consumer and Manufacturer Perceptions", 25, *Journal of Consumer Affairs*, 68-83.

Kessler, F. (1943). "Contracts of Adhesion - Some Thoughts About Freedom of Contract", 43, *Columbia Law Review*, 629-642.

Kessler, F. (1964). "The Protection of the Consumer Under Modern Sales Law, Part 1", 74, *Yale Law Journal*, 262.

Kim, C.S., Djamaludin, I. and Murthy, D.N.P. (2001). "Warranty Cost Analysis with Heterogenous Usage Intensity", 8, *International Transactions in Operational Research*, 337-347.

Kutner, W.R. (1977). "Consumer Product Warranties Under the Magnuson-Moss Warranty Act and the Uniform Commercial Code", 62, *Cornell Law Review* 738.

Lassar, W., Folkes, V., Grewal, D. and Costley, C. (1998). "Consumer Affective Reactions to Product Problems When The Timing of Warranty Expiration Varies", 42, *Journal of Business Research*, 265-270.

Law Commission (2002). *Unfair Contract Terms – A Consultation Document* (London: The Stationery Office).

Law Society (1992). "Consumer Guarantees", 30, *Law Society's Gazette*, 15-16.

Lawson, R.G. (1992). "Guarantees: the present law and proposals for change", *Solicitors' Journal*, 770-771.

Leder, M. and Shears, P. (1996). *Consumer Law* (4th edition) (London: Pitman Publishing).

Lee, S.W. (1976). "The Magnuson-Moss Warranty Act: Consumer Information and Warranty Regulation", 51, *Indiana Law Journal*, 397-415.

Liu, R. and McClure, P. (2001). "Recognising cross-cultural differences in consumer complaint behaviour and intentions: an empirical examination", 18, *Journal of Consumer Marketing*, 54-74.

Llewellyn, K.N. (1936). "On Warranty of Quality, and Society", 36, *Columbia Law Review*, 699.

Llewellyn, K.N. (1937). "On Warranty of Quality, and Society: II", 37, *Columbia Law Review*, 341.

London Economics (1997). *Consumer Detriment under Conditions of Imperfect Information - OFT Research Paper 11* (London: Office for Fair Trading).

Loomba, A.P.S (1998). "Evolution of Product Warranty: A chronological study", 4(2), *Journal of Management History*, 124-136.

Lowe, D. (1986). "Vehicles and Manufacturers' Warranties", 2, *Road Law,* 142-145.

Lowe, R. and Woodroffe, G. (1999). *Consumer Law and Practice* (London: Sweet & Maxwell).

Lutz, N.A. (1989). "Warranties as Signals under Consumer Moral Hazard", 20, *RAND Journal of Economics*, 239-255.

Lutz, N.A. and Padmanabhan, V. (1995). "Why Do We Observe Minimal Warranties?", 14(4), *Marketing Science*, 417-441.

Lutz, N.A. and Padmanabhan, V. (1998). "Warranties, Extended Warranties and Product Quality", 16, *International Journal of Industrial Organisation*, 463-493.

Macaulay, S. (1979). "Lawyers and Consumer Protection Laws", 14, *Law and Society Review*, 115-171.
Macaulay, S., Kidwell, J. and Whitford, W. (1995). *Contracts: Law in Action Volume I* (Michie).
MacMillan, C. (2000). "A Birthday Present for Lord Denning: The Contracts (Rights of Third Parties) Act 1999", 63, *Modern Law Review*, 721-738.
McDaniel, S. and Rao, C.P. (1982). "Consumer Attitudes toward and satisfaction with warranties and warranty performance - before and after Magnuson-Moss", *Baylor Business Studies*, 47-61.
McMeel, G. (1997). "Contractual Intention: The Smoke Ball strikes back", 113 *Law Quarterly Review*, 47.
Malinvaud, P. (2002), "Article 6", in Grundman, S. and Bianca, C.M. (eds), *EU Sales Directive - Commentary* (Oxford: Intersentia).
Micklitz, H.W. (1997). "Ein einheitliches Kaufrecht für Verbraucher in der EG?", 8, *Europäische Zeitschrift für Wirtschaftsrecht*, 229.
Micklitz, H.W. (1999). "Die Verbrauchsgüterkauf-Richtlinie", 10, *Europäische Zeitschrift für Wirtschaftsrecht*, 485.
Micklitz, H.W. and Amtenbrink, F. (1995). "Legal Guarantees - German Civil Law in the light of the Green Paper", *Consumer Law Journal*, 117.
Micklitz, H.W. and Howells, G. (1999). *Consumer Guarantees in Central and Eastern Europe - Approximation, Harmonisation and Compatibility with European Union Law* (Louvain-la-Neuve: CDC Publications).
Miller, C.J., Harvey, B.W. and Parry, D.L. (1998). *Consumer and Trading Law: Text, Cases and Materials* (Oxford: Oxford University Press).
Moore, E.M. and Shuptrine, F.K. (1993). "Warranties: Continued Readability Problems After the 1975 Magnusson-Moss Warranty Act", 27, *The Journal of Consumer Affairs*, 23.
Moorthy, S. and Srinivasan, K. (1995). "Signaling Quality with a Money-Back guarantee: The Role of Transaction Cost", 14(4), *Marketing Science*, 442-466.
Morel, K.P.N., Poiesz, T.B.C. and Wilke, H.A.M. (1997). "Motivation, Capacity and Opportunity to Complain: Towards a comprehensive model of Consumer Complaint Behaviour", 24, *Advances in Consumer Research*, 464-469.
National Consumer Council (NCC, 1989a). *Competing in Quality - A consultation paper* (London: NCC).
National Consumer Council (NCC, 1989b). *The Consumer Guarantee - Final Report* (London: NCC).
National Consumer Council (NCC, 1997). *Unfair Trading - Recommendations for reform of Part III of the Fair Trading Act* (London: NCC).
Nyer, P.U. (2000). "An Investigation Into Whether Complaining Can Cause Increased Consumer Satisfaction", 17(1), *Journal of Consumer Marketing*, 9-19.
Office of Fair Trading (OFT, 1984). *Consumer Guarantees - A discussion paper* (London: OFT).
Office of Fair Trading (OFT, 1986). *Consumer Guarantees - A report* (London: OFT).
Office of Fair Trading (OFT, 1989). *Servicing and Repairs* (London: OFT).
Office of Fair Trading (OFT, 1994). *Extended Warranties on Electrical Goods* (London: OFT).
Office of Fair Trading (OFT, 1996a). *Consumer Dissatisfaction* (London: OFT).
Office of Fair Trading (OFT, 1996b). *Price Transparency in the Sale of Extended Warranties by Electrical Retailers* (London: OFT).
Office of Fair Trading (OFT, 1996c). *Unfair Contract Terms Bulletin*, 1 (London: OFT).

Office of Fair Trading (OFT, 1996d). *Unfair Contract Terms Bulletin*, 2 (London: OFT).
Office of Fair Trading (OFT, 1997a). *Unfair Contract Terms Bulletin*, 3 (London: OFT).
Office of Fair Trading (OFT, 1997b). *Unfair Contract Terms Bulletin*, 4 (London: OFT).
Office of Fair Trading (OFT, 1997c). "Supplementary Memorandum: Consumer Complaints Relating to Defective Goods and Guarantees", Appendix to House of Lords (1997), p.42-43.
Office of Fair Trading (OFT, 1998). *Unfair Contract Terms Bulletin*, 5 (London: OFT).
Office of Fair Trading (OFT, 1999a). *Unfair Contract Terms Bulletin*, 6 (London: OFT).
Office of Fair Trading (OFT, 1999b). *Unfair Contract Terms Bulletin*, 7 (London: OFT).
Office of Fair Trading (OFT, 1999c). *Unfair Contract Terms Bulletin*, 8 (London: OFT).
Office of Fair Trading (OFT, 2000a). *Unfair Contract Terms Bulletin*, 9 (London: OFT).
Office of Fair Trading (OFT, 2000b). *Unfair Contract Terms Bulletin*, 10 (London: OFT).
Office of Fair Trading (OFT, 2000c). *Unfair Contract Terms Bulletin*, 11 (London: OFT).
Office of Fair Trading (OFT, 2000d). *Unfair Contract Terms Bulletin*, 12 (London: OFT).
Office of Fair Trading (OFT, 2000e). *Consumer Detriment* (London: OFT).
Office of Fair Trading (OFT, 2001a). *Unfair Contract Terms Bulletin*, 13 (London: OFT).
Office of Fair Trading (OFT, 2001b). *Unfair Contract Terms Bulletin*, 14 (London: OFT).
Office of Fair Trading (OFT, 2001c). *Unfair Contract Terms Guidance* (London:OFT).
Office of Fair Trading (OFT, 2001d). *Unfair Contract Terms Bulletin*, 15 (London: OFT).
Office of Fair Trading (OFT, 2001e). *Unfair Contract Terms Bulletin*, 16 (London: OFT).
Office of Fair Trading (OFT, 2002a). *Unfair Contract Terms Bulletin*, 17 (London: OFT).
Office of Fair Trading (OFT, 2002b). *Extended Warranties on Domestic Electrical Goods - A report on an OFT investigation* (London: OFT).
Oral Evidence, Minutes of Evidence - Appendix to House of Lords (1997). *Consumer Guarantees - Tenth Report of the Select Committee on European Communities*, 4 March 1997 (London: HMSO).
Padmanabhan, V. (1995). "Usage Heterogeneity and Extended Warranties", 4, *Journal of Economics and Marketing Strategy*, 33-53.
Palfrey, T. and Romer, T. (1983). "Warranties, Performance and the Resolution of Buyer-Seller Disputes", *Bell Journal of Economics*, 97.
Perry, M. and Perry, A. (1976). "Service Contract Compared to Warranty as a Means to Reduce Consumer's Risk", 52(2), *Journal of Retailing*, 33.
Price, L.J. and Dawar, N. (2002), "The Joint Effects of Brands and Warranties in Signalling New Product Quality", 23, *Journal of Economic Psychology*, 165-190.
Priest, G.L. (1981). "A theory of the consumer product warranty", 90, *Yale Law Journal*, 1297-1352.
Priest, G.L. (1982). "The Best Evidence of the Effect of Products Liability Law on the Accident Rate: Reply", 91, *Yale Law Journal*, 1386-1401.
Purohit, D. and Srivastava, J. (2001). "Effect of Manufacturer Reputation, Retailer Reputation and Product Warranty on Consumer Judgments of Product Quality: A Cue Diagnosticity Framework", 10, *Journal of Consumer Psychology*, 123-134.
Ramsay, I. (1981). "Consumer Redress Mechanisms for Poor-Quality and Defective Products", 31, *University of Toronto Law Journal*, 117-152.
Ramsay, I. (1984). *Rationales for Intervention in the Consumer Marketplace* (London: Office of Fair Trading).
Ramsay, I. (1991). "Consumer Law and the Search for Empowerment", 19, *Canadian Business Law Journal*, 397-411.
Ramsay, I. (1993). "Consumer Law and Structures of Thought - A Comment", 16, *Journal of Consumer Policy*, 79-94.
Rao, C.P. and Weinrauch, J.D. (1976). "Consumer Perceptions and Satisfaction with major appliance warranties", *Baylor Business Studies*, 17-27.

Rasor, P.B. (1982). "The History of Warranties of Quality in the Sale of Goods: Contract or Tort? - A Case Study in Full Circles", 21, *Washburn Law Review*, 175-218.

Reich, N. (1996). *Europäisches Verbraucherrecht* (Baden-Baden:Nomos).

Reitz, C.R. (1978). *Consumer Protection under the Magnuson-Moss Warranty Act* (Philadelphia: ALI ABA).

Richardson, W. and Morris, D. (1988). "Towards More Effective Consumer Marketplace Interventions - A Model For Improvement of OFT Codes of Practice", 11, *Journal Of Consumer Policy*, 315-334.

Richins, M.L. (1983). "Negative Word-of-Mouth by Dissatisfied Consumers: A Pilot Study", 47, *Journal of Marketing*, 68-78.

Richins, M.L. and Bronislaw, J.V. (1985). "Seeking Redress for Consumer Dissatisfaction: The Role of Attitudes and Situational Factors", 8, *Journal of Consumer Policy*, 29-44.

Riegert, R.A. (1990). "An Overview of the Magnuson-Moss Warranty Act and the Successful Consumer-Plaintiff's Right to Attorneys' Fees", 95, *Commercial Law Journal*, 468-485.

Roe, T. (2000). "Contractual Intention Under Section 1(1)(b) and 1(2) of the Contracts (Rights of Third Parties) Act 1999", 63, *Modern Law Review*, 887-894.

Ross, H.L. and Littlefield, N.O. (1978). "Complaint as a problem-solving mechanism", 12, *Law and Society Review* 199-216.

Rothschild, D.P. (1976). "The Magnuson-Moss Warranty Act: Does It Balance Warrantor and Consumer Interests?", 44, *George Washington Law Review*, 335-380.

Saving, T.R. (1995). "Legal Implications of Imperfect Information In Consumer Markets - Comment", 151, *Journal of Institutional and Theoretical Economics*, 52-57.

Saxby, C.L., Tat, P.K. and Johansen, J.T. (2000). "Measuring Consumer Perceptions Of Procedural Justice In a Complaint Context", 34, *Journal of Consumer Affairs*, 204-216.

Saxe, D.B. and Blejwas, D.I. (1976). "The Federal Warranty Act: Progress and Pitfalls", 22, *New York Law School Review*, 1-28.

Schermaier, M.J. (ed.) (2003). *Verbraucherkauf in Europa – Altes Gewährleistungsrecht und die Umsetzung der Richtlinie 1999/44/EG* (Munich: Sellier ELP).

Schwartz, A. (1995). "Legal Implications of Imperfect Information In Consumer Markets", 151, *Journal of Institutional and Theoretical Economics*, 31-48.

Schwartz, A. and Wilde, L.L. (1983). "Imperfect Information in Markets For Contract Terms: The Examples of Warranties and Security Interests", 69, *Virginia Law Review*, 1387-1485.

Schwartze, A. (2000) *Europäische Sachmängelgewährleistung beim Warenkauf* (Tübingen: Mohr Siebeck).

Scott, C. and Black, J. (2000). *Cranston's Consumers and the Law*, 3rd edition (London: Butterworths).

Shieh, S. (1996)."Price and Money-back Guarantees as Signals of Product Quality", 5(3), *Journal of Economics and Management Strategy*, 361-377.

Shimp, T.A. and Bearden, W.O. (1982). "Warranty and other extrinsic cue effects on Consumers' Risk Perceptions", 9, *Journal of Consumer Research* 38-46.

Sims, V.K. and Goddard, R.J. (2002). "Controlling Contractual Discretion", 61, *Cambridge Law Journal*, 268-271.

Smith, C. (1977). "The Magnuson-Moss Warranty Act: Turning the Tables on Caveat Emptor", 13, *California Western Law Review*, 391-429.

Speidel, R.E. (1987). "Warranty Theory, Economic Loss and the Privity Requirement: Once more into the void", 67, *Boston University Law Review*, 9-58.

Spence, M. (1977). "Consumer Misperceptions, Product Failure and Producer Liability", 44, *Review of Economic Studies*, 561-572.

Srivastava, J. and Mitra, A. (1998). "Warranty as a signal of quality: The Moderating Effect Of Consumer Knowledge On Quality Evaluations", 9, *Marketing Letters*, 327-336.

Staudenmeyer, D. (1999). "Die EG Richtlinie über den Verbrauchsgüterkauf", 52, *Neue Juristische Wochenschrift*, 2393-2397.

Stephens, N. and Gwinner, K.P. (1998). "Why Don't Some People Complain? A Cognitive-Emotive Process Model Of Consumer Complaint Behaviour", 26(3), *Journal of the Academy of Marketing Science*, 172-189.

Steyn, J. (1997). "Contract Law: Fulfilling The Reasonable Expectations of Honest Men", 113, *Law Quarterly Review*, 433-442.

Stoljar, S.J. (1952). "Conditions, Warranties and Descriptions of Quality in Sale of Goods - I", 15, *Modern Law Review*, 425-445.

Stoljar, S.J. (1953). "Conditions, Warranties and Descriptions of Quality in Sale of Goods - II", 16, *Modern Law Review*, 174-197.

Sullivan, T.J. (1980). "Innovation in the Law of Warranty: The Burden of Reform", 32, *Hastings Law Journal*, 341-401.

Tan, S.J and Leong, W.Y. (1999). "Warranty Strategy: a solution to hybrid product woes?", 16, *International Marketing Review*, 40-64.

Tan, S.J., Lee, K.S. and Lim, G.H. (2001). "Warranty and warrantor reputations as signals of hybrid product quality", 35, *European Journal of Marketing*, 110-132.

Taylor Nelson Sofres (2001). *Report into Extended Warranties* (Gerrards Cross: Taylor Nelson Sofres).

Tenreiro, M. (1995). "Guarantees and After-Sales Service: Brief analysis of the Green Paper presented by the European Commission", *Consumer Law Journal*, 79.

Tenreiro, M. (1996). "La proposition de directive sur la vente et les garanties des biens de consommation", *Revue européene de droit de la consommation*, 187.

Thogersen, J. (2000). "Pysochological Determinants of Paying Attention to Eco-Labels in Purchase Decisions: Model Development and Multinational Validation", 23, *Journal of Consumer Policy*, 285-313.

Thomas, R. (1984), "Codes of Practice in the United Kingdom and the Consumer Interest", 7, *Journal of Consumer Policy*, 198-202.

Thomas, R. (1988). "Alternative Dispute Resolution - Consumer Disputes", 7, *Civil Justice Quarterly*, 206-219.

Trebilcock, M.J. (1969). "Consumer Protection in the Affluent Society", 16, *McGill Law Journal*, 263-296.

Trebilcock, M.J. (1972). "Manufacturers' Guarantees", 18, *McGill Law Journal*, 1-44.

Tur, R. (1982). "Litigation and the Consumer Interest; the Class Action and Beyond", 2, *Legal Studies*, 135-171.

Twigg-Flesner, C. (1999a). "Consumer Product Guarantees and Insurance Law", *Journal of Business Law*, 279-285.

Twigg-Flesner, C. (1999b). "The E.C. Directive on Certain Aspects of The Sale of Consumer Goods and Associated Guarantees", 7, *Consumer Law Journal*, 177-192.

Twigg-Flesner, C. (1999c). "Network Liability for Manufacturers' Guarantees - Remedying Legislative Shortcomings With A Legal Jigsaw", *Journal of Business Law*, 568-580.

Twigg-Flesner, C. (2000a). "New Rules for Guarantees: For better or worse?", 10 (3), *Consumer Policy Review*, 100.

Twigg-Flesner, C. (2000b). "The Unfair Terms in Consumer Contracts Regulations 1999 - New Powers for the Regulators and the Consumers' Association", 11, *Utilities Law Review*, 41.

Twigg-Flesner, C. (2002), "Dissatisfaction Guaranteed? The Legal Issues of Extended Warranties Explored", *Web Journal of Current Legal Issues* <http://webjcli.ncl.ac.uk/2002/issue4/twigg-flesner4.html>

Twigg-Flesner, C. (2003), "New Remedies for Consumer Sales Transactions: A Change for the Worse?", forthcoming.

Twigg-Flesner, C. and Bohling, H. (1999). "Insurance Regulation: When a Warranty is Not a Guarantee", 9, *Consumer Policy Review*, 193.

Twigg-Flesner, C. and Bradgate, R. (2000). "The E.C. Directive on Certain Aspects of the Sale of Consumer Goods and Associated Guarantees - All Talk and No Do?", *Web Journal of Current Legal Issues* No.2 <http://webjcli.ncl.ac.uk/2000/issue2/flesner2.html> .

Udell, J.G. and Anderson, E. (1968). "The Product Warranty as an element of Competitive Strategy", 32, *Journal of Marketing*, 1-8.

Vandegrift, D. (2001). "Quality-assuring price and breach of express or implied warranty", 19, *Contemporary Economic Policy 186-196.*

Voss, G.B. and Ahmed, I. (1992). "Extended Warranties: A behavioral perspective", 19, *Advances in Consumer Research*, 879-886.

Weatherill, S. (1994). "Consumer Guarantees", 110, *Law Quarterly Review*, 545-549.

Weatherill, S. (1996). "Consumer Guarantees and the Development of the Internal Market", in Lonbay (ed.) *Enhancing the legal position of the European Consumer* (BIICL: London).

Wein, T. (2001). "Consumer Information Problems – Causes and Consequences", in Grundmann, S., Kerber, W. and Weatherill, S. (eds), *Party Autonomy and the Role of Information in the Internal Market* (Berlin: de Gruyter).

Whincup, M. (1996). "Comment on *Bowerman v ABTA*", 4, *Consumer Law Journal*, CS6.

Whish, R. (2001). *Competition Law*, 4th edition. (London: Butterworths).

White, M.B. (1986). "Retail Sellers And The Enforcement Of Manufacturer Warranties: An Application of the Uniform Commercial Code to Consumer Distribution Systems", 32, *Wayne Law Review*, 1049-1102.

Whitford, W.C. (1968). "Law and the Consumer Transactions: A Study of the Automobile Warranty", 63, *Wisconsion Law Review*, 1006-1098.

Whitford, W.C. (1973). "The Function of Disclosure Regulation in Consumer Transactions", 68, *Wisconsin Law Review*, 400-470.

Whitford, W.C. (1982). "Comment on a theory of the Consumer Product Warranty", 91, *Yale Law Journal*, 1371-1385.

Wiechens, K. (2001), "Arbitrating Consumer Claims under the Magnuson-Moss Warranty Act", 68, *University of Chicago Law Review*, 1459-1486.

Wiener, J.L. (1985). "Are warranties accurate signals of product reliability?", 12, *Journal of Consumer Research*, 245-250.

Wightman, J. (1999). "Good Faith and Pluralism in the Law of Contract", in Browsword, R., Hird, N.J. and Howells, G. (eds) *Good Faith un Contract: Concept and Context* (Aldershot: Ashgate).

Wilhelm Consulting (1997). *Study on the possible economic impact of the proposal for a directive on the sale of consumer goods and associated guarantees.*

Wilhelmsson, T. (ed.) (1993). *Perspectives of Critical Contract Law* (Aldershot: Dartmouth).

Wilkes, R.E. and Wilcox (1976). "Consumer Perceptions of Product Warranties and their implications for retail strategy", 4, *Journal of Business Research*, 35-43.

Williamson, O.E. (1995). "Legal Implications of Imperfect Information in Consumer Markets - Comment", 151, *Journal of Institutional and Theoretical Economics*, 49-51.

Willett, C. (1991). "The unacceptable face of the Consumer Guarantees Bill", 54, *Modern Law Review*, 552-560.

Willett, C. (1992). "Consumer Guarantees, Citizen's Charter's and Access to Justice", 11, *Civil Justice Quarterly*, 99-105.

Willett, C. (1993). "The Quality of Goods and the Rights of Consumers", 44, *Northern Ireland Legal Quarterly*, 218-232.

Willett, C. (1999). "Good Faith And Consumer Contract Terms", in Browsword, R., Hird, N.J. and Howells, G. (eds) *Good Faith In Contract: Concept and Context* (Aldershot: Ashgate).

Williston, S. (1908). "What Constitutes an Express Warranty in the Sale of Goods", 21, *Harvard Law Review*, 555.

Wisdom, M.J. (1979). "An Empirical Study of the Magnuson-Moss Warranty Act", 31, *Stanford Law Review*, 1117.

Zollers, F.E., Hurd, S.N. and Shears, P. (1999). "Consumer Protection in the European Union: An analysis of the Directive On the Sale of Consumer Goods and Associated Guarantees", 20, *University of Pennsylvania Journal of International Economic law*, 97-131.

Index